Prince Eugene of Savoy

Prince Eugene of Savoy

A Genius for War Against Louis XIV and the Ottoman Empire

James Falkner

Now, 'Murmur Tales of Iron Wars'[1]

Pen & Sword
MILITARY

AN IMPRINT OF PEN & SWORD BOOKS LTD.
YORKSHIRE - PHILADELPHIA

First published in Great Britain in 2022
and reissued in this format in 2024 by
PEN & SWORD MILITARY
An imprint of
Pen & Sword Books Ltd
Yorkshire – Philadelphia

ISBN 978 1 52679 942 5

A CIP catalogue record for this book is available from the British Library

Typeset in 11/13.5 & Ehrhardt MT Std by SJmagic DESIGN SERVICES, India.

Printed and bound in the UK by CPI Group (UK) Ltd.

Pen & Sword Books Ltd incorporates the imprints of Pen & Sword Archaeology,
Atlas, Aviation, Battleground, Discovery, Family History, History, Maritime, Military,
Naval, Politics, Social History, Transport, True Crime, Claymore Press, Frontline
Books, Praetorian Press, Seaforth Publishing and White Owl

For a complete list of Pen & Sword titles please contact
PEN & SWORD BOOKS LTD
47 Church Street, Barnsley, South Yorkshire, S70 2AS, England
E-mail: enquiries@pen-and-sword.co.uk
Website: www.pen-and-sword.co.uk

Or

PEN AND SWORD BOOKS
1950 Lawrence Rd, Havertown, PA 19083, USA
E-mail: Uspen-and-sword@casematepublishers.com
Website: www.penandswordbooks.com

Contents

List of Maps

List of Illustrations

B&W Plates

1. Prince Eugene of Savoy, c. 1700. Imperial field commander and President of the War Council in Vienna.
2. Duke Victor-Amadeus of Savoy.
3. Eugene's mother Olympia Mancini, Countess de Soissons, c. 1670.
4. Emperor Leopold of Austria, c. 1680.
5. 'Turken Louis': Louis-Guillaume, Margrave of Baden, sponsor and supporter of the young Eugene.
6. Count Ernst Rüdiger von Starhemberg, staunch defender of Vienna in 1683.
7. Field Marshal Guido von Starhemberg, a close colleague of Eugene, who later became a severe critic.
8. The fortress of Belgrade, viewed from across the Danube.
9. Emperor Joseph I, a great supporter of Eugene.
10. Emperor Charles VI of Austria, Habsburg claimant to the throne of Spain.
11. Nicholas de Catinat, Marshal of France.
12. François de Neufville, Duc de Villeroi, Marshal of France.
13. Louis-Joseph de Bourbon, Duc de Vendôme.
14. Louis-François, Duc de Boufflers, Marshal of France.
15. Claude-Louis-Hector de Villars, Marshal of France.
16. Grand Vizier Kara Mustapha, Ottoman commander defeated at Vienna in 1683.
17. Gräfin Elenore Batthyány, close friend of Eugene.
18. An Ottoman janissary.
19. The Hôtel de Soissons, where Eugene was born.
20. Eugene's Winterhof Palace in Vienna, where he died.

Colour Plates

1. Prince Eugene of Savoy c. 1730.
2. The Austrian siege of Buda (Ofen), 1686.
3. The Second Battle of Mohacs, 12 August 1687.
4. A battle for a river crossing in Hungary, c. 1690.

Introduction

The magnificent equestrian statue of Prince Eugene standing in the centre of Vienna bears the stirring inscription 'To the glorious conqueror of Austria's enemies'. True enough, but in his youth Eugene had been intended by the Sun King, Louis XIV of France, for a career in the Church. This was against his nature and inclination, and so the young adventurer fled to Austria to offer his services, and his unbloodied sword, to the Habsburg emperor, Leopold I. At the time a formidable army, sent by the sultan in Constantinople, was at the gates of Vienna, and the safe deliverance of the city in the summer of 1683, and the repulse of what had every appearance of a major Ottoman incursion into central Europe, was an extraordinary feat of arms. The young exile played a gallant part in the drama, attracting favourable attention and setting himself firmly on the way to renown. Eugene proved to have a naturally aggressive talent for soldiering, and in the years that followed he campaigned hard and although an outsider rose rapidly in rank, scoring significant military successes, most notably the astonishing victory in 1697 over the Ottoman army at Zenta on the river Tisza in Hungary.

By the onset of the long war for the throne of Spain just four years later, Eugene ranked as Emperor Leopold's foremost military commander. He was appointed as President of the Imperial War Council, the *Hofkriegsrat*, and in this role formed a renowned partnership, and a lasting friendship, with Queen Anne's Captain-General, John Churchill, 1st Duke of Marlborough. The Englishman famously brought his army to the Danube to share with Eugene the victory over the French and Bavarians at the Battle of Blenheim (Höchstädt) in August 1704. The military and political shape of Europe changed forever that day, and the two comrades continued to work in close harmony throughout the hard years of campaigning that led to the weary peace achieved at the Treaties of Utrecht, Rastadt and Baden in 1713 and 1714. Although arguing his point from a position of relative weakness, Eugene's persuasive participation in the complex negotiations to bring about this long-overdue peace was significant, and widely acknowledged.

Eugene was a prince in his own right, being a member of the junior branch of the ruling noble house of Savoy, with a natural, perhaps almost brash, self-confidence that stood him in good stead through long years of demanding service to three successive Habsburg emperors. Perhaps understandably it is his famous partnership with Marlborough for which he is best known in

Western Europe, and particularly so to the British reader, but this is to see only half of the picture. Eugene's daring march to Turin in the high summer of 1706, moving unchecked around the flank of a large French army to go to the relief of his beleaguered cousin, Duke Victor-Amadeus II of Savoy, must rank at least with Marlborough's famous march to the Danube, and yet then the duke's opponents had largely been in the dark as to his real intentions. Not so with Eugene, as his opponent, that veteran the Duc de Vendôme, was aware of his goal, and yet failed utterly to prevent what stands as an almost unique achievement. Demanding campaigns against stubbornly resilient France lay ahead, and resurgent Ottoman power on the wide grassy plains and marshy wastelands of south-eastern Europe would in time have to be confronted again. There, in unforgiving terrain for large-scale military operations and facing formidable opponents, Eugene achieved major victories on an astonishing scale, such as those at Peterwardein in 1716 and the capture of Belgrade in the following year. As with Zenta, Blenheim and Turin, these successes were regarded as simply the wonders of the age and Eugene pre-eminent amongst the military commanders of the day. He drove his men hard, and often recklessly drove himself, but while demanding much and forgiving little, the affection and trust felt by his shabby and ill-equipped soldiers for their strange, unimpressively stooped and singular commander enabled them repeatedly to achieve great things against daunting odds.

Lying like a shadow over Eugene's whole career was the chronic inability of the treasury in Vienna, the *Hofkammer*, to properly fund the army as the Austrian empire grew. Despite such a handicap, over an active military life spanning almost 53 years Eugene's military talents at both a strategic and a tactical level were amply and repeatedly demonstrated. His eye for ground, a sense of what his opponents might attempt, and his driving, sweeping energy, were all remarkable, and no contemporary was regarded as fully his equal. If age and ill-health at last took their toll and his powers in the field and his influence at court faltered, it was still understood that what military success Vienna enjoyed could largely be attributed to his efforts. In that sense he had proved to be a true warlord for the House of Habsburg, and amply worthy of his salt. That was not all, for Eugene's achievements in the diplomatic field were considerable, if less dramatic than those in battle, and he could be both formidable and persuasive in negotiation, and established an effective intelligence-gathering system throughout the courts and chancelleries of Europe. The advice he tendered to Leopold I, and subsequently to his sons Joseph I and then Charles VI, was well-judged, but often not heeded as being out of tune with the views of narrow and naturally conservative factions at the Imperial court, while it should be acknowledged that much of what he proposed was simply not achievable given the persistently threadbare state of finances in Vienna.

Eugene was well rewarded and became a very wealthy man, an avid collector and notable patron of the arts, amassing a huge library, a private menagerie and a collection of pictures and *objet d'art* at his various palaces, most particularly the magnificent Belvedere and Winterhof in Vienna. A lifelong bachelor, with persistent rumours as to his private life that accompany such a single state, Eugene was nonetheless fond of agreeable female company, but cared little to provide details of such liaisons for the edification of those who wished to gossip about him. Intriguingly, while fiercely protective in life of his reputation, in death Eugene appeared to care little for his legacy, having nurtured hardly any fresh talent to follow his lead in command of the army. There were amongst his private papers no diaries, no journals, no 'reveries' or idle thoughts, no testament, will, or indeed gifts of money, pensions or bequests for friends and long-time servants, or any directions as to what should be done with his huge art collection and library. In this curious way, it seemed that he had little interest in things he could no longer use and enjoy.

It is worth mentioning that Eugene was never that at ease in using the German language, his preferred means of expression being French. He was born and raised in Paris of course, with a noble Savoyard father serving in the king's army, and a devastatingly beautiful but scandalously meddling mother who hailed from Italy. Italian he knew and some Latin, of course, and he also had some Spanish, but spoke little English. His letters were invariably written in French, and as this was the *lingua franca* (no pun intended) in the polyglot armies of the time, this was perhaps no great handicap. Still, the relative lack of fluency in German might explain to some degree the difficulties Eugene had in dealing with the complex and devious intrigues in Vienna, although to make too much of this would be a mistake, as both French and Italian were much in favour at the Imperial court. More tellingly, perhaps, the elegant and subtle skills of the nimble courtier were not his, and although he could be charming and gregarious, he was also bluntly impatient, bordering on the rude, and would not easily dissemble, cajole and flatter as well as others who played this game more astutely. Like many great men he did not suffer fools gladly, and made this plain, but this was not the way to make friends, enlist supporters and establish alliances. As a consequence, when his opponents in Vienna were in the ascendant he would easily slip out of favour with the emperor of the day, although such estrangement never lasted long, as his talents were too great to lie idle.

That Eugene achieved so much in the widest sense, despite all this, and in the face of entrenched hostile interests and open self-seeking at court, says much for his energy and abilities. This was a dangerous and shifting time in the politics of Europe, and it is appropriate to notice that he always saw his sword as devoted to the service of the Habsburgs, to whom he had sworn allegiance, rather than of Austria. When in 1736, long acknowledged as the pre-eminent Great Captain of the age, Eugene died and left the scene, a gap appeared that could not be filled. The fortunes of Vienna flagged thereafter, as it was found that no-one of his merit, brilliance and stature was at hand to step forward and take up the reins that he had held so long and so well, as the greatest servant that the House of Habsburg would ever have. Lesser men lost no time in bungling renewed conflict in Hungary against the Ottomans, and not until the talents of Field Marshal Maximilian von Browne in the service of Emperor Charles VI's daughter Maria-Theresa in the 1740s and 1750s, would Eugene's like be seen again in Austria, and even then the comparison appears to be rather pale.

Like Marlborough, Eugene left no memoirs, although a number of entertaining works so described are available, but these are really more accounts of his reminiscences, recalled and retold with varying degrees of veracity by others, and accordingly have to be treated with caution. Still, they relate to what did indeed happen, and have a value as such in telling a story. Nonetheless, it is apparent that for all the histories of his life and campaigns, various biographies, the copious official papers in the Austrian *Kriegarkiv*, the continued interest in this most unusual soldier and the almost unequalled reputation as a great commander that he enjoys, Eugene remains something of an enigma. Sir Winston Churchill lamented in the 1930s that there was no adequate biography of him in English, although Malleson and MacMunn had valiantly tried, and Henderson and McKay also addressed this lack in the 1960s and 1970s, but these later works do not concentrate, as much as one would perhaps wish, on the vital military sphere. It is this gap that I have tried to address with this book, looking to 'murmur tales of iron wars', with an account which largely concentrates on Eugene's epic career as a commander and campaigner, within the wider political setting of a rapidly-expanding Austrian Empire. An extraordinary man, whether on the battlefield or in the council chamber, in almost equal measure gallant, courageous, generous and warm, but also hard, unforgiving, tactless and as flawed as the next, we glimpse Eugene as a figure standing almost in the shadows, but undeniably a great 'Feldherr', the true master of the field.

Chronology of the Life of Eugene

1663   Born in Paris at the Hotel de Soissons
1673   His father, the Duc de Soissons, dies
1683   Takes service with Emperor Leopold. At the Ottoman siege of Vienna
1686   With the Duke of Lorraine at the capture of Buda
1687   Present at the Battle of Berg Harsan (2nd Mohacs). The Hungarian throne made hereditary for the House of Habsburg
1688   Serves under the Elector of Bavaria at the capture of Belgrade
1689   Wounded at the siege of Mainz
1690   Campaigns in Italy with his cousin, Duke Victor-Amadeus II of Savoy
1697   Victorious against the Ottomans at the Battle of Zenta
1699   Treaty (Peace) of Carlowitz between the Ottomans and Austria, Poland, Venice and Russia
1700   Death of King Carlos II of Spain. Outbreak of the Great Northern War
1701   In command of Austrian forces in northern Italy
1702   Formal outbreak of the War of the Spanish Succession
1703   President of the Imperial War Council in Vienna. Hungarian revolt begins
1704   With Marlborough at the victory of Blenheim (Höchstädt) in Bavaria
1705   Commands in Italy at Battle of Cassano. Death of Emperor Leopold
1706   Triumphant at the lifting the siege of Turin. Made Viceroy of Milan
1707   At the siege of Toulon with Victor-Amadeus.
1708   With Marlborough at the victory of Oudenarde and the siege of Lille. Mother dies
1709   Successful with Marlborough at Tournai, Malplaquet and Mons. Charles XII of Sweden defeated at Poltava
1710   Eugene's political opponent, Prince Salm, retires from court in Vienna
1711   Death of Emperor Joseph I. Marlborough dismissed by Queen Anne
1712   Eugene in London. Defeated at Denain by Marshal Villars.
1713   Treaty of Utrecht. Pragmatic Sanction issued by Emperor Charles VI
1714   Treaties of Rastadt and Baden agreed. Death of Queen Anne
1715   Death of Louis XIV. Duc d'Orleans becomes Regent of France
1716   Eugene appointed Governor-General of the Austrian (Southern) Netherlands. Victorious at Peterwardein on the Danube
1717   Captures Belgrade from the Ottomans. Spain attacks Sardinia

1718   Peace of Passorowitz confirms Austrian gains in the east. Treaty of
       Quadruple Alliance formed between Great Britain, France and Austria
1719   Treaty between Austria, Hanover, Prussia and Saxony
1720   Treaty of Madrid agreed between Spain and Austria. Charles VI
       abandons his claim to the Spanish throne.
1721   Death of Charles XII and end of the Great Northern War
1723   Ostend Trading Company formed
1724   Eugene resigns as Governor-General of the Austrian Netherlands
1725   First Treaty of Vienna between Austria and Spain
1726   Treaty agreed between Austria and Russia
1729   Spain agrees Treaty of Seville with Great Britain and France
1731   Second Treaty of Vienna between Austria and Great Britain
1733   Outbreak of the War of the Polish Succession.
1734   Eugene commands the Imperial forces on the Rhine
1734   End of the War of the Polish Succession
1736   Archduchess Maria-Theresa marries Duke Francis-Stephen of Lorraine.
       Eugene dies in Vienna
1737   Renewed war with the Ottomans, with Belgrade subsequently
       lost by Austria
1740   Emperor Charles dies. Maria-Theresa looks to succeed to the
       Imperial throne

Note on Terminology, Nomenclature and Dating

The prince is variously referred to as Eugene or Eugen, the latter being the usual German rendering of his name; his letters were usually signed off as 'Eugen von Savoyen' or 'Eugene de Savoie'. I have chosen to use Eugene, as being most commonly found in English, although Henderson chose Eugen. Where it seemed appropriate, I have occasionally used the term 'the prince' as he moved through a tangled European scene sprinkled with other princes large and small, dukes, margraves, barons and counts.

Looming large in that scene was the Holy Roman Empire, a largely German body and quite different from the Habsburg (or Austrian) Empire, although to a degree entwined. The Habsburgs were the hereditary rulers of the Austrian Empire, but only by long custom leaders of the Holy Roman Empire, and the 'emperor' had to be elected by the relevant constituent parties, all of whom had their own ambitions to further. Therefore, references in the text to 'Imperial' forces or troops can be confusing, but refer to those of the Holy Roman Empire when operating in the West, but of the Habsburg/Austrian Empire when operating (with the assistance of allies, most often German), at the command of Vienna in Italy and Hungary. See the Appendix for more details on this complex puzzle.

Many accounts of the campaigns in Hungary and along the Danube refer to Vienna's adversaries as being the Turks, but I have chosen to employ the term 'Ottomans', the 'Ottoman Empire', and occasionally the 'Sublime Porte' (high-gate – a title commonly used to describe the inner court in Constantinople at the time). Many of the sultan's most active and trusted servants and subjects were not 'Turks' from Anatolia, but hailed from the Balkans and south-eastern Europe, and the Sublime Porte was often more interested in taxpayers and capable soldiers than converts.

Where it seemed appropriate, I have corrected to modern usage, sensitively it is hoped, some of the curious and inconsistent spelling and grammar in contemporary quotes, and where additional detail seemed to be useful this is given in [brackets]. The spelling of place names in Eastern Europe varies widely, even today, but I have largely followed modern practice when these are given in English, although some occasional inconsistency may still be noted. The Gregorian Calendar (New Style) at this time was in use in most of continental Europe, and this was ten days in advance of the Julian Calendar (Old Style) still used in Great Britain (eleven days from 1700 onwards). As almost all the events described here took place on the continent, New Style has been used throughout, unless indicated otherwise.

Chapter 1

A Little Priest – Eugene and Louis XIV

Eugene-François was born in the Hotel Soissons in Paris on 18 October 1663, the youngest boy amongst seven children. His father was Eugene-Maurice Prince of Savoy-Carignan and Comte de Soissons, so the boy was of noble stock, with paternal great-grandparents that included Duke Emanuel of Savoy, and Catalina, the youngest daughter of King Philip II of Spain. His Italian-born mother, Olympia née Mancini, was the niece of the young Louis XIV's chief minister Cardinal Jules Mazarin who in 1647 had introduced her and her two lively sisters, Marie and Laura, as impecunious but glitteringly attractive young women to the delights of the French court. 'See those little girls,' one courtier wrote rather cynically, 'who are now not rich; they will soon have fine chateaux, good incomes, splendid jewels, beautiful silver services, and perhaps great dignities.'[1] Olympia, devastatingly good-looking in the dark-eyed Italian style and utterly charming when she chose to be, became something of a brittle force at court, as did Marie who even briefly had aspirations of marriage with the king, before his mother and the cardinal put a stop to things: 'Proof of [Queen] Anne's and Mazarine's [*sic*] mastery.'[2]

Olympia was nicknamed 'The Snipe', avidly fond of malicious gossip, a game played widely in Versailles and Fontainebleau, but often indulged in overly freely, and the Mancini girls' heady influence at court waned after a while. In 1654 Marie was married to the Italian Count Colonna, and three years later Mazarin found a good and prudent match for Olympia, in the form of the Comte de Soissons, a well-regarded soldier who had fought for the Crown in the civil war widely known as the Second Fronde, and been entrusted with delicate diplomatic missions abroad.[3] His main passion was hunting and the chase, when not on campaign with his regiment, and he was complacent and polite enough not to worry too greatly what his lively young wife was doing when he was away from home, and in this period that was not unusual. In time, though, Olympia's liking for gossip became too much, and in March 1665 she and her husband were instructed to leave the court and go to their estates in the country and live quietly. They were soon allowed to return, together with the outward appearance of matrimonial harmony, and Olympia once more became a centre of revelry, amusement and entertainment, but early in 1673 Soissons died unexpectedly while travelling to resume campaigning under Marshal Turenne. His widow then very foolishly picked a quarrel with the king's latest favourite, Athenaïs the Marquise de Montespan, and was also in contact with Catherine Deshayes, known as 'La Voisin', who reputedly and notoriously traded in witchcraft and poison, and by that reckless association involved in intrigues of a very risky nature. 'Madame la Comtesse de Soissons,' wrote an acquaintance at court, 'asked if she [La Voisin] could win back for her a lover who had deserted her; this lover being *a great prince*.'[4] Talk of this kind was dangerous, for in the feverish atmosphere in Paris almost amounting to hysteria arising from the 'Affair of the Poisons', it might before long be suggested that Soissons, complacent though he was but still inconveniently in the way, had perhaps not died of natural causes after all.

Olympia had friends enough to be warned, and in January 1680 she ignored a summons to go for questioning, and found it best to travel to Brussels in the Spanish Netherlands, with the presence of mind to take with her all her jewels and money, having no intention of eking out a living in exile as a pauper. No attempt was made to impede her journey, which cannot have been inconspicuous for her coach was drawn by a team of eight horses with coachmen clad in her own livery, and the indications were that Louis XIV had enough fondness for her to just want her to go, and leave it at that. This flight was undoubtedly prudent, as Olympia had excited the dislike of some powerful people, amongst them the formidable Minister for War, François-Michel le Tellier, Marquis de Louvois, and of course de Montespan, and if remaining in France witnesses would perhaps have been found ready to swear that she had indeed poisoned her husband. While La Voisin and her alleged accomplices in crime were tortured and burned at the stake, the suspicions against Olympia were soon generally held to have been groundless, but she was not permitted to return to Paris, maintaining instead her *salon* in Brussels. In her absence, 16-year-old Eugene and his sisters, straightened for funds but lordly in genteel poverty, were entrusted to the care of their paternal French-born grandmother, Marie de Bourbon, Princess of Carignan.

Two of Eugene's brothers, Louis Julius, the Chevalier de Savoy, and Emanuel Philibert, the Comte de Dreux, had gone to take service with their second cousin Duke Victor-Amadeus II in Turin. The eldest boy, Thomas Louis, had already been appointed to be colonel of the prestigious Regiment de Soissons, but his career flagged, reputedly because Louis XIV had amorous designs on his wife, the beautiful Urania, who was admirably unresponsive to his approaches. Eugene, as the youngest son of minor nobility, and with something of a cloud hanging over the family courtesy of his mother's erratic behaviour, was inevitably destined for a career in either the Church or the army. His grandmother favoured the former, as apparently did the king, and for a time the young man wore a tonsure and was known, only part-jokingly, as the 'Abbé de Savoie' or the 'Little Abbé de Carignan'.[5] However, he became keenly interested in mathematics and was enthralled by reading of the exploits of the renowned Marshals of France, so that in 1683 he announced that the Church was not for him, and that he wished to become a soldier in the royal service. Marie de Bourbon was not impressed, but with little money to speak of, a career had to be found, and in February 1683 Eugene appealed directly to the king to be appointed to the command of a company in his army. He had enlisted the help of the raffish Prince Louis-Armand Conti, son-in-law of Louis XIV and a nephew of the great military commander Condé, but Eugene's slight boyish figure, with a stooped and almost frail physical build, failed to impress, and the request was brusquely refused. He characteristically did not take the refusal well, and showed it, but at the French court manners were everything, and the king afterwards recalled that 'The request was modest, but the applicant was not. Nobody ever ventured to stare me in the face so insolently, like an angry sparrow-hawk.'[6] Whether a less naïve Eugene would have been more successful had he shown a little more polish in making his request, or in dealing with the refusal, can never be known, but that the Minister for War so disliked his mother must have told against his prospects.

While this was unfolding, one of his brothers, Louis Julius, had gone to take command of a regiment of dragoons in the army of Emperor Leopold I of Austria and was killed at Petronell while fighting the Ottomans. News of his death reached Paris on 23 July 1683, and this seemed to act as a spur to action, too much of a coincidence otherwise, for three days later Eugene left Paris clandestinely in company with Conti, and the two took horses for the Rhine and the border with the patchwork lands of the Holy Roman Empire. Louis XIV was furious when he learned that they had absconded, but probably more so over his son-in-law rather than Eugene who seemed to be no great loss. The king's agents were soon in pursuit and overtook the pair in Frankfurt am Main, where Conti was persuaded to return to France, but Eugene refused to do so, and was allowed to go on his way. With expectations of the support of his cousin, Louis-Guillaume, Margrave of Baden (a nephew of Marie de Bourbon and already an established commander in the Imperial service), Eugene had firm hopes of a warm welcome in Vienna.

At Frankfurt, the two friends parted on good terms, and Conti gave Eugene a purse of gold coins and a valuable ring as a keepsake, which was just as well as he had little money of his own. The young adventurer was not further delayed and was greeted in early August by Louis-Guillaume in Passau, and introduced to his uncle, the highly influential Hermann of Baden, newly appointed President of the Imperial War Council. On 14 August 1683, the Spanish envoy to Vienna, Marquès Carlo-Emanuele de Bergomanero, who took a benevolent interest in the young fugitive, presented Eugene to Emperor Leopold, 'The most virtuous and pious monarch of his time', with the warm recommendation of his cousin as a promising young man.[7] Eugene had Habsburg blood, and was related to Victor-Amadeus of Savoy, with whom Leopold wished to form an alliance, and his mother's origins also helped, as many of the best commanders in Imperial service were Italian, all of which did the rather unimpressively slight young man no harm in the emperor's estimation, and the first steps had been taken on a precarious ladder leading to renown. Another officer had already been appointed to the command of

Eugene's deceased brother's regiment, and however much he may have wished it he could hardly have expected to receive such an appointment for himself, being both inexperienced and an unknown quantity. Still, his enthusiasm was clear, and Leopold was pleased to accept him as a volunteer to serve under the tutelage of Baden and he swore 'To devote all my strength, all my courage, and if need be, my last drop of blood, to the service of your Imperial Majesty'.[8] Eugene could prove himself in action, and any deficiency in knowledge and training would be soon put to rights without too great a risk. Should he fail, then not a great deal would have been lost and he could be packed off back to France to explain himself to Louis XIV. As it was, this moment was one of acute peril and distress for Austria and the House of Habsburg, for a turning point had just been reached outside the walls of Vienna. The Ottoman Empire was in expansionist mode, posing a potent threat almost without parallel in European history, and coincidentally offering bright opportunity for someone as active and ambitious as the young Eugene.

Chapter 2

Vienna – The Golden Apple

For generations the Ottoman rulers in Constantinople had expanded their dominion and influence progressively into the Balkans and south-eastern Europe. Often, but not always, this was deliberate policy, but there was little capability to fight two major wars simultaneously, and the sultans and their grand viziers were alert to tension with Sassafid Persia in the east, and to growing Muscovite pressure in the Caucasus. Nonetheless, in a form of mission creep, the ambitious activities of strong-willed local beys and governors, pursuing their own ambitions, obliged the Sublime Porte, with varying degrees of enthusiasm, to provide support for their ventures. The resulting repeated clashes were inevitable, with the powerful Hungarian, Serbian, Moldovian, and Wallachian princely houses, the Venetian Empire, and latterly the Habsburg Austrians, all with their own interest and ambitions. Stunning Ottoman successes, and occasional setbacks, were followed by intervals of uneasy peace, while the last big gains for the Ottomans, in establishing suzerainty over the principality of Transylvania, only came as late as the 1660s.

A formal 20-year treaty was in place between Vienna and Constantinople, the result of an unexpected Ottoman defeat in August 1664 at the Battle of Mogersdorf, near to St Gotthard on the river Rába, where the sultan's field commander had famously mistaken the long-haired volunteer French cavaliers for 'young girls', but this agreement for peace was due to be renewed or re-negotiated. The Ottomans complied with the agreed treaty terms, in the main, but crucially, for Austria, power politics were in play, and with Vienna's attention firmly drawn to the threat from Louis XIV's France in the West, the opportunistic activities of an aggressive 'war party' in Constantinople, led by Sultan Mehmet IV's ambitious grand vizier, reached a peak, with the chance to take advantage of this Austrian distraction.

Ottoman troops intervened in 1681, and again the next year, to assist revolt against Austrian rule and burdensome tax-gathering in those north-western parts of Hungary under the control of Vienna. At heart, there was a long-standing problem, linked to money, for the emperor: 'Given Leopold's inability to overcome administrative inefficiency and corruption, he was forced to rely on the extraction of more and higher taxes.'[1] Hungarian rebels, driven to seek sanctuary with local Ottoman governors, were tolerated, especially as their habit of raiding across the border as freebooting bands of Kuruks (Crusaders) was an expensive

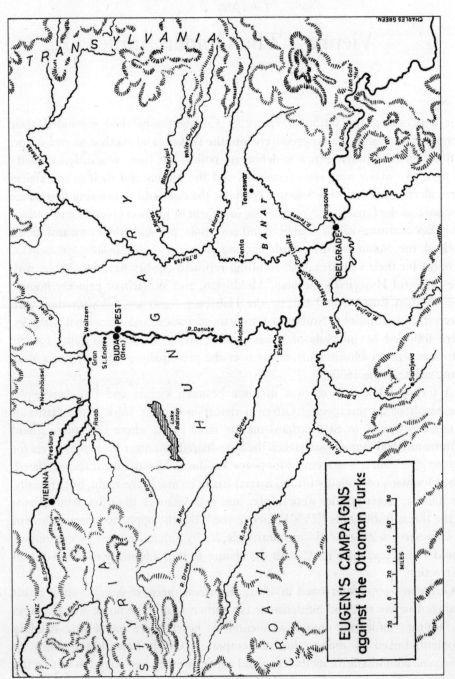

Map 1. Eugene's Campaigns against the Ottomans.

distraction for Vienna. Matters in Persia and the Caucasus were quiet for the time being, and this encouraged the sultan to be adventurous, when his grand vizier, 'Black' Kara Mustapha, an adopted member of the influential Kuprülü family, saw what seemed to be a fine opportunity to push a fresh campaign of conquest against Habsburg-held territory. A large and magnificently-equipped Ottoman army was reliably reported to be gathering around Adrianople, moving then on to Belgrade, with the 'Tugh', a five-horsetail war standard, hoisted aloft as a sure sign of impending operations.

The principal concern in Vienna remained that of the renewed threat from France, for Louis XIV was striving to gain more Spanish-held territory in the Low Countries, and might well turn his attention to the Rhine frontier and the more exposed German states of the Holy Roman Empire. Leopold and his ministers believed that the sultan could be bought off, and that taking gains obtained by negotiation, he would renew the 20-year-long peace treaty. This proved to be a severe misjudgement, and earnest efforts to avert renewed conflict by Austrian emissaries in Constantinople proved fruitless, even though significant territorial concessions were hinted at. French influence at the Sublime Porte was strong, as it suited Louis XIV very well to have Leopold's attention diverted to the East. One additional alarm that might have sounded in Vienna, but apparently did not, was the ratification of a treaty agreed in 1681 between Constantinople and the Muscovite tsar, so that the borders of the sultan's domains on the river Dneiper, the Crimea and the Caucasus would remain untroubled for the foreseeable future. The Tartar irregular cavalry that the Ottomans found so terrifyingly useful would, accordingly, be available to go on campaign. However, Leopold was neither unaware of the growing threat, nor inactive, and a partial counterbalance was achieved with the timely agreement for a treaty of alliance between Austria and Poland, in the event of an Ottoman attack.

The Ottoman army moved in grand array northwards along the line of the Danube, with Sultan Mehmet at the head. He and his huge retinue soon took their leave, for the role of field commander was held by Kara Mustapha, a man of great experience and ruthless skill, who had recently campaigned brilliantly against the Venetians in the Morea region in Greece. While accounts of the numbers the grand vizier had under his command vary, it was clear that it was a formidable force, with informed opinion in Vienna estimating a solid core of almost 40,000 regular troops.[2] These comprised a strong corps of professional foot soldiers, the renowned Janissaries, 'Seasoned warriors fully armed and accoutred ... marching in close formation and brandishing their weapons',[3] who together with superbly mounted regular cavalry regiments, the Sipahis, were the backbone of the army: 'The best of the Ottomans, but there were never enough of them.'[4] There was also a well-equipped and highly-trained corps of artillery, and a substantial body of skilled engineers, many of whose officers were veterans recruited from Western Europe. The immensely valuable pontoon bridging train, which ensured the army's mobility when encountering the wide and hard-to-ford rivers and marshes of the Danubian Basin, also had its own close escort to ensure its security.

The regular Janissaries and Sipahi cavalry were fine but expensive, and relatively few in number with concurrent garrison duties elsewhere in the Ottoman Empire as part of their remit, so that not all were available to go on campaign at any one time. Accordingly, much reliance was placed upon provincial troops, the Timariots, whose land-holding tenure depended both upon tax-gathering ability and local policing, with the occasional provision of military service to the sultan proportionate to the size of their estates. Then there were the irregular horsemen from the plains of Wallachia, Moldovia and Transylvania, and the wild Tartars. With these skilful riders working a like deadly cloud ahead of the main force, spreading confusion and terror, the striking power of Ottoman armies was notable, but it was also true that while such irregulars performed well when raiding and in the headlong attack, their best days were past. They proved to be irresolute when stoutly confronted, and it was noted that 'Gone were the days when the Ottoman cavalry, surging through the passes and thundering across the plains of south-east Europe, could demolish the chivalry of the nations'.[5] The appearance of great Ottoman war strength could be misleading, and has misled many since, as much depended upon early success leading to further success, while one keen observer who watched the grand vizier's army leave Belgrade that fateful summer reckoned rather scornfully that he could count on only 20,000 good fighting men.[6] Leaving to one side the ferocious Tartars and their like, the regular Ottoman regiments and their Timariot comrades were supported as they approached Vienna by some 40,000 locally-raised levies brought to the field by the pashas and the beyerbeys (military governors), who owed military service to the sultan. Once more, the principal strength of these troops was in the attack, but they were patchily trained and often ill-equipped, and noted for wavering when things were not going well. 'The musketeers of the western infantry, firing in line [four deep], were not easily thrown into the panic which the "Turkish Fury" found it fairly easy to engender in earlier days.'[7]

So, a significant part of the grand vizier's army comprised locally-raised troops, with equipment, loyalty and discipline of doubtful quality, and some Ottoman commanders were even reluctant to trust their Christian levies with firearms at all, although in most cases they were as reliable as their Muslim neighbours in battle. Still, Colonel Jean-Martin De La Colonie, who encountered them on many fields, remembered that 'Their troops are a mob collected from the populations of the Grand Seigneur [sultan], which his Viceroys or Governors of the various provinces are required to gather'.[8] Although the logistical administration of Ottoman armies was admirable, the command and control arrangements for the locally-raised troops was ill-defined, with their leaders, men akin to potentates in their own region, having a tendency to go their own way to the detriment of overall efficiency. 'The state had encouraged provincial governors to enrol militias to keep order, but they were tempted to use them to defy the [Sublime] Porte . . . The Porte winked at this, for without these levies it might have no army.'[9] Still, the pace that was set in 1683 was impressive, for 'Ottoman armies moved like tides',[10] and it must have seemed to nervous observers that a colourful yet immensely threatening caravanserai was on the approaches to central Europe. However, the often-repeated claims of an overwhelmingly vast host threatening Vienna have to be treated with caution, as the resources of the Ottoman Empire were finite, and other potential theatres of war, although quiet for the moment, could not be entirely ignored, and the 'Ottoman state was far from being an armed camp'.[11]

Whatever the true numbers, on 29 June 1683, after 19 years of comparative peace, the Ottoman army entered Habsburg territory, soon joined by troops under the sultan's Transylvanian vassal, Prince Michael Apafi. With the open co-operation of the Hungarian rebel leader Imre Thököly, the key fortress of Györ on the river Rába was reached two days later, and Kara Mustapha demanded the submission of the Imperial garrison. This, in effect, constituted a formal declaration of war as the summons was bound to be refused, and Vienna's misjudgement of this Ottoman determination to press forward almost proved fatal to Leopold and the fortunes of the House of Habsburg on the Danube. The appointed Imperial commander, Duke Charles IV of Lorraine and Bar, had inspected the defences of Györ in May and been satisfied, but his own army was only slowly gathering, and all but minor decisions had to be referred to the Imperial War Council in Vienna, where Hermann of Baden was being obstructive. Lorraine proposed to move to threaten an Ottoman-held fortress, perhaps either Neuhäusel or Esztergom, but time was lost in consultation, and when he did advance against Neuhäusel, the operation miscarried. In the meantime, the Ottomans continued on their way towards Vienna, ignoring secondary garrisons and outposts, so that Lorraine had to conform and fall back, covered by a rearguard under the command of the Margrave of Baden.

By the end of June Vienna was under imminent threat, and the night sky was lit by the glare of burning villages creeping ever closer to the city. On 7 July, the Ottomans attacked Lorraine's forces near to Schloss Petronell some 25 miles from the city, and were only held after severe fighting, during which Prince Eugene's older brother, Julius Louis, was mortally wounded. Despite this local success, Kara Mustapha's advance could not be halted, and the duke withdrew to a fresh position at Leopoldstadt and the adjacent islands on the Danube. Lacking support, he then fell back to Jedlesee only three miles from the defensive walls. Leopold, his pregnant wife and the entire court had in the meantime gone to Passau, 175 miles to the west, to direct the campaign from the relative safety of that town. This move brought a degree of scorn on to the emperor's head, 'Cursed, abused and even damned',[12] having encouraged everyone to stand firm before making off himself. However, with no pretensions to be a great field commander, his presence would have been an unhelpful distraction for the 10,000 troops and militia under Count Ernst Rüdiger von Starhemberg, the commander of the garrison left to hold Vienna.

The city was invested and under a close siege by 14 July, but the Duke of Lorraine moved to the north bank of the Danube, first to Krems, and then reached out to attack and rout Thököly's Hungarians who were on the point of seizing Pressburg. Lorraine then moved back to Stammersdorf where he mauled an Ottoman detachment under the command of the Pasha of Grosswardein. In the meantime, disease and hunger were taking hold in the besieged city, with a citizenry fearful of what would happen next. Von Starhemberg smuggled out a message to Lorraine pleading for relief, but this letter fell into the hands of Kara Mustapha. With sardonic humour he sent his own reply, calling on the garrison to submit on good terms, but 'If the people of Vienna doubt the Grand Vizier's clemency they will soon experience the direct impact of his divine wrath'.[13] However, he was reluctant to incur the heavy casualties that an outright assault would entail, and the siege operations proceeded at a deliberate pace, although a number of probing attacks, together with highly skilful sapping and mining, were made on the outer defences.

The grand vizier had miscalculated, however, both in assessing the stubborn nature of the garrison under von Starhemberg's able command, and the resourcefulness of the princes of central Europe, so often at loggerheads with each other, when roused and faced with this kind of external threat. Reinforcements from the various parts of the Holy Roman Empire arrived on the Danube, piece by piece, and on 30 August Lorraine effected a junction near to Ober-Hollabrun on the Tullnerfeld with a relieving army, in part commanded by King John Sobieski of Poland. The forces necessary to lift the siege of Vienna were at last at hand, with troops from Bavaria, Saxony, Franconia and Hanover taking the field alongside numerous individual adventurers and volunteers (including a number of French officers). Time was pressing, as the Ottoman miners had now breached the defensive walls closest to the Hofburg Palace, and furious and gallantly-pressed assaults there were only beaten off by von Starhenberg's rapidly dwindling garrison with the greatest difficulty.

On Sunday, 12 September 1683, the attack was launched by the combined forces of Lorraine and Sobieski, now estimated at 85,000 strong.[14] General Jablonowski brought forward the Poles on the right of the advancing army, the Prince of Waldeck led the Imperial Franconian and Bavarian troops in the centre, while Lorraine rode with the Saxons and Austrians on the left, hard against the banks of the Danube. The advance of the Poles was delayed by difficult ground, and progress was only made after a laborious reconnaissance in which Eugene took part.[15] Nonetheless, the vigour with which the attack was eventually made was remarkable, and Eugene rode with Baden and his cavalry. Kara Mustapha was hardly unaware of this approach, and yet his besieging army, deployed as it was on low ground between the city walls and the Kahlenberg feature, was thrown into confusion. The grand vizier only paused long enough to have the throat of his favourite concubine slit, rather than that she should fall into enemy hands, before riding away with his cavalry. Amongst the haul of prisoners, weapons, guns, standards, banners, tentage, campaign materiel, draught animals and camels, pontoon bridging train and treasure-chest that the Austrians and their allies seized in the abandoned camp was a stock of fine coffee. The happy discovery led over time to Vienna's well-deserved reputation for fine cafes and coffee houses (the first such establishment, stirringly named 'The Blue Bottle', was opened by a Polish soldier, a veteran of the siege). Meanwhile, having attempted without success to pass the blame for the defeat on to his subordinate commanders, several of whom he had executed including the venerable governor of Ofen (Buda), the grand vizier was strangled with a silk scarf in Belgrade on 25 December. 'Am I to die?', he asked his body servant. 'It must be so,' 'So be it.'[16]

On 7 October, during the pursuit of the Ottoman army, the Polish cavalry were roughly handled at Párkány on the left bank of the Danube, opposite to Gran, but two days later Baden led a successful assault on the place, and Eugene again took an active part. With the onset of poor weather, Sobieski took his cavalry back to Poland, and the campaign for the year, which had seen such an astonishing outcome for the future of Europe, came to a close. Eugene, as a youthful volunteer, clearly played a minor role in the huge drama that was the deliverance of Vienna, but clad in the easily-recognized russet-brown coat and dark cuirass that would become his trademark, his conduct in the fighting over the Kahlenberg feature to the Burgtor on 12 September, where he was lightly wounded by an arrow through the hand, was noticed. The young adventurer was fortunate to have taken part in the campaign, to be formally congratulated by Lorraine for his valour and presented with the gift of a pair of golden spurs, brought to the notice of the emperor, and having plainly done well.

On 14 December, the appropriate tangible reward came when Eugene was appointed to the command of the Kufstein Dragoons, a regiment then in Gran but raised in the Tyrol, his predecessor having been killed in the fighting outside the walls of Vienna; the commission was dated and signed by Leopold while he was in Linz, and may still be seen in the Ost-Akriegsarkiv in Vienna. Such an appointment, with the rank of colonel, marked the real start of the prince's progress as a military commander, certainly a good step for one so young, and could prove lucrative with the perquisites and allowances that came with the role assessed, it was said, to be equal to that of a margravate in the Empire. Still, for the time being Eugene was hard pressed to afford the equipment, horses, servants and baggage necessary for a regimental commander, even one of such middling rank, obliged to sell the ring given to him by the Prince of Conti at their parting in Passau, and to rely upon loans and gifts of money from Baden to make ends meet.

After such defeat for the Ottomans before Vienna, a robust advance in 1684 by the Austrians and their allies might have cleared the Hungarian border provinces. This was particularly so as Constantinople was increasingly concerned with tensions on the border with both the Persians and the Venetians in the Adriatic, neither of which would have counted for too much had the campaign against

Vienna gone otherwise than it did. In March 1684, with the encouragement of Pope Innocent XI, an alliance was formed between Austria, Poland and Venice, known as The Holy League, to drive the Ottomans back in south-eastern Europe and the Balkans. For the time being, Leopold's attention could safely be devoted to the east, as the recently concluded Treaty of Ratisbon (Regensburg) acknowledged territorial gains made by Louis XIV, with peace coming to the Rhine frontier. Consequently, in June that year, the Duke of Lorraine made a determined advance upon Buda.

This apparently late start to the campaign was unavoidable, as the spring meltwaters of the Danube and adjacent tributaries had to subside to allow armies to operate effectively unhampered by the wide inundated floodplains and extensive muddy riverbank marshes common at the time. The ability of the armies to bridge rapidly and effectively was crucial, hence the vital importance of the pontoon bridging train to any commander. Despite a new setback at Gran, where General Hallwyl was roughly handled and Baden had to hurry to his support, Lorraine took Visograd and defeated an Ottoman force at Waitzen, and then moved to invest Buda itself. The Ottomans mounted a spirited attack at Szente Endre, but were repulsed, and it was a well-judged charge led by Eugene with his dragoons that helped to seal the success that day. Once again, his aggressive valour, bravery and apparently natural skill on the battlefield was noted with approval.

The city of Buda, on the right bank of the Danube, with the much smaller town of Pest on the far shore, had been in Ottoman hands since 1541 and as their military headquarters in Hungary would be stoutly defended. The siege of the place was begun on 14 July with the digging of the trenches, while an attempt by a relieving force to disrupt the works was beaten off eight days later, with Eugene's conduct commended in Lorraine's report of the affair to Vienna. The siege operations were not well handled, however. Logistical support was poor and the army was under-strength, with supply lines that were harried by fast-moving Ottoman horsemen. Things dragged on in foul weather in the face of a tough resistance by the well-supplied garrison, until the arrival of the chill months of winter when the siege was abandoned and the troops sent off to their comfortless billets.

Eugene took the opportunity of the necessary lull in activity to visit his cousin in Turin early in 1685, and managed to secure further loans to finance the recruiting and re-equipping of his regiment. In the summer the campaign was renewed with vigour, and Lorraine was successful in an action at Gran on 16 August 1685, where Eugene's dragoons were again hotly engaged. Count Aeneas Caprara stormed the Ottoman outpost at Neuhäusel on the river Nitra, some 76 miles from Vienna, three days later and in this way, the path towards Buda was properly cleared. Eugene once more attracted favourable attention for his skill in handling cavalry, and Baden continued his interest in his protégé, taking the opportunity to recommend him once more to Leopold, with the warm congratulatory words, 'Sire, this young man will with time occupy the place of those whom the world regards as great leaders of armies.'[17] Remarkably, but almost entirely due to his own efforts (assisted by the benevolent interest of his cousin, of course), Eugene was made a major-general in the Austrian service at the end of 1685, while aged only 22. However, to suggest that he was particularly influential in these campaigns would clearly be mistaken as he was still a relatively junior officer, although establishing a nicely growing reputation.

Once again, preparations for the next campaign got off rather slowly, and only in the third week of June 1686 had the meltwaters subsided enough for Buda to be properly invested once more. Austrian siege techniques were gradually improving, and the works were opened before the defences, with the first of the parallel trenches being dug next to an old bath-house. Lorraine led the covering army, while the Elector of Bavaria, Max-Emmanuel Wittelsbach, commanded the siege operations themselves, the main attack going in through the suburb which became known as Raizenstadt, between the Blocksberg and Speissberg features. A spirited sortie by the garrison was driven back by troops led by Eugene, who impetuously followed them into a part of the city itself, where his men got badly cut up for their trouble, the Ottoman garrison, under the energetic command of Abdi Ali Pasha, putting up a fine defence. They threw back a major assault on 27 July, and another on 3 August; on both occasions losses were severe, with Eugene twice lightly wounded and his horses killed.

On 14 August, an attempt was made to raise the siege by the Ottoman field army commanded by Grand Vizier Sari Suleiman Pasha, and only driven off after stiff fighting. Eugene was selected by Lorraine to take the news of this fresh success to Vienna. He lingered in the city just one day, and returned to the army in time to be present when Buda fell to assault on 2 September 1686, 'It was over by 5 o'clock in the afternoon',[18] when Abdi Ali Pasha, a most able soldier who had held out for an admirable 78 days, was killed scimitar in hand along with most of his loyal garrison. An enthusiastic sack of the city then took place, with the massacre of many of the inhabitants, and Eugene was amongst those officers unable or unwilling to restrain the soldiers. Brutal as this was, it was nonetheless the custom when a fortress would not submit and had to be stormed with all the attendant cost. Baden was sent with cavalry and dragoons to follow the grand vizier as he withdrew, and Eugene accompanied his cousin southwards to the river Drava. Making the most of the disarray amongst their opponents, the towns of Simontornya, Caleza, Funfkirken, Sziklos and Kaposvar were swiftly taken by the margrave, and the famous bridge at Esseg (Osijeck) burned. Enough had been done, the Austrians and their allies were becoming overstretched, the countryside was ravaged and bare of supplies, and the campaign for the year came to a close. One important consequence was that the Transylvanian Diet, which had attempted to remain neutral, was induced to acknowledge Habsburg overlordship and accept Austrian garrisons, and to provide funds to help finance Vienna's forces in the field. To further crown the success that summer, Imre Thököly's Hungarians were routed by the Neapolitan Count Antonio Caraffa, so that the rebel leader fled to seek Ottoman protection in Belgrade.

With campaigning for the year at an end, Eugene went with Max-Emmanuel and other officers to Venice, where a tour of the huge arsenal was undertaken to watch cannon being forged, and the naval dockyard to see warships being launched, together with a mock sea battle. The notoriously dissolute and riotous Venetian carnival was also in progress, but apparently held out little attraction for the ambitious young soldier. Eugene was no prude, but he was intent on making his way in a determined fashion in a still most uncertain world, albeit at the expense of other amusements. All that he had achieved might yet turn to dust, and tiring rather quickly of the delights offered by the city, he hurried back to Vienna to rejoin the army, and take up his regimental command once again.

The fresh campaign in 1687 proceeded well enough at first for Lorraine, despite tension with both Baden and Max-Emmanuel over who had authority, as the two younger men felt that the duke was too cautious. The Ottoman field army, still commanded by Grand Vizier Sari Suleiman Pasha, had taken up a position on the Danube below Buda near to Mohács, the site of the great Ottoman victory over the Hungarian princes in 1526. On 12 August, the Battle of Berg Harzan (2nd Mohács) was fought. Lorraine deftly deployed his army to invite an attack, while holding a strong force ready to make a counter move once the energy of his opponents was spent. This tactic worked well: the pasha's attacks were valiant and full of vigour, but severely punished by well-controlled musketry, while the Ottoman cavalry was so hampered by wooded ground that many riders dismounted to close with their opponents on foot. The strongly entrenched Austrian position held firm, and at a carefully judged moment, squadrons of armoured cuirassiers swept forward onto the pasha's flanks, and the day was won. Eugene had command of a brigade of cavalry, and was amongst those who broke into the Ottoman camp to set up the Imperial eagle standard. Claude-Louis-Hector, Comte de Villars, and James Fitzjames, Duke of Berwick, both of whom as Marshals of France would meet him on battlefields in later years, were present on the day, and Villars remembered that he liked what he saw of Eugene, and that he had a lot of courage and common sense. This fresh Ottoman defeat was so severe that the grand vizier feared to face the anger of his troops, and fled to Constantinople armed with numerous plausible excuses, but this did not save him.

Sent once again to convey the glad news of victory to Leopold, Eugene was rewarded with a portrait miniature set in diamonds, together with the subsequent promotion to marshal lieutenant (approximately equivalent to lieutenant general). He returned to the army without delay, and although rivalry between the senior commanders hampered the campaign, matters were pressed forward and much of Slavonia between the Drava and Sava rivers occupied, while the Ottoman-held fortress of Erlau was invested and submitted to Count Caraffa in December.

The fortress of Munkács, the last remained place of importance in eastern Hungary, and which under Helena Zriny (redoubtable wife of the rebel leader, Imre Thököly) had once defied a three-year-long siege, was captured on 6 January 1688. Baden and Max-Emmanuel had in the meantime left the army, apparently resentful that their efforts were not sufficiently valued, and Eugene had the useful concomitant chance, with other aspiring middle-ranking commanders, to shine. King Carlos II of Spain sent word of his appointment to the prestigious Order of the Golden Fleece in recognition of his successes in recent campaigns, and the intricate emblem of that order is prominent on the breast in later portraits of the prince, secured on a golden chain thoughtfully provided by Victor-Amadeus. At the duke's suggestion, the pope also bestowed on Eugene the revenues of two wealthy abbeys in Piedmont, which certainly helped to alleviate his inconvenient shortage of ready funds. He even found time to visit his mother Olympia, who long harboured a wish that he should enter the service of Spain in the Low Countries, but the trip was not an unqualified success, and her coincidental plans for his advantageous marriage to a Spanish lady of good fortune came to nothing.

The Duke of Lorraine diplomatically claimed illness and gave up the command of the army, to avoid risking the loss of the large contingent of Bavarian troops who would follow Max-Emmanuel if he went back to Munich. The elector promptly resumed active campaigning with appropriate energy and drive, aiming to take Belgrade, 'The White Castle', regarded as the key to the lower Danube, an entry port for any army moving along the line of the river and a city in Ottoman hands since 1522 when Suleiman the Magnificent took the place. The level of the waters in the region having fallen sufficiently, on 28 July 1688 the Imperial army moved forward, and uncontested crossings of the Drava and Sava rivers were safely accomplished. The Ottomans had made little effort to impede the progress of their opponents, but the garrison in Belgrade was strengthened in good time and the suburbs flattened to allow better fields of fire against any attempt at a siege.

As the campaign gathered pace, Eugene was sent forward with an advance guard of six infantry battalions and his own dragoons, to take up a position to cut off the garrison from further reinforcement or ready relief. The city was properly invested on 10 August, and the heavy guns began their battering work five days later, with a bombardment that lasted for all of three weeks. Yegen Osman, the Ottoman commander, refused the offer of a huge bribe to give the city up, and on 5 September two breaches in the main defensive walls were deemed to be practical (that is, capable of being entered by a soldier walking unaided and with both hands on his musket), and a storm was attempted the following morning, with Max-Emmanuel leading his troops forward on foot. Once past the breach, an undetected secondary defensive line was met, and the attack slowed, until Count Heinrich von Starhemberg urged his troops onwards, and the defenders overwhelmed after bloody fighting with bayonet, sword and musket butt. In this final assault Eugene received a heavy scimitar cut across the forehead, cleanly splitting the visor of his helmet, but despite the wound and a spent musket ball strike just above the knee, he was able to fell his assailant before being taken to receive treatment. So severe was the injury that his life was at first despaired of and he had to be taken back to Vienna, so that he was not fully recovered until the following January. In the meantime, the garrison had prudently submitted as prisoners 'at discretion' rather than being offered good terms. The loss of Belgrade was a distinct further blow for the Ottomans, and their hold was lost on much of northern Bosnia, where 'Turken Louis' Baden in his martial prime conducted a skilful secondary campaign that summer and autumn, and roundly defeated the pasha of that region. Even Semendria with its massive fortifications, close to the pass known as the 'Iron Gates' on the border of Wallachia, was abandoned to the confident Austrian advance.

Eugene, although frustrated in convalescence, could look back and reflect with satisfaction on almost six years of active service fighting against the Ottomans. The young exile had undoubtedly done very well, being highly regarded by the emperor and many at his court in Vienna, having acquired an enviable reputation in the army as a hard fighter and dependable commander with natural and aggressive skill. He had also gained a great deal of valuable experience in coalition warfare, observing how such diverse and combative talents as Lorraine, Baden, Caraffa and Max-Emmanuel worked together, more or less in harmony, to gain a common goal. Significantly, amongst the tactical lessons learned had been the way in which the furious attacks of the Ottoman troops could be held and thrown back, as once their wild energy was spent, there seemed to be nothing left in the locker. Not that the fighting abilities of the sultan's soldiers had lessened: their courage was seldom in doubt, but the ability and tactics of their opponents had improved. At the heart of this was the value of the disciplined musketry of well-trained foot soldiers, added to the striking power of armoured cuirassiers, when operating under the hand of cool-headed commanders.

Late in 1688 Louis XIV sought once more to extend his own borders at the expense of his neighbours, using as a pretext a dispute over the Electoral-Archbishopric of Cologne, and renewed war in the West was the inevitable result. Eugene was amongst those who felt that the capture of Belgrade offered a timely chance to strike an agreement with the Sublime Porte, so that the fresh threat in the West could be addressed. He wrote to Victor-Amadeus in Turin on 28 November that 'Most people believe that we want to continue the two wars, although anyone with any sense who has the public good at heart is furious about it'.[19] In this he was perhaps for the first time, but certainly not the last, openly offering criticism of the emperor and his advisers, but being just one middle-ranking commander amongst many others, his views as yet carried little weight at court. With a stubbornness for which Leopold was well known, he decided on fighting two campaigns at the same time after all, and refused a promising request from Constantinople for a formal cessation of hostilities in Hungary. 'For reasons which to ordinary men were hard to understand, he resolved to fight the war with the [Sublime] Porte whilst he repelled the invasion of the French.'[20]

This was courting trouble, as finances in Vienna were wretched, and with multiple commitments weighing heavily on the *Hofkammer*, the treasury, Leopold could only belatedly despatch sufficient troops to the Palatinate in June 1689. There were, nonetheless, certain contrary attractions for what he did, as the Ottoman Empire was in something of a state of crisis, with Sultan Mehmet being deposed in the aftermath of the loss of both Buda and Belgrade, added to the defeat at Berg Harsan and the abandoning of Semendria. There was growing unrest in parts of Serbia, Wallachia and Moldovia, while Transylvania now openly acknowledged Vienna, so that the opportunities for Austria to gain additional territory in the East held a certain allure. To fight wars on two fronts with inadequate funds was plainly not ideal, but Victor-Amadeus of Savoy would be persuaded, partly as a result of a diplomatic mission to Turin entrusted to Eugene, to abandon his previous agreement with Louis XIV and ally himself to Austria, together with the Maritime Powers (Holland and England), Spain and Denmark. In this way the League of Augsburg, the remarkable Grand Alliance which in time would have to be re-forged to fight a war for the throne in Madrid, was brought into being.

With considerable effort, no fewer than four Imperial armies were mustered and equipped, after a fashion, to campaign in the summer of 1689. The Margrave of Baden commanded the troops still confronting the Ottomans in Hungary, while in the West the Duke of Lorraine was entrusted to recover Mainz from the French. The Elector of Brandenburg (who would soon be permitted to style himself 'King in Prussia') was with the army on the lower Rhine, with the task of driving the French out of the disputed Archbishopric of Cologne. Meanwhile, Max-Emmanuel led the Imperial forces on the upper Rhine, covering Franconia and Swabia, and Eugene served in this army. He must surely have reflected on the curious way that fate worked, in that some years after fleeing the court in Versailles, almost a refugee, he was now a commander of repute and facing French troops in the field for the first time. The elector soon left Count Aeneas Caprara to look after matters on the upper Rhine and took a detachment of his army to join in the operations to recover Mainz, where on 4 August Eugene was wounded once again, receiving a glancing musket ball strike to the head. He was fit enough, however, to take part in the storm of the covered way on 6 September, with the French troops submitting three days later. The garrison in Bonn were granted terms shortly afterwards, and the campaign for the year came to a close, so that Eugene was able to be present at the coronation in Frankfurt of the emperor's eldest son as King of the Romans. In consequence, the young Archduke Joseph could expect his almost automatic accession to the Imperial throne in due course.

To general regret, the Duke of Lorraine, regarded as the most capable of Leopold's senior field commanders, died in April 1690. It was now evident that the forces deployed by the emperor had not been strong enough everywhere, with the Ottomans recovering their balance in Hungary. A reconstituted army commanded by the new grand vizier, Surmeli Ai Pasha, dramatically recaptured both Semendria and Belgrade, and summoned the nobility of Transylvania to once again acknowledge the sultan as their overlord. What had been achieved on the Danube since the saving of Vienna appeared to be slipping away. Matters did seem brighter in northern Italy, when in July Victor-Amadeus confirmed his alliance with Vienna, and Eugene was placed in command of troops sent to campaign alongside his cousin in Piedmont. He had just 5,000 men, two cavalry regiments, two regiments of foot and his regiment of dragoons, and this was the start of a long association with Italy. The key fact was that Savoy-Piedmont offered strategic advantages for both Austria and France, so either power could use the duchy as a sallyport when moving to attack the other, and conversely if the region was dominated by an opponent, ready passage would be barred. At first Eugene's frank opinion of some of the troops with whom he was allied was less than complimentary, and – speaking of the Italian units recruited from the Spanish-ruled duchies of the Milanese and Lombardy – he wrote that 'Every day their one aim is to do nothing. They see difficulties in every proposal, and I doubt if there is a place in the whole of Piedmont which they could be sure of holding.'[21]

Eugene's opponent in Italy was General Nicholas Catinat, an able soldier who could be counted on to make few mistakes. On 17 August 1690, he marched to Saluzzo to threaten both the flank of the Savoyard army and their depots and magazines in the region. In response, the following day Victor-Amadeus took up a position at Staffarda beside the river Po, where the French commander threw his weight across difficult and marshy ground against the left of his opponent's army, and drove him from the field in great confusion with the loss of 4,000 men, eleven field guns and a huge quantity of stores. Eugene, slightly wounded again, did what he could to stem the rout, but almost none of his own troops were on the field and there was little that he could do. Catinat took advantage of the success to ravage the countryside around, before leaving garrisons in the principal towns of the region, and falling back within France with his army to find winter quarters. The fighting in the campaign had been spasmodic. Although the French had achieved a great deal, Eugene did manage in a sharp and bloody little encounter to overtake and scatter a French detachment that had been busy pillaging Rivoli. Many of those with whom he had to campaign were of a meeker stamp and not keen to take risks, and the prince was frustrated at this lack of vigour. Such an attitude prevented advantage being taken of any temporary numerical superiority enjoyed over the French, and this would become a recurring theme, but not everyone had his energy or thirst for success and promotion. The goad, apart from his evident daring skill, was that unlike others Eugene would long remain a man in a hurry. He settled his troops securely in winter quarters in Montferrat, where the French-supporting ruler was uncooperative, and there were a number of rumours that attempts were made to abduct or even assassinate him.

Eugene still had command of a force inadequate to achieve very much, and his troops were poorly-equipped and often unpaid, and he reflected bitterly that the emperor should either have no army in Italy or take the trouble to maintain a strong one there. He went to Vienna early in March 1691 to ask for more resources, and these were promptly granted, a surprisingly welcome result that would not often be repeated. On this occasion he had the valuable support of the Imperial Vice-Chancellor, Graf Leopold Wilhelm von Königsegg, and the Court Chancellor Graf Theodor Strattmann, able men who enjoyed the trust and favour of Leopold. It was decided to increase the army in northern Italy to 20,000 troops, but such an augmentation, drawn as it must be largely from the German electorates of the Empire, required a more senior commander than Eugene, and this role was offered to Elector Max-Emmanuel. However, the fire and drive that he had once shown on campaign against the Ottomans had faded, and his performance in northern Italy would soon match that of Count Antonio Caraffa, who also seemed to have lost his touch. Eugene was particularly damning of the count, and he wrote that 'I know no one who is less of a soldier, and who understands war so little'.[22]

French troops and resources were being diverted elsewhere, although Catinat had deftly taken Villafranca, Montalban and Nice from Victor-Amadeus in the spring of 1691, but Eugene decided that a vigorous counter-offensive into southern France could produce results. Almost inevitably this was too ambitious a project for his colleagues (with good reason, it might be said), so he went off to Vienna yet again to request an interview with the emperor on the subject. Gaining access to the innermost circles at court was never simple, even for a field commander with a growing reputation, but Eugene at last secured an audience, although Leopold was unconvinced of the merits of an incursion into France. Catinat meanwhile had moved to threaten the town of Cuneo on the river Stura, but the garrison held out and on his return to the army Eugene marched to relieve the place. Pressing ahead with his cavalry, he found that his rapid approach had so alarmed the French commander of the besieging troops, the Marquis du Bulonde, that on 28 June 1691 he had withdrawn and left his camp stores behind to be looted. Catinat promptly had him arrested for not putting up a fight, but he was released soon afterwards.

With Cuneo secure, Eugene withdrew to meet the reinforcements, 12,000 Bavarians, Protestant Swiss and Huguenots, promised him in the spring, all marching smartly to war with Max-Emmanuel at their head. With this augmentation of strength, the allies, Austrian, Imperial and Savoyard, were some 40,000 strong and more than enough to challenge Catinat, although the commander of the Spanish/Italian troops with the army, the Marques de Legañez, at first proved rather uncooperative. Max-Emmanuel ordered an advance up the river Po to Carignano, and the French cautiously fell back towards Saluzzo, although Eugene with his cavalry managed to savage their rearguard while on the march. Catinat went into a strongly-entrenched camp, and it was

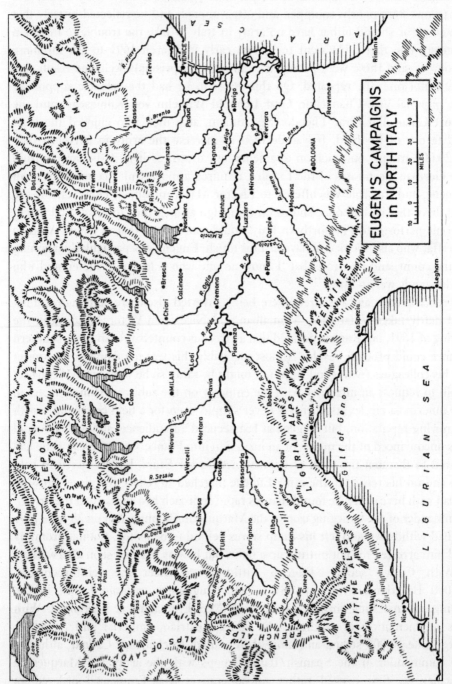

Map 2. Eugene's Campaigns in Italy.

clear that either a frontal attack or blockade were equally unlikely to succeed. At a council of war Eugene suggested a manoeuvre against Catinat's communications, but it was decided that a siege of the French garrison in Carmagnola should be undertaken instead. This was successfully done, but in the meantime Catinat, who would soon be made a Marshal of France, adroitly slipped away to Pinerolo on the Chisane river and out of the grasp of the allies, eventually taking up a new defensive position close to Susa. Attempts to prepare a siege either of Susa or Pinerolo proved fruitless, and to Eugene's frustration the months of autumn were spent unproductively. No sooner, however, had the allied commanders taken their men off to their winter quarters, than Catinat sprang into action, and on 29 December forced the garrison in Montmélian to submit. The oddly hesitant actions of Max-Emmanuel, compounded initially by the indecisiveness of Caraffa and the surprising awkwardness of de Laganez, had resulted in a very plainly sterile campaign that year.

Once his troops were in quarters, Eugene returned to Vienna to make what preparations he could for the campaign in 1692. Leopold had in the meantime transferred Caraffa to campaign on the Rhine, and Max-Emmanuel had gone to take up the lucrative post of Governor-General of the Spanish Netherlands. The overall command of the allied army in northern Italy devolved on to Duke Victor-Amadeus, while Count Aeneas Silvius Caprara, a tough soldier and notorious looter in Hungary, was appointed by Vienna to lead the Austrian and Imperial troops. This was not quite the snub it at first appeared, for Eugene still lacked rank as an army commander, no matter what skill was on display, and for the time being had with rather bad grace to serve under Caprara, and employ what patience he could muster.

The French field army still occupied a good position between Susa on the river Dora and Pinerolo, and a question arose, despite Catinat's relative weakness in numbers, whether an outright attack might still be too hazardous. An alternative move, superficially promising as it seemed, was to mount a raid into southern France through the valley of the Barcelonette, and this course was agreed on. With a detachment under Count Johán Pálffy remaining in Piedmont to observe the French, and General Pianezza blockading Casale on the river Po, the remainder of the allied army, almost 30,000 strong, was divided into three columns for the march. Eugene had the command of the cavalry vanguard of the column led by the Marquis Parella, moving by way of Saluzzo, Castel Delfino and Col de Longet and on into the Val de Queyras, overlooked by the formidable Vauban-designed fortress of that name. The operation was initially a success, with the Barcelonette occupied and the towns of Embrun and Gap taken after some sharp fighting in mid-August. Eugene, slightly wounded once again, pressed for a further advance against Grenoble, but his fellow commanders were reluctant to go so far forward, and at this point Victor-Amadeus was struck down a fever that developed into smallpox, and for a time his life was despaired of. Once recovered, the duke returned to Turin to convalesce, and the army went with him, as the fire had unsurprisingly gone out of the enterprise and had he died, there would be a disputed succession in Savoy.

Louis XIV was busy campaigning in the Low Countries, and his reaction to the raid into southern France was dismissive, as the fortifications of Embrun and Guillestre were demolished and the town of Gap put to the torch, but that was all that was achieved. Eugene's disappointment that not enough had been attempted was acute, if a little unreasonable, and he went to Vienna once again to press for a more vigorous campaign in the coming year. He urged that Pinerolo be secured as a preliminary to a fresh advance on the Barcelonette, as that would deny Catinat easy access southwards across the river Chisane. This was in vain, as the attention of the court was now concentrated on affairs in Hungary and on the Rhine, and Eugene got only a scant hearing for his plans for Italy. Had he been more involved in wider strategic considerations, he would perhaps have better recognized the reasons for this, but for the moment his outlook was narrowly focussed. Still, the emperor did promote him, at the age of just 30, to be the youngest of the more than twenty field marshals in the Austrian service, but he still had to continue to serve with Caprara in command for the time being.

The campaign in Italy dragged once more, supplies and forage were scarce, the region had been much fought over and accordingly picked clean. The ill-equipped Austrian troops and their allies only took the field at Carignano in June 1693, and having taken the fortress of San Giorgio near to Casale lost time in an unproductive siege of Pinerolo, a project only of real value had a fresh advance into France been in prospect. René de Froulay, Comte de Tessé, commanded the garrison, and he was an astute commander who would not give up the fortress lightly. In the meantime, Catinat moved with his reinforced army in late June from Fenestrelles to Bussoleno, seeming to threaten Turin, and Victor-Amadeus took alarm and promptly raising the siege of Pinerolo, just as the French anticipated, The marshal was nimbler, taking up a position in late September between the village of Orbassano and the rather larger Marsaglia, to the south-west of Turin. From a position of advantage, he was plainly challenging his opponents to fight. Victor-Amadeus decided on a frontal attack on 4 October, with Caprara and himself on the right, Eugene commanding the Austrian regiments in the centre, and the Spanish/Italians on the left under the Marques de Legañez. Catinat handled his troops very well, and in fierce fighting repulsed the effort on the allied left, which in turn threatened Eugene's advance. When the right of the allied army also began to give way under French pressure, he had no choice but to conform and fall back in whatever order could be managed. The battle at Marsaglia, which lasted just four hours, was a clear defeat for the allies who abandoned twenty guns on the field, and much to the credit of Catinat. The fighting had been hard, and his own losses were such that a vigorous pursuit could not be attempted as his opponents fell back to Turin, but he did move to recapture San

Giorgio without difficulty. Little had been achieved during the campaign, and even Catinat's success at Marsaglia was hollow in a way, as he had been obliged to let Victor-Amadeus get away and regroup at leisure. This was accomplished well enough for an advance on Montcalieri to be undertaken before winter closed the campaign once more. As it was, the duke was quietly contemplating renewing his alliance with Louis XIV, and in the meantime showed little appetite for any decisive moves.

On the wider scene, matters in the East were of more pressing concern, and so Caprara was posted back to Hungary, and Eugene was at last to command the Austrian and Imperial forces in northern Italy for the 1694 campaign. This was highly significant, his first such appointment to lead an army, and yet in conference in Turin, he found Victor-Amadeus obstinately reluctant to attempt anything much against Catinat. Frustrated at what little could be done, and suspicious of his cousin's motives despite the family connection, Eugene reported his concerns to Vienna, but nothing could be proved. Double-dealing was in play, though, and Catinat wrote that year, that 'We certainly received, apparently by virtue of our understanding with the duke or with one of his ministers, information, always accurate, regarding the contemplated movements of the enemy'.[23] Only in March 1695 could Eugene recapture San Giorgio and re-establish a close blockade of Casale, but the campaign proceeded slowly, with Victor-Amadeus still evasive, and the fortress only submitted on 9 July. Attention then turned back to Pinerolo, but the plans to seize the place had been divulged to the garrison commander, Tessé, and perhaps understandably little was achieved as the summer weeks sped by. Eventually, and in frustration, Eugene left the army encamped before Casale, and once again went to Vienna to urge either reinforcements and adequate supplies, or if they were unavailable, even an abandonment of the campaign in northern Italy altogether. This was too much for Leopold, and after fruitless discussions he was sent back to Turin, even more sure of his cousin's change of allegiance, a fact that the duke would declare in June 1696. Hampered in what could be done, Eugene manoeuvred to cover Milan, now with the welcome support of the newly invigorated Marques de Legañez. The formal switch by Victor-Amadeus to renew his alliance with Louis XIV took place on 29 August 1696, with his appointment in September to command the French and Savoyard troops facing Eugene and de Lagañez, surely a quite extraordinary event with the duke having been commander-in-chief of two directly opposing armies in the space of a few weeks. Those who had dealt with Victor-Amadeus in the past might not have been too surprised at his *volte-face*, for he often tried to ride two horses at the same time, and only occasionally fell off. It should also be said, however, that Savoy-Piedmont had been devastated by repeated campaigns, and to ally once more with Versailles might well have been seen in Turin as the best way to gain a respite for his weary people.

Eugene had little option but to withdraw his outnumbered troops from contact with the French and their new ally, but as it proved, the war had run its course, and by the Treaty of Vigaveno that October, France, Savoy, Spain and Austria agreed an armistice in Italy. Louis XIV's treasury was under strain, stringent measures for increased taxation had produced less than expected, and the finances in Vienna were certainly no better. The League of Augsburg fractured in the process, and almost a year later, a general agreement for peace was negotiated, known as the Treaty of Ryswick, which brought to an end what was usually remembered as the Nine Years War. Leopold typically delayed the signing until the last moment, pointlessly casting for ways to carry on with the conflict. In the end it had to be recognized that Louis XIV's ambitions for the time being had been curbed, and accordingly much achieved and to be welcomed. French troops had been obliged to fall back to the left bank of the Rhine, restrained in northern Italy and removed from the Duchy of Lorraine, while the accession of William III to the throne in London was at last formally acknowledged in Versailles. Seen objectively, the French king had played high and lost high, although much unfinished business littered the European scene, and renewed conflict would not be far off.

Chapter 3

The Triumph of Zenta

While Eugene was striving with only modest success in Italy, significant reverses had taken place in the East, after Emperor Leopold refused Ottoman overtures to conclude a formal peace treaty, or even agree to a mutually beneficial truce. In 1690, a reinvigorated campaign under the robust leadership of Sultan Mustapha II routed exposed Austrian detachments and most dramatically recovered both Semendria and Belgrade. He then advanced on the fortress of Essegg (Osijek) on the river Drava in Slavonia, but the garrison under the command of Guido von Starhemberg put up an admirable defence, enabling the Margrave of Baden to march up in time to relieve the place. A sharp engagement then took place at Salankament in August 1691, where 'Turken Louis' won the day, although his supply train was overrun and burned, with the Ottomans driven off the field. Baden then moved to occupy Grosswarden but was unable to make any further progress towards recovering Belgrade, and his poorly supplied operations were thereafter rather aimless, with neither side achieving or losing a great deal, although the key Danubian fortress of Peterwardein was held, for the time being, against a well-directed Ottoman blockade.

Despite a welcome increment in funds, when Leopold supported the creation of Duke Ernest-Augustus of Brunswick-Luneburg as an elector of the Holy Roman Empire in return for the payment to Vienna's coffers of 750,000 florins, it was claimed that it was not possible to pay or supply the troops in Hungary. Conditions in the army were now not at all good: 'The heat, the gnats and scarcity of food were very severe . . . I was never in a more dreadful place.'[1] Aeneas Caprara continued his militarily pointless policy of looting, while Baden appeared to lose much of the energy and zeal for which he had so recently been known and in 1695 stood down as field commander. In an effort to reinvigorate the flagging efforts to retake Belgrade, the command of the Imperial army on the Danube was given to Fredrick-Augustus, 'Augustus the Strong', the Elector of Saxony. This proved to be a mistake, as he was a lacklustre commander, quite unlike Baden on a good day, and was beaten in battle by the sultan at Olasch near to Temesvár in the Banat in August 1696. Providentially, Frederick-Augustus was then elected as King of Poland, on the death of the renowned John Sobieski, giving up the command of the army and converting to Catholicism in the same breath, and many officers were thoroughly glad to see him go. With the Ottoman urge to recover lost territory clear and strong, it was at last evident to Vienna that something drastic had to be done. This something was the appointment of Prince Eugene, on 5 July 1697, to take up the command of the army in the East, a role of the highest importance to Leopold and the Austrian Empire, and of course, to his own subsequent career and reputation. So, it might almost be said that his hour had come. The appointment of one so comparatively young, just 33 years old, was controversial, and there was much shaking of grey heads at court when it was announced, but crucially Graf Ernst Rüdiger von Starhemberg, then the President of the Imperial War Council (and stalwart defender of Vienna in 1683), was in favour, writing warmly of Eugene that 'I do not know anyone who has more understanding, experience, application and zeal for the Emperor's service, or with a more generous and unselfish temper, and possessing the esteem of his soldiers'.[2]

Eugene reached the army's encampment at Esseg during the second week of July 1697, taking with him the helpful advice of the emperor that he should act with caution and not on any account to run risks. He found on his arrival a good deal of mismanagement and lack of discipline in the army, and the troops were ill-clad and poorly fed, with chronic arrears of pay, while many senior officers were absent without proper authority or on the flimsiest excuses. As before, Eugene's restless energy soon rectified much of the lack in stores, munitions and provisions, while the officers were summoned back to their posts, and morale rose steadily. The supply of money from Vienna remained uncertain, which surprised no-one, but under his firm control much improved remarkably quickly. Previously scattered detachments of troops, lacking support and liable to be picked off as Count Auersperg had recently been at Bibacz, were brought in and concentrated ready to press the summer campaign forward with proper vigour. An added complicating factor, however, was that renewed unrest amongst the much-abused and weary peasantry of upper Hungary alarmed Vienna, so that Prince Charles Vaudémont of Lorraine, a close friend of Eugene, had to be detached with a substantial force to restore and maintain order. In consequence, metaphorically at least, he was constantly having to look over his shoulder to see how Vaudémont was faring.

Sultan Mustapha was, it seemed, riding something akin to the crest of a wave after recent successes against weak Imperial detachments at Bibacz, Lugos, Ulas and Cenei. He took the field in 1697 with an army reported to be close on 100,000 strong (effectives, plus thousands of supporters and camp followers), although such a suspiciously neat figure should be treated with caution. The sultan moved forward from the mustering point at Belgrade to cross the Danube at Páncsova on 19 August, once more exercising personal command rather than entrusting it, as was more usual, to his grand vizier. At first, he divided his forces, with one corps going with the Danubian river fleet to Salankament demonstrating a potential threat to Peterwardein, while the corps he kept under his own eye moved northwards along the left bank of the Tisza towards the Murusel river, and the approaches to Transylvania. Such a splitting of Ottoman forces in this way might seem rash, but the sultan was typically moving quickly, so the risk was fairly small if he was able to keep his opponent in doubt over his true intentions, and as long as he also retained the ability to concentrate once more. As in days gone by, he looked to summon local levies to join the campaign, and pick off Austrian detachments, but narrowly missed the opportunity to intercept sixteen squadrons of cavalry, perhaps 3,000 riders under the command of the French émigré Count Jean-Louis Bussy-Rabutin, which were marching from Transylvania to join Eugene.

Meanwhile, Eugene had moved north towards the Austrian-held fortress of Szegedin to effect a combination of forces with Vaudémont and Bussy-Rabutin, and in doing so achieved a total active strength of just over 50,000 troops (the combined army included 12,000 Hungarians under the Palatine Paul Esterharzy, and 11,000 Serbian militia). Sultan Mustapha was not yet aware of this concentration, his light cavalry for once having failed to provide the necessary details in good time. He had, however, combined his own army once more, after crossing to the right bank of the Tisza and turning southwards towards Peterwardein and driving an Austrian detachment under General Dietrich Nehem out of Titel, at the confluence of the Tisza with the river Beg. Eugene was alert to the danger and force-marched around his opponent to counter the threat to Peterwardein, so that, finding the road to that fortress unexpectedly barred, Mustapha began to retrace his steps in the direction of Szegdin. Eugene marched to shadow his movements, keeping just out of reach but neatly hampering the sultan's options, constrained as he now was with the wide marshy margins of the Danube on the one hand, and the equally difficult marshes of the Tisza on the other. He had little room in which to manoeuvre freely to deploy his superior strength, in a region devastated by previous campaigns, with forage and fodder almost negligible, and, even allowing for the usual excellent administrative 'tail' of Ottoman armies on campaign, it was not somewhere Mustapha could linger for long.

With little to be gained by remaining west of the Tisza, on 6 September the sultan sought to break away and put some distance between his army and that of Eugene, but in doing surrendered what initiative he retained in the campaign. The move was noted by General Nehem, who promptly reported it to Eugene. Thinking that the way eastwards to Ottoman-held Temesvár and the Banat region, where he would have more room to manoeuvre, would now be clear, the sultan marched northwards along the right bank of the Tisza, tearing down the long bridges over the stagnant marshes at St Thomas and Syrec behind him to impede any immediate pursuit. This work of destruction was in vain for despite the weariness of his hard-marching troops, Eugene had turned northwards. After quickly repairing the bridges, he moved to close with the Ottoman army, which with all its baggage, guns, camp followers and gear was now static and found in a hastily-built defensive encampment while waiting to get across the Tisza. After a gruelling forced march, the prince reached Becse on 10 September, and learned that the Ottomans were still halted close to the burnt-out village of Zenta, on the near bank of the river. A clear opportunity beckoned to force an action on his opponents with a wide water obstacle at their back, and at a hastily convened council of war, all the senior officers agreed with Eugene that an all-out attack should be mounted as soon as it could be done.

A senior Ottoman officer, Djafa Pasha, had the misfortune to be captured while conducting his own reconnaissance of Eugene's movements, and he was persuaded to describe in detail the layout and intentions of the sultan's army. Quite how he was induced to comply so readily is not known, but there was probably little choice offered in the matter. He confirmed that pioneers had laid a massive planked bridge on sixty boats moored bank-to-bank across the Tisza, and an encampment on the far side was being made ready to receive the main body of the army once it had crossed. Sultan Mustapha, accompanied by his entourage, a field battery and most of his regular cavalry, had already crossed the river, while the rest of his artillery and baggage trains were ready and preparing to follow, covered by the Ottoman infantry under the command of the grand vizier, Elmes Mehmet Pasha. These troops, who after their customary practice had constructed palisade defences, in effect formed a strong rearguard, and all being well they should be able to hold their ground, allow the baggage and impedimenta of the army to get over the river, and following on concentrate once more, ready to fight with full strength. It was clear, however, that unaware of how close Eugene's army was, the sultan had made a tactical error, and while the position at the river's edge was apparently strongly held, it was now packed with foot soldiers, irregular cavalry, artillery pieces limbered-up and ready to move, draught animals, camp followers and baggage wagons, with little space in which the fighting troops could properly form or manoeuvre. If the sultan's infantry did not stand their ground and were pushed back away from their palisade defences, only the steep banks and fast-flowing water of the wide river awaited them, as there would be little chance to get over the planked bridge in good time and decent order. Nor could they be readily supported from the far bank; even if such a move was to be attempted, there was now no room for the sultan's regular cavalry to properly deploy should they venture back across the bridge.[3]

On the morning of 11 September 1697, the opportunity was plain to Eugene, with nothing more to be considered, but at this critical and exciting moment, with so much in the balance, and his troops hurrying forward from the line of march, a courier reputedly arrived from Vienna with a message warning Eugene on no account to risk a major battle. If this was indeed so, the slip of paper was put away and ignored, as he arranged his troops, labouring in the dusty summer heat, deployed for battle into six columns, each comprised of heavy cavalry and infantry. There was little time for hesitation: victory awaited if the Ottomans could only be engaged while they were both cornered and divided. Whatever advantage in numbers the sultan had enjoyed was now gone, and Eugene had achieved his own local superiority by overtaking the opposing infantry, with few supports, while waiting to cross the river. The command of the right of his army was entrusted to the veteran Graf Sigbert Heister together with Count Bussy-Rabutin and General Ernest Bagni, while the reliable Guido von Starhemberg commanded on the left together with Prince Vaudémont, General Anton Gutterstein and Count Leopold Schlick. With a tactical formation half-moon in shape, initially over 4,000 yards wide, both Heister and von Starhemberg had, rather like their opponents, flanks which rested secure on the respective banks of the Tisza as they moved forward. The key difference was that the Austrians and their allies were advancing, all arms deployed, to envelop the Ottomans, who were forced to fight at a disadvantage with a dramatically flawed tactical disposition.

Eugene, as commander-in-chief, naturally took post in the centre with Prince Charles Commercy, Graf Hermann of Baden and his chief gunner General August Börner. Despite the wonderful prize that was offered, almost beyond the wildest dreams of these seasoned campaigners, nothing was rushed or put in jeopardy by faulty arrangements even though the precious hours of afternoon sped by, and Börner's sixty guns were hauled into position with great effort and the ammunition carts placed close at hand. If a degree of impatience was nonetheless noted in Eugene's demeanour, as reported, this was only to be expected at such a critical moment, as he was about to engage in a major action as undisputed army commander for the first time, and the chances for a major success were simply breath-taking.

The unexpected approach of Eugene's army, in full battle array with the light guns to the fore, was soon observed by the grand vizier, and squadrons of irregular cavalry were sent by the Hungarian rebel Imre Thököly sweeping out of the defensive perimeter to slow the Imperial advance, but Eugene anticipated the move, and a brigade of Saxon dragoons from his second line was sent to drive them off. This was done without great difficulty, and the dragoons then dismounted to go forward in support of the infantry as they closed with the Ottoman defences. The opening which allowed these horsemen to easily venture forth in this way is shown on contemporary plans as a gap in the defensive palisades, and may also have served as a convenient weak spot identified by Eugene during his advance. The sultan's gunners, who had been preparing to cross the river when their turn came, had hastily unlimbered their pieces and opened a fierce and well-directed cannonade, but Börner's artillery replied with such vigour that the well-ordered advance of Eugene's infantry, although gaps were torn in their ranks, was not slowed to any great degree. The single Ottoman battery on the far bank of the Tisza also opened fire, but it would later be learned that Mustapha had left much of his heavy artillery in Belgrade, so as to allow his field army to move all the faster. This was a laudable aim, but he had been outmanoeuvred and caught at a critical disadvantage by Eugene, and this lack of ordnance was a handicap, although whether to eventual outcome would have been any different may be doubted.[4]

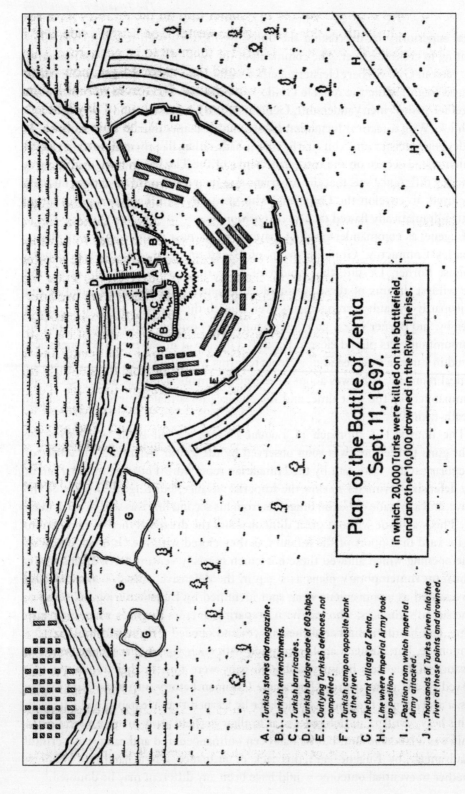

Plan of the Battle of Zenta
Sept. 11, 1697.

in which 20,000 Turks were killed on the battlefield,
and another 10,000 drowned in the River Theiss.

River Theiss

A...Turkish stores and magazine.
B...Turkish entrenchments.
C...Turkish barricades.
D...Turkish bridge made of 60 ships.
E...Outlying Turkish defences, not completed.
F...Turkish camp on opposite bank of the river.
C...The burnt village of Zenta.
H...Line where Imperial Army took up position.
I...Position from which Imperial Army attacked.
J...Thousands of Turks driven into the river at these points and drowned.

Map 3. The Battle of Zenta, 11 September 1697.

The bank of the Tisza on the right of the Ottoman position, where the Sipahi cavalry had picketed their horses the previous day, was less steep than that on the left, and as his troops moved forward, Guido von Starhemberg found that he was able to move infantry and dismounted dragoons led by Count Schlick across a stretch of low water there without much trouble. His wading troops took firm possession of an unoccupied 40-yard-long sandbank nearby, and this move was surprisingly uncontested, neatly uncovering the pasha's right flank. So much had thus been achieved by Eugene's rapid advance, but all was still to play for, and with just two hours of daylight remaining hesitation might yet mean that everything would be lost. He seized the moment and ordered a full attack, and the Ottoman commanders faltered, apparently distracted by von Starhemberg having so readily turned the flank of their position. Eugene's infantry, their long lines of levelled bayonets glittering in the late afternoon sun, valiantly brushed off their steadily mounting casualties, and swarmed over the palisaded defences, smashed in places by the fire of Börner's gunners. The Ottoman baggage wagons had been hauled around and chained together for defence, as had been learned by the experience of long years of hard fighting in Hungary, but the vigour of the Austrians and their allies was such that this secondary barricade was also soon overrun. The Grand Vizier's soldiers, most notably the ranks of Janissary matchlock-men, fought with their customary vigour, and for a short while the issue remained in doubt, but their cohesion steadily crumbled under the weight of the attack, their musketry was poor and ill-directed, while contrary to shouted orders many threw down their pieces in frustration, to make better use of the scimitar. Gradually but certainly, under the remorseless pressure of Eugene's musketeers, grenadiers and dismounted dragoons, the Ottoman foot soldiers were pushed back in a rapidly tightening mass towards the river.

Sultan Mustapha, observing from the far bank of the Tisza the unfolding peril to his rearguard and baggage train, hastily sent back across the pontoon bridge five squadrons of his Timariot cavalry to their support. Such a move, which might in other circumstances have been well judged, had the unfortunate effect of jamming any movement over the swaying and pitching bridge, which was itself now under a withering fire from Börner's gunners. However unlikely it might have been at this late stage, any intended withdrawal in good order for the Ottoman infantry was now not possible, and in the growing confusion command and control slipped away, as prudently did Imre Thököly who managed to escape. In desperation and growing confusion the pasha's soldiers began to crowd back towards the bridge, and all cohesion was lost as Imperial cuirassiers in their blackened armour, the matchless heavy cavalry of Eugene's right wing under Bussy-Rabutin's steady hand, with horse pistols, carbines and long swords plied with vigour, were sent forward to press into what was fast becoming an uncontrollable mass of fugitive infantrymen and their camp followers.

As so often in a pitched battle that had tumbled out of control, a point was reached at which nothing could be done to rectify matters. 'Defence turned to retreat, retreat to rout, rout to slaughter.'[5] Large numbers of the fleeing Ottoman soldiers were pushed or threw themselves into the river, seeking in desperation to escape, but although they flung aside their weapons many were swept away or drowned. Grand Vizier Elmes Mehmet Pasha was killed, surrounded by a fallen ring of loyal body servants and personal guards, as were the Governors of Anatolia and Bosnia, and the Aga-Vizier of the Janissaries who alone that evening had stood fast as a body and died almost to a man. Eugene's troops were outraged to discover the mutilated bodies of their own comrades, who had been taken prisoner and then brutally tortured to death, so that little mercy or quarter was shown, and in the slaughter senior Ottoman officers – pashas, viziers and beyerbeys, men of note, reputation and standing – offered in vain the promise of vast ransom rewards if spared, before they were bayonetted or cut down. 'The soldiers got so worked up to such a pitch that they spared no-one, and butchered all who fell into their hands.'[6] The slaughter was too intense and ghastly to last long, and Eugene's soldiers gathered in over 4,000 prisoners at the end of the day. A precise estimate of the losses in the Ottoman army that day is impossible to now calculate, the Sublime Porte never obliged by providing such figures, but reports generally credited at the time put the total casualties a little improbably at 30,000 killed, including those who were drowned in the Tisza, as their customary loose-fitting clothing dragged them down into the fast-flowing water. 'The men,' it was recorded by Eugene, 'could stand on the dead bodies as if on an island in the water.'[7]

In the setting sun of that extraordinary day, Sultan Mustapha watched in despair from the far bank as much as a half of his effective strength was destroyed by Eugene's remorseless attack, and hardly more than 1,500 fugitives reputedly managed to escape over the bridge. In the gathering darkness he fled eastwards with his cavalry, hoping to reach Temesvár and from there to the security of the fortress walls of Belgrade. Abandoned in the process was his supply train, gun park, all tentage, campaign gear and ordnance, seven horse-tail standards, and a vast war chest containing the unbelievably fabulous sum of three million piastres. That the massively constructed and immensely valuable pontoon bridge over the Tisza was lost too hardly needs mentioning, and Eugene's troop found in the abandoned encampment and at the water's edge over 9,000 loaded wagons and 1,500 head of cattle. Also taken were thousands of camels, in use both as draught animals and some rather comically intended to have light artillery pieces mounted on their backs, all of which rather perplexed the soldiers as to what to do with them. Count Glockensperg, with a detachment of Austrian light cavalry, was sent to keep the defeated sultan and his cavalry under observation as they went, but Eugene felt the need to do little more while his next moves were considered. However, the Ottoman Danube flotilla, which had been intended to assist with operations against Peterwardein, evaded capture and on learning of the disaster at Zenta, adroitly slipped downstream with all haste.

The victory was astonishing, achieved by Eugene with daring, dash and skill and at relatively modest cost, as no more than 2,500 casualties were all that his army could list.[8] Sultan Mustapha's own miscalculation played a significant part in his defeat, that was clear, but the magnitude of the success gained by Eugene did not brook of argument, and he had taken the risk and reaped the appropriate reward. This was a decisive triumph on a grand scale. In almost unprecedented fashion the Ottoman field army in south-eastern Europe had been broken beyond hope of ready repair, and the defeat 'Marked irrevocably the decline of the Ottoman Empire'.[9] Prince Vaudémont was sent spurring to Vienna with the news, almost unbelievable as it would seem to those who heard it, of victory in the east and people walked about as if in a daze on learning of such a dramatic thing. 'The sun,' Eugene wrote rather lyrically to Leopold, perhaps consciously invoking the Gideon of the Old Testament, 'had been unwilling to go down before it had witnessed the full triumph of your Imperial Majesty's glorious arms.'[10] He also mused, with wry humour, that he could not have hoped for such a complete success had he faced his old adversary Marshal Catinat that day.

The season was too advanced to permit a move against either Temesvár or Belgrade, tempting though this must have been, so after securing the fortresses in the immediate region, Eugene with 7,000 troops swept on a raid across the rivers Drava and Sava to clear out Ottoman detachments in Bosnia and Serbia. Concurrently, Count Bussy-Rabutin was sent with his cavalry to probe the line of the Danube to test what resistance might be offered, but was warned not to press on too far. On 23 October, Eugene briefly occupied and thoroughly sacked Sarajevo – 'Burning everything to our right and left'[11] – after the garrison fled on his approach, but not before having fired on his emissaries trying to offer good terms for a submission. He re-crossed the Sava on 5 November to reach Essegg the next day, from where he directed that his troops be sent to winter quarters. Bussy-Rabutin meanwhile had met little opposition, penetrated as far as the Iron Gates on the Danube downriver from Belgrade, and even taking the town of Ujfralanka and burning Pánscova, before safely making his way to rejoin the main army.

Prince Eugene returned to Vienna to tremendous acclaim, and on 17 November handed to Emperor Leopold the Great Seal of the Ottoman Empire, a trophy never before gained in battle, taken from the hacked body of the grand vizier on the field of Zenta. Amongst the honours and gifts that were presented to Eugene as the hero of the hour, was a richly jewelled sword, the emperor's promise of a grand estate in Hungary (quite which one was not defined) and a commemorative medal struck by the Imperial Mint honouring both victor and victory. Amidst all the acclamation, however, there were those at court who viewed the success with a degree of jealousy and spite. Many long-established and well-entrenched vested interests were at risk, as a man of such energy and almost reckless daring might cast others into the shadows and make an uncomfortable colleague and companion in the council chambers of the Empire. The Imperial War Council even impertinently announced that, after careful consideration of the circumstances, Eugene was to be congratulated rather than censured for risking so much, surely an interesting insight into the stony mind-set of the veterans in the highest circles at court, who by now had, it would be said, become 'A council of ancients, stalked by death'.[12]

There was little chance that Ottoman fortunes in Hungary and the middle Danube Basin could be quickly restored, but the sultan must have been heartened to learn that the Venetian fleet had been soundly defeated by the Dey of Algiers at Tenedos, while in the east his commanders had taken the key town of Basra on the Tigris from the Persians. However, continued tension with Russia partly explained why Mustapha had been unable to call on many of the ruthlessly effective Crimean Tartars to take part in his recent campaign, and the lack of timely information obtained concerning Eugene's rapid movements prior to Zenta was significant. Rebuilding his main field army on the Danube with an exhausted treasury would be slow, but could be done, and the sultan appointed as his new grand vizier Hussein Koprili Pasha, a most able man and devoted servant of the Sublime Porte. Within a year, a fresh force had been assembled under his command, enough to at least shield Belgrade from immediate attack, and that was something of an achievement in the grim aftermath of the catastrophe at Zenta. Sharp skirmishing ensued, and when Eugene advanced again from Peterwardein in the spring of 1698, with an army flushed with victory but still short of money and supplies, he found the new grand vizier's dispositions sound enough to deter any immediate attempt to retake the city. The prince could do little more than to manoeuvre and try and entice his opponents to come out and fight, which they were little inclined to do. Ominously, he also had to put down a mutiny in some of his own regiments arising from a lack of pay, which he did with considerable severity, thirty-two of the mutineers, all veterans of Zenta, being executed.

In January that year the Sublime Porte had agreed to accept the mediation of the British ambassador in Constantinople, Lord William Paget, as a preliminary to formal negotiations for a cessation of hostilities with Vienna and the Holy League. Austrian delegates and those of the Ottomans were joined by English, Dutch, Venetian, Russian and Polish emissaries in complex discussions at Carlowitz, just across the Danube from Peterwardein. Despite the unhelpful intervention of Tsar Peter, who hoped to gain a port on the Black Sea through the efforts of others, peace terms were eventually agreed in October and the treaty itself was signed by the Ottoman plenipotentiary, Rami Reis Effendi, at 11.45am on 26 January 1699, the precise time his astrologers had determined to be most propitious. The Peace of Carlowitz was of immense significance, as Constantinople had previously never seen a need to negotiate formally with European powers, and 'The [Ottoman] government was fully aware that it no longer could dictate its place in the early modern Europe world order, and that it now had to bargain with equal or even more powerful states'.[13]

Venice secured control of Dalmatia and regained much of the Morea in Greece, but relinquished its hold on Corinth, while the port and fortress of Azov was eventually and reluctantly ceded to the tsar. The region of Podolia was returned to Poland, while most significantly, everything won by Vienna since the fateful days of 1683 was confirmed, with new frontiers for the Austrian Empire established along the line of the rivers Sava, Drava and middle Danube. The devastated Bácksha region between the Danube and the Tisza, Little (western) Wallachia and the principality of Transylvania were secured from Ottoman overlordship, although Belgrade and the Banat remained in their hands. Still, such an achievement meant an extraordinary extension of Vienna's power, influence and territory, the establishing of a military frontier, and effectively re-balancing the Habsburg centre of gravity from the West to the East. Of almost equal importance to Vienna, unrest in Hungary could henceforth only ever be a local matter, largely unaffected by mischief-making in Constantinople. This was the aggregate work of many commanders and their long-suffering men, but the Sublime Porte's formal recognition of such enormous gains was the direct result of Eugene's victory at Zenta, and he was rightly celebrated as becoming one of the foremost captains of the age. All the same, the final setting of the new border was not simple, as the existing maps were often contradictory and open to interpretation and dispute. It took two years for Count Luigi Marsigli, acting for Vienna, together with the Ottoman official Ibrahim Pasha, to physically ride the length of the new border and agree the details largely based upon physical features such as major rivers, passes and mountains.[14]

Amongst the results of these successes was an outpouring of renewed self-confidence in Vienna, and almost a mania amongst the gentry and nobility for building grand houses on the site of the long-abandoned Ottoman siege works. Eugene was not immune to this enthusiasm, having already acquired a large plot of land to the south-east of the city walls on which he now had constructed a summer palace which became known as the Belvedere, with views over the nearby Kahlenberg battlefield. The emperor had also granted him an estate in Hungary of course, and he was able to pay off long-standing debts, while buying a large house and estate on the 50-mile-long island of Czepel on the Danube below Buda. Clearly, the victory at Zenta had appropriate benefits, but Leopold was never mean when rewarding his servants. Eugene would take a careful interest in the demands of good husbandry on his growing estates; they had been hard won and were clearly to be nurtured. He encouraged the improvement of the soil and the agricultural methods used by his tenants, who found that as long as they paid their rents promptly, they were fortunate in their new landlord after so many years of war, uncertainty and want.

Although he never married, Eugene was not immune to feminine charms, and when not out on campaign had shared a house for a time, perhaps even a bedchamber, with the magnificently-titled Princess Franziska von Sachsen-Lauenberg. Nuptials between the two were clearly not in the wind, and the complicated plan devised by his wayward mother, Olympia, still living in comfortable exile in Brussels, to marry her famous son off to a wealthy Spanish lady had come to nothing. Her meddling in this way, which may well have been intended to be helpful, was not at all appreciated but Eugene remained fond of his parent, or his childhood memory of her at any rate, during their long years of separation. There remains a sense that he avoided cultivating close personal associations which might distract or impede his career as a field commander, and while agreeable enough when he chose to be, even in repose his mind would often seem to be elsewhere. He had friends, that is certain, but few real intimates, although when his older brother, Louis, turned up in Vienna with his family soon after the Zenta campaign, poor and almost as a vagrant having been dismissed and meanly deprived of a pension by Louis XIV, Eugene helped to secure for him a command in the emperor's army. Three years later Louis was killed fighting the French, so that the prince then undertook to look after the welfare of his niece and three nephews as their mother, the once-beautiful Urania, had immured herself in a convent and seemed to have forgotten them. Back in France Eugene's sisters lacked a guiding hand with their mother sybaritically enjoying herself in Brussels, and they led rather raffish lives attracting a fair amount of criticism for their behaviour at the Hotel de Soissons in Paris, before sinking into fairly comfortable obscurity.

Matters rarely stood still for long, and Vienna having contended for many years with threats from both East and West to the interests of Austria, the Habsburg Monarchy and the Holy Roman Empire, a great deal had been achieved with slim resources and against formidable odds. Evidently, while the ambitions of the sultans in Constantinople had been settled, for the time being at any rate, the danger posed by the ambitions of King Louis XIV was only dormant. Most particularly, a problem that had been troubling the courts and chancelleries of Europe, and festering for some time suddenly came to an acute head. Soon after the victory at Zenta and the welcome agreements of the Peace of Carlowitz, Eugene would be called upon to undertake another task as great, perhaps even greater, in the service of Emperor Leopold.

Chapter 4

A Death in Spain

On 1 November 1700, the last of the Spanish Habsburgs, King Carlos II, died at the Escorial Palace outside Madrid. He was childless and had no surviving brothers or sisters, and so the question of who should succeed him, and inherit the vast Spanish Empire, had been for some time an increasingly urgent one. French influence at the Spanish court was strong, and to many of the nobility this interest seemed the best prospect that the empire should not, by default, be divided amongst contending candidates for the crown. However, the 1697 Treaty of Ryswick, which brought to an end the Nine Years War, had contained the provision that Prince Joseph-Ferdinand Wittelsbach, young son of the Elector of Bavaria and Maria-Antonia, Emperor Leopold's daughter, should succeed to the Spanish throne if Carlos had no child at the time of his death. This agreement was enshrined in what became known as a First Partition Treaty in October 1698, with valuable parts of the Spanish Empire – Luxembourg, Milan, Naples and Sicily – apportioned to the other rival claimants, French and Austrian, in recompense. While it might have been thought by France, England and Holland to be a neat solution to the problem, neither the nobility in Madrid or Emperor Leopold in Vienna were closely consulted on the matter, and the whole arrangement fell to pieces when the prince died unexpectedly of smallpox in February 1699.

There were left two principal contenders for the throne, in the form of Archduke Charles, second son of the emperor, and Philippe Duc d'Anjou, second eldest grandson of King Louis XIV. Their fathers, Leopold and Louis, the Dauphin of France, would each set aside their own claims, derived as they were from their respective Spanish-born mothers.[1] As an aside, Duke Victor-Amadeus of Savoy also tried to advance his own claim, on the basis of his Spanish grandmother, but little attention was paid to this. The position of the duke was in any case a strange one, as his daughter Adelaide was married to the eldest grandson of Louis XIV, the Duc de Bourgogne, and would in time expect to become Queen of France at her husband's side, but that this would never happen could not be foreseen. No-one relished the thought of renewed war, and a Second Partition Treaty was negotiated between France and the Maritime Powers, Britain and Holland, in the spring of 1699. This set out that Archduke Charles should have the throne when it became vacant, while France would receive, by way of compensation for the lost hopes of the Duc d'Anjou, valuable concessions of Spanish-held territory in Italy. This arrangement, reached once more without consultation with the ailing Carlos and his nobles, would of course entail the division of their empire, something greatly resisted in Madrid. Nor was Leopold impressed. With the threat to the East fading, he was inclined to be more assertive in dealing with the West, and protested that too much was being given away to France. 'It was characteristic of Leopold that his obstinacy was not accompanied by activity: though his refusal to accept the treaty was senseless, unless he was prepared to fight for what he wanted.'[2] The emperor miscalculated, and failed to appreciate the growing strength of French influence in Madrid.

As he sank onto his deathbed, Carlos drafted a new will, which offered the soon-to-be vacated throne to Anjou, and only if he, or his younger brother the Duc de Berry, refused would that same offer then be made to Archduke Charles. 'In the event that we should have no heir, the said Duke of Anjou is to succeed to all our kingdoms and lordships, not merely those belonging to the Crown of Castile, but also those of the Crowns of Aragon and Navarre, and *to all our possessions both within and without Spain*' [author's italics].[3] That was clear enough, and perfectly legitimate even if the will was drawn up under a degree of persuasion, as some suspected. No matter, the Spanish Empire was a prize of enormous worth, and those in the rival camps, Versailles and Vienna, felt it worth fighting for if they could not get their own way in any other manner. When the long-awaited news of the death of Carlos on 1 November 1700 and of the details of his last will were conveyed to the French king and his court at Fontainebleau, Louis XIV, although initially hesitant, felt unable to resist the offer of the throne to his grandson.

War might yet have been avoided, even though Leopold was still anxious to press his own son's claim, in particular due to the strategic importance to Vienna of Spanish-held territories in Italy. Affronted when both Britain and Holland acknowledged the French claimant to the throne, as did Elector of Bavaria Max-Emmanuel and his brother the Archbishop of Cologne, the emperor protested the validity of the will and, as he saw it, of an attempt to disinherit the late king's nearest eligible relation, young Archduke Charles. Things were considered very differently in France, but efforts at diplomacy faltered, in part because early in 1701 French troops were sent to occupy the Spanish (southern) Netherlands, and Louis XIV then outraged opinion in England by appearing to meddle in plans for the Protestant succession to the throne in London. There was a certain grim inevitability about the whole matter with war declared in May 1702 on France and the French claimant to the Spanish throne by a reforged Grand Alliance composed of Austria, Holland and Britain. In time both Portugal and Savoy would join them to confront France and the Bourbon (French) faction in Spain, while Max-Emmanuel, as Governor-General of the Spanish Netherlands, chose to formally ally himself to Louis XIV. This last move was seen in Vienna as a betrayal by the elector, and much resented by his father-in-law Leopold.

In the meantime, the only parts that of the Spanish Empire that Austria could try to secure without assistance were those in Italy, principally the Milanese, but perhaps also Naples and Sicily. Leopold claimed that Milan, as an Imperial fief, had reverted to the Holy Roman Empire on the death of Carlos II, and just as Louis XIV had thought it legitimate to occupy the Spanish Netherlands to secure the region for his grandson, so Leopold could occupy Milan to ensure stability there on behalf of his own son. At least that was how the rather specious argument ran, and Austrian troops moving into Italy would therefore be enforcing established rights and not trespassing on the territory of others. It was also seen as important to support Victor-Amadeus, who otherwise might soon see Savoy-Piedmont full of French troops, although the duke had still to declare his intentions, for all his close family connection with Versailles. The Imperial War Council was in agreement that action be taken, and Leopold gave the necessary instructions for Milan to be occupied, and on 21 November 1700, almost as soon as the news was known in Vienna that Louis XIV had accepted the offered throne on behalf of his grandson, Eugene was appointed to the command in northern Italy. Predictably, few preparations had been made for such a venture, and there was exasperating delay in mustering and equipping the necessary troops. While Vienna fumbled, Victor-Amadeus permitted a French army to move through the Alpine passes into the valley of the river Po, and accordingly the situation that Eugene would face was not promising. In February 1701, troops under Marshal de Tessé occupied Milan together with the key fortresses of Mantua, Peschiera, Legnano and Modena, and King Philip V (as d'Anjou was now styled) in Madrid, was acknowledged in both Naples and Sicily. To complicate things further, Victor-Amadeus achieved something of a coup by marrying his youngest daughter to Philip, and formally renewed his alliance with France.

In May 1701, at Rovereto on the river Adige, to the south of Trento in the Tyrol, Eugene took the field with Guido von Starhemberg and Prince Charles Commercy, August Börner again as his chief of artillery, and Prince Charles-Thomas de Vaudémont in command of the cavalry (rather inconveniently, Vaudémont's father was Madrid's appointed governor in Milan). For once, Vienna had been able to concentrate forces and attention on mustering just one army for operations, and despite shortages Eugene's troops were in good shape, and they were 'The choice of all the Emperor's forces'.[4] No formal state of war yet existed between Austria and France and Spain, but this nicety was not allowed to delay things, and Eugene's first task to was to get the army into more open country and the great valley and plains of the river Po. He faced powerful French, Savoyard and Spanish/Italian forces, known to be in superior numbers and now under the able command of Marshal Catinat, who had the firm intention of blocking any Austrian advance from the constricted mountain passes. The marshal saw the most critical point as the pass at Chiusa di Verona on the Adige, some 10 miles from that city, and established a strong blocking position there. Eugene had no intention of confronting his opponent head-on, and in the last week of May moved eastwards into the inhospitable Terragnolo and Fredda valleys. The snowy roads were almost mountain paths more than anything else, and even the light Austrian guns had to be dismantled to be dragged along by teams of soldiers, while the heavier artillery had to be left at Rovereto for the time being. Vaudémont's cavalry went by way of the Val Duga, while an 8,000-strong detachment under General Guttenstein observed the French and their allies still in position covering Verona, to keep their attention away from Eugene's movements. So successful was this, that as late as the end of May, Catinat had failed to discover what his opponent was doing, and still expected an attack on his covering position at Chiusa di Verona.

Disregarding faint protests from neutral Venice, Eugene emerged from the passes on 3 June, and encamped with 22,000 men on the heights of Breonio near to Vicenza, and the heavy artillery was then called forward, along a track widened and improved by impressed civilian labour. Two days later, he moved forward to St Antonio, only 24 miles from Verona itself, and the right flank of Catinat's dispositions was turned. Justifiably proud of such a daring achievement, Eugene wrote to Leopold that 'It was amazing that an army and its artillery had crossed such dangerous and precipitous mountains where there had been no roads before'.[5] The exploit was widely applauded, as the terrain crossed had been deemed impractical, and the Marquis de Langallerie, in his entertaining memoirs, wrote that 'It was looked upon as a prodigy, the glory of which was attributed to the conduct and bravery of Prince Eugene'.[6] Catinat had been wrong-footed; in effect his army was facing the wrong way, thinking that the only route the Austrians could take would be through Rivoli and along the eastern shore of Lake Garda. He was still unsure in which direction his opponent would strike next, and accordingly strengthened his hold on all the main crossing places over the river Adige. In this way he had to split his forces, a wasteful exercise which left him weak everywhere and strong nowhere.

Eugene nimbly sidestepped and marched southwards to Castelbardo, where an advanced detachment under the command of Count Johan Pálffy was to throw a pontoon bridge across the Po. The crossing was made without difficulty at Occhiobello, with Eugene moving on to Arcole, but Catinat was soon aware of the shift southwards, intended perhaps to threaten Modena, where the duke had just declared for the French claimant to the Spanish throne. The marshal manoeuvred towards Ostiglia to divert Eugene's attention, but left a detachment under General St Fremont near to Carpi on the river Secchia. The prince learned of this dividing of his opponent's forces and turned swiftly to cross the Secchia on the night of 8 July. In the early dawn of the following day he overran St Fremont's exposed forward post at Castagnaro and advanced on Carpi, where his advance guard, formed by the Neuberg Cuirassier Regiment, was engaged by French troops on approaching the town. Things rapidly escalated into a general engagement, with St Fremont badly outnumbered and his troops, who behaved well under the pressure at first, being forced back as Count Tessé came up with reinforcements.

Acting with great skill, Tessé allowed St Fremont's soldiers through his own well-ordered ranks, and by presenting a bold front brought Eugene's pursuit to a halt. The French and their allies were overstretched and had to give way, but the withdrawal was in good order, while the Austrian troops took possession of Carpi and looted the hastily-abandoned French camp with appropriate relish. Eugene, who had taken a spent musket ball to the knee, moved forward on 10 July to San Pietro di Legnano, which had been evacuated during the night. The withdrawal of his opponents effectively left him in undisputed possession of the whole territory between the Adige and Mincio rivers while, had he chosen to do so, he could turn to re-cross the Po and threaten Parma, Modena, Bologna or even Ravenna, if they declared or persisted in their support for the French claimant in the conflict. For the moment, the strategic initiative lay with Eugene, despite his comparative lack of numbers. 'Retreat became necessary,' Catinat wrote to Versailles, to explain why he had fallen back behind the Mincio, in the process leaving the Duke of Mantua exposed to attack, adding rather lamely that the movement was 'accomplished in excellent order'.[7] Louis XIV's rather testy response was that Eugene's troops were 'Marching through a country that is unknown to them; they have neither magazines nor safe places, yet nothing stops them . . . I have warned you that you are dealing with an enterprising young prince, he does not tie himself down to the rules of war.'[8] We can suspect, but never know, how much the king now regretted having rejected the young Eugene's request for a commission in his army.

Eugene next confronted the French on 18 July at Villa Franca, but the position they held was too strong, and he cast about for a better opportunity. Nine days later, as night came on, he moved towards the small town of Salionze on the Mincio, to the left of Catinat's position, and began to prepare pontoon bridges. This construction was completed by noon the following day, and the crossing made without hindrance, with a small French detachment prudently withdrawing, so that Eugene advanced rapidly to Castiglione. Victor-Amadeus had now joined Catinat in the field, and was at least nominally in command of the army, ordering a further withdrawal to the Oglio river after agreeing to strengthen the garrison in Mantua. A new position was occupied at Fontanella to the south of Bergamo, where Catinat learned that he was to be replaced by François de Neufville, Duc de Villeroi, a close confidante of the French king and well known to Eugene in his youth. The change would be a mistake as events would show, as Villeroi – 'Very brave, very honest and a good friend, agreeable in society and magnificent in everything'[9] – nonetheless lacked the required touch to handle a battle in full progress, but all the same he took up the command in late August.

The combined French, Savoyard and Spanish/Italian army was now some 50,000 strong, while Eugene still had no more than 32,000 troops, deployed in an advanced position on the eastern bank of the Oglio. For the moment Mantua could be ignored, and on 23 August his cavalry crossed the river without interference to feel out their opponent's dispositions, but finding no immediate opportunity to strike, the prince drew back and deployed into a good defensive position near to the small fortress of Chiari. So often aggressive and energetic in manoeuvre and attack, he plainly knew that there was more than one way to win a battle, and was in effect inviting an attack while he held a position of considerable strength. Villeroi and Victor-Amadeus obliged by taking the bait on 1 September 1701 with a crossing of the Oglio, an uncontested move that should have caused concern, and then without finesse they made a sharp frontal assault on the entrenched Austrian position. Eugene had warned his commanders that the soldiers were not to waste their precious and by now scarce ammunition by firing at too great a range, and this was strictly enforced. As the attack went in a number of Eugene's troops wavered, before rallying and holding firm, and despite the gallantry of the attackers, who made several brave but unavailing attempts, all was in vain and Villeroi was repulsed with the loss of nearly 2,000 killed and wounded, or left as prisoners. The Austrians, by comparison, suffered much more lightly, and as so often accounts on this score vary, but a widely reported figure of only about 350 casualties, including a small handful taken prisoner, seems most likely.

Impressed by the energy and bravery of his opponents, and feeling that they might come on again, Eugene delayed making a report, but on 4 September, he wrote to Vienna of the day's action that 'My post at Chiari, notwithstanding its excellence, was nearly forced by the unparalleled impetuosity of the French . . . Never did I witness such valour.'[10] Victor-Amadeus and Villeroi pulled their mauled army back into an entrenched position at Urago, from where Eugene could see little prospect of driving them out without correspondingly severe losses. Louis XIV was distressed when reports of the bloody repulse at Chiari were received. 'The number of casualties is much greater than you had indicated . . . I am hurt to lose so many brave men in one affair.'[11] Although there remained a significant disparity in numbers between the two armies, Eugene retained the initiative, and Johán Pálffy's cavalry raided the French and Savoyard supply convoys on several occasions, while Vaudémont overtook and severely handled a Spanish/Italian cavalry brigade at Cassano, capturing nine standards and their baggage train. The autumn weather was worsening, though, and so too was the Austrian logistical situation, with forage for the horses being in particularly short supply. The problem was not only his own, and Villeroi complained to Versailles that 'We have provisions for only two days remaining. The weather is bad, the rains are continuous, the roads are in a frightful condition.'[12] It seemed that Eugene was simply going to stand his ground for the time being, so on 12 November Villeroi withdrew his army across the Oglio to take up winter quarters around Milan. Eugene did open an artillery bombardment of the marshal's rearguard, slightly wounding Catinat, who had lingered with the army offering advice which was mostly ignored. This injury afforded the displaced marshal the excuse he needed to leave with dignity, and go back to Versailles where, although predicting yet more failure, he was kindly received by the king.

On 4 December Eugene took Canneto on the Oglio after a short siege, allowing the French garrison commander to surrender on generous terms which he did not really deserve. A move was then made to Macaria where Villeroi's troops were forced to abandon their encampment nearby at Torre d'Oglio, but a week later Tessé, always dangerous, surprised and routed an Austrian detachment under a Lieutenant-Colonel Mercy. Eugene's response was to consolidate his position by occupying Borgoforte, Goernolo, Ostiglia and Ponte Milino in Mantua. On 16 December, he took the fortress at Guastalla on the river Po after brief but sharp fighting, but decided that enough had been achieved in the campaign and his troops went into winter quarters in Mantua, billeted as rather unwelcome guests.

One by-product of Eugene's run of modest successes was the encouragement given to Britain and Holland in reaching the agreed terms of the Grand Alliance with Austria. In effect their aim was still to achieve a division of the Spanish empire on broadly equitable terms between the rival claimants. The newly-proclaimed King in Prussia was also impressed, as was the King of Denmark, while minor Italian states were discouraged from allying themselves too closely or openly to the French. The Duke of Modena allowed Eugene access to the arsenal at Brescello with enormous amounts of arms, munitions and ordnance, while the Princess of Mirandolo declared for Archduke Charles, and asked for the loan of some cavalry to help expel a French detachment. Nonetheless, the prince's supply situation worsened when Pope Clement XI supported the French claimant and issued an edict that Austrian troops and their allies should not be given assistance. In a curious parallel, Villeroi was also unsure that the French position in northern Italy could be maintained, especially as the local gentry and citizens in the Milanese were lacking in sympathy and support for him and his hungry troops, and the wholesale levying of 'contributions' by the French.

The whole region remained of prime interest for Emperor Leopold, and it was known in courtly circles in Vienna that 'Spain was scarce worth the having, unless accompanied with the dominions of Italy'.[13] By gaining ground in the Po valley, assuming that those gains could be held, the division of the Spanish empire could be said to have begun. The importance of these events was not lost on John Churchill, Earl of Marlborough, soon to be appointed to command the Anglo-Dutch armies, and he wrote 'We are here in great expectation of the success that may be in Italy, . . . The strengthening of Prince Eugene must not be neglected.'[14] However, despite repeated appeals to Vienna, he was kept short of money, munitions, casualty replacements and supplies throughout the months leading to the 1702 season for campaigning. What slim funds were provided were devoted by Eugene to buying food for his men in their overcrowded billets in Mantua, where morale was in danger of slipping. Deciding that action was to be preferred to inaction, he ignored the convention that campaigning was not practical during the winter months, and mustered his troops in mid-January 1702, to strike without warning at the major French-held fortress of Cremona, 48 miles to the south-east of Milan, near to the junction of the river Adda with the Po.

Cremona was strongly held by French troops, and Villeroi had established his headquarters there over the winter. Prince Commercy, who knew the place well, described the street layout to Eugene, drawing attention to a minor drainage channel usually not guarded. The Duc de St Simon wrote afterwards that 'Eugene ascertained that there was at Cremona an ancient aqueduct which extended far out into the country, and which started from the town in the vault of a house occupied by a priest'.[15] On 28 January, Guido von Starhemberg was sent with a 4,000-strong detachment to Ostiano, with instructions to close in on Cremona from the north, while Prince Charles Vaudémont with some 5,000 men approached the Po Gate of the city from the south-west. Three days later, Eugene joined von Starhemberg, but although the weather was bad, with heavy rain and roads clogged with icy slush, in the early morning of 1 February the attacking force was in position, apparently undetected by the garrison. A Major Hoffman with 200 men went forward and gained entrance to the city by crawling through the unguarded channel, followed by more troops under the command of Count Kufstein and Count Nassary. While these detachments made their quiet way through the outer defences, Eugene had Count Claude Mercy close up to the Margherita Gate on the northern side of the city, which Hoffman's men had secured and thrown open. They moved rapidly through the sleeping streets to open the Po Gate, and the defences were laid bare, so that Austrian troops began to pour into the city, but the alarm was given, bells rang, firing began, and the clamour grew with all the rapid and startling intensity of sudden hand-to-hand street fighting.

Villeroi had only returned to Cremona the night before, to be abruptly roused from his slumbers by his valet coming in and shouting that the Germans were in the town. Throwing on his clothes and ordered his papers to be burned, the dishevelled marshal rode to the main guard-post to try and rally the defence, but was hauled off his horse and taken prisoner by a Captain MacDonnell, an Irish soldier of fortune in the Imperial service. The offer of a handsome bribe was refused, and the captain took Villeroi to where von Starhemberg was directing the assault (it was rumoured that he had actually been taken while still dressing, but the more generously inclined accepted that the French commander had been in action in the street). Ironically enough it was a number of Irish troops in the French service who eventually drove the Austrians back from the Po Gate, Mercy being wounded and taken prisoner. As the garrison recovered from their surprise, they fought very well, particularly those under the immediate command of the Marquis d'Entragues, and Eugene lacked the numbers on hand to overwhelm them. 'D'Entragues was a bold and skilful soldier,' St Simon wrote, 'with a great desire to distinguish himself . . . and kept up a defence so obstinate, that he gave time to all the town to awake.'[16] The loss of the Po Gate undermined the assault, Vaudémont was delayed and could not get his troops through, and Eugene saw by the early afternoon that there was nothing more to be gained. He withdrew with his prisoners, prominent amongst them, of course, the unfortunate Villeroi who received appropriately courteous treatment while being escorted to Ostiano. Some 1,200 of the garrison were listed as casualties or captured, while Eugene had lost almost 700 killed and wounded in the attempt, and left a similar number behind as prisoners. A daring and brave effort, which fell well short of success, but the unique capture of a Marshal of France, albeit while attempting gallantly to restore matters, was news received with astonishment in Versailles.

Eugene had achieved a neat if limited and rather expensive success at Cremona, and the exploit was a sensation when reports circulated throughout Europe. Villeroi was conducted to comfortable and honourable captivity in Graz, where he was soon released and returned to Versailles, while a recovered Count Mercy was released under the same arrangement. Villeroi sent Eugene a draft of money to cover the expense of his keep while a prisoner, but the chit remained uncashed. The new problem for Eugene, stemming from all this, was that Louis XIV replaced Villeroi with a field commander of a very different stripe, in the form of Louis-Joseph de Bourbon, Duc de Vendôme. A bruising and dangerous soldier (incidentally a relation of Eugene on both sides of the family), he could be trusted to take the French campaign forward in ways his rather dilettante predecessor had not: 'He neglected details too much . . . but in the days of battle, he repaired everything by a presence of mind and by inspiration of genius which danger always aroused in him.'[17] Before Vendôme could arrive, the subordinate French commanders, intimidated by Eugene's daring raid on Cremona, pulled back from the Oglio and took up a fresh defensive position behind the river Adda. With this withdrawal, and only Cremona left as the last major French-held city in the region, the Austrian lines of communication and supply back through the Tyrol were made more secure. Not that Eugene had much hope of ready reinforcement or resupply, as Vienna was still slow to respond to his requests. The blockade of Mantua could continue due to the French withdrawal, but an added frustration was Leopold's growing interest in securing Naples in the south. With little warning, Eugene was instructed to detach 10,000 troops, under the command of Prince Commercy, to seize the city and region from the hands of the French claimant to the Spanish throne. Such a distraction would hamper any ability to press the main campaign onwards and he protested vigorously, so that the emperor gave way with very bad grace. Fresh supplies, money and troops still failed to arrive, and given the prevailing tense atmosphere between court and camp Eugene was probably not that surprised.

Vendôme reached Milan on 18 February 1702, and soon had almost 80,000 men, French, Savoyard and Spanish/Italian, under his command, so that he could comfortably outnumber his opponent by almost three to one by the time that the spring campaign got under way. Eugene still had troops blockading Mantua, and could not immediately put his full force in the field, and that he was seriously overstretched was evident. He had not been well for some weeks, but was just about able to hold the line of the rivers Mincio and Oglio and maintain a grip on Mantua, but the lack of money and supplies hampered his ability to do more. Eugene's protests to the emperor and Graf Heinrich von Mansfeld, the newly-appointed President of the Imperial War Council, at this state of things were blunt, but unavailing. Johann Pálffy, veteran Hungarian campaigner, uncritically loyal and a highly skilled cavalry commander, was sent to Vienna to plead for men, guns, ammunition and money. He was also to ask that Archduke Joseph, Leopold's eldest son, should come to Italy, to put fresh heart into the soldiers, but instead he was sent to join the campaign on the Rhine. In the meantime, Eugene had make do with what he had to hand, but the tone in the messages from the court in Vienna was hostile. 'I would be more disturbed,' he wrote, 'if I did not know that nowadays criticism is universal and that so far as it is directed at me it comes from people who like to puff themselves up with brave words, but who have not the smallest understanding.'[18] He offered to resign his command if Leopold no longer had confidence in him, but this was ignored, and the gesture was more as a mark of protest than anything else.

The weeks of early spring were quiet, a relief for Eugene as he was still not well, while trying to ready his threadbare troops for the coming campaign. It seemed that Vendôme proceeded with a degree of caution that hardly fitted the circumstances and 'Had the enemy begun operations in March as they should have done,' Eugene reported, 'I do not know what would have happened'.[19] On 4 May 1702, the French commander marched at last, looking to relieve Mantua by crossing the Po near to Cremona and feinting at first towards Brescello, then retracing his steps, he re-crossed the river and bridged the Oglio at Pontevico eleven days after setting off. Eugene realized soon enough what was intended, but had not the strength to contest the passage of the Oglio, and instead drew his army up into a good defensive position at Canneto. On 19 May, Vendôme approached, and learned that one of the main redoubts protecting the gates at Mantua had been lost, so that the fall of the city seemed imminent. He moved quickly, turned Eugene's position with a flank march and neatly raised the blockade of the city, so that Eugene had to fall back and take up a fresh position between Montanara and Curtatone, with flanks resting respectively on the rivers Po to his left and the Mincio to the right. With dispositions that could not be easily turned, if Vendôme did attempt a crossing, to either left or right, there was a good chance that Eugene could attack while the operation was in progress and his opponent's forces divided and vulnerable. With the shorter interior lines, he could concentrate quickly and look to defeat one or other of the advancing detachments in detail before Vendôme could respond effectively.

Vendôme was astute enough not to be caught, and he drew his army up on ground fronting the marshy stretches of the Mincio, and the two armies settled down to watch each other, while their commanders considered their next moves. Eugene's first choice of action was a novel one, and on 10 June he despatched a raiding party under the Marquis Davia, his Adjutant-General, to try and abduct Vendôme in the house he occupied at nearby Rivalta, but the expedition was discovered and nothing came it. Perhaps having secured one French army commander at Cremona, Eugene hoped to lay hands on another and by figuratively removing the head, so ruin the French campaign for the year. Vendôme was furious when he learned of what had been attempted, and in retaliation bombarded Eugene's headquarters in Curtatone so heavily that he was obliged to move to Montanara. He did, however, establish a strong post observing the Porta Pradella, the main western gate of Mantua, and drove off an attempt to retake the feature.

The new French-born King of Spain, Philip V, arrived in Vendôme's camp to see how the campaign was progressing, accompanied as might be expected by a considerable and elegant entourage who added not one bayonet to the army's strength. They had to be fed and watered in appropriate style, and forage found for their horses, so that they were a considerable distraction. There was, however, the enticing prospect of achieving a victory under the approving eye of the young king, and Vendôme sprang into action, dividing his army by sending a detachment to threaten Guastalla and Brescello in the Duchy of Modena, while maintaining a strong force to confront Eugene, who could not be sure quite what was intended, but countered by sending a cavalry brigade under the Marquis Visconti to observe the French movements, but Visconti was caught unawares and badly mauled in a small but lively battle at Santa Vittoria near to the river Tassone. Matters might have been worse had it not been for the good conduct of the Herbeville Dragoon Regiment, that came up in time to support Visconti and prevent a complete rout from taking place.

Eugene was not that dismayed, at what was really just a minor, if irritating, setback. It was apparent by the force with which Visconti was attacked that Vendôme had now split his army, and if the prince moved with equal speed he might overtake and do serious damage to one or other of the detached portions before it could concentrate once more. Leaving just enough men to maintain the watch on Mantua, he broke up his entrenched camp and crossed to the south bank of the Po on 1 August. Vendôme, who had marched to take almost uncontested possession of both Reggio and Modena, moved in response towards a fresh position south of the river, and late in the evening of 14 August he reached the small town of Luzzara. His attention initially centred on forcing the submission of the small garrison there, but he soon had to deploy to meet Eugene's approach. In fact the French commander had been outmanoeuvred, and the prince found what he had sought for some weeks, as his opponent was in close proximity with a divided army, having given away his superiority in numbers, finding himself in the open and having to stand and fight with what he had to hand.

Eugene halted his army at Riva, just over a mile from Luzzara, and was in position by the mid-afternoon of 15 August 1702, with Prince Commercy commanding on the right and von Starhemberg on the left, while Prince Vaudémont with the cavalry formed the second line and reserve. The attack went in without delay, but with rather a lack of finesse as no attempt was made to find and turn a flank, and Eugene was apparently concerned that his opponent might yet combine his full strength once more, or slip away before he could be properly engaged. The two commanders could each field between 25,000–30,000 men, and Eugene having been successful in luring Vendôme into the open, hoped to make his approach undetected, but this proved impossible, and a French battery on the far bank of the Po to his right harassed the troops as they advanced. A close-range musketry contest quickly developed, each side attempting to beat down the other with the weight of their fire, and the fighting grew rapidly in intensity, with Commercy well forward and valiantly directing his troops when he fell mortally wounded, so that his men wavered until Eugene came up to encourage them onwards. The attack on the left was also hotly contested, and it took Vendôme's personal intervention (a parallel of Eugene's behaviour on the other side of the field) to steady the French troops as von Starhemberg's well directed attack came thrusting in. 'The fight was raging with extraordinary fury, Vendôme rushed forward, rallied his men and led them on himself.'[20] Despite this, the French right wing was gradually pushed back towards their own encampment, as Vaudémont fed his second-line troops into the conflict, but night was approaching, and a mist rising from the marshy waters of the nearby river further obscured observation. Eugene's attack could not be maintained in the failing light and he reluctantly halted his men, in possession of much of the field, but tantalizingly short of victory. In the darkness, he sought and found the lifeless body of his friend, Commercy, throat and breast pierced by French musket balls, and was seen to stand in crestfallen silence for some time.

With the dawn it was clear that the armies were fought out and neither commander sought to renew the battle, so that the moment for Eugene to snatch a victory had passed. Apart from some sporadic artillery exchanges, almost for the sake of form, the opposing soldiers gathered in their wounded from the previous day's action, and by and large ignored each other, other than shouting some not-unfriendly banter. Accounts of the casualties suffered vary, as is often the case, but there is general agreement that at Luzzara Vendôme lost some 3,000 men, and Eugene slightly fewer, although some suspect reports claim that his killed and wounded were less than half those of the French, which seems unlikely given that he did most of the attacking on the day.[21] In the meantime, Vendôme received the news that both the towns of Luzzara and Guastalla had submitted to his summons, and so in his typical fashion he claimed in his despatch to Versailles that he was the victor. Eugene could also, just about, claim a success as he had undoubtedly frustrated the French commander's wider intentions to save Mantua, and in mid-September he received a letter of congratulation from the Earl of Marlborough, in what was the first of many such messages:

> The victory which Your Highness has just won over the enemy gives me an excellent opportunity which I cannot miss of congratulating you upon it as I indeed do from the bottom of my heart. It is a successor to the great actions in which Your Highness has participated since arriving in Italy, and which have been so valuable to the common cause.[22]

The armies maintained their positions at Luzzara, each seeming to be waiting for the other to make a move, but Vendôme was sufficiently impressed by the vigour shown by Eugene that he attempted little more before marching his army off to their own winter quarters on the river Adda on 3 November. On the way he took the opportunity to seize the towns of Governolo and Borgoforte, and Eugene was not able to prevent him doing so.

The campaign for the year, apparently so indecisive, was anything but, as Eugene with the smaller army, poorly supported and ill-provisioned, had foiled his opponent's plans, then outmanoeuvred and mauled him in open battle. For all the loss of a number of towns, mostly of secondary importance, the Austrian position in northern Italy had been held, and command of the confluence of the Po and Mincio rivers maintained. Eugene took his troops to find quarters at Carbonara on the Po, and then to Mirandola and Modena, from where he continued to urge the emperor in Vienna to support an army on which such hopes rested, but now comprising little more than 20,000 men, and visibly wasting away through neglect. 'We are at the end of November,' he wrote, 'and the troops have not received their pay for the previous winter, let alone the summer.'[23] How Eugene kept his army together at all in the circumstances is something of a wonder, but surely says much for his force of personality, as well as the stout stubbornness of his men, who seldom failed to rise to the occasion.

An astute English observer wrote of 'Prince Eugene being strangely neglected by the court of Vienna'[24] but Leopold had his own problems, amongst which was the necessity to sustain not two but three major campaigns, the one in Italy under Eugene and another on the Rhine where Louis-Guillaume, Margrave of Baden, faced Claude-Louis-Hector, Duc de Villars. The margrave had been beaten in battle at Freidlingen, by which Villars gained his baton as a Marshal of France. To add to this, Max-Emmanuel, Elector of Bavaria, had in August 1702 after openly allying himself to Louis XIV, become active on the upper Danube, taking possession of the free city of Ulm, and threatening to close the passes through the

Tyrol along which Eugene's army really should have been sustained. Of course, to add to all this, always at the back of the mind of those in Vienna, there was concern about ongoing instability in Hungary, and even that the Ottoman threat might reappear.

Eugene again threatened to resign his command unless his troops were properly provisioned, but this seems not to have been taken seriously, and so in late December he left von Starhemberg in temporary command and took the road to Vienna to plead his case in person. On 8 January 1703, he arrived in the city, to the acute discomfort of von Mansfeld at the Imperial War Council, who had been anxious to keep him well away from anywhere he could relate tales of corruption, peculation and fraud in the supplying of the war, not only in Italy but also on the Rhine. Baden faced similar problems, and Archduke Joseph had witnessed this at first hand. Appropriate reports were made to Vienna, but nothing much was done to rectify things; the self-serving machinery of Imperial government was not to be easily moved. Matters would come to a particular head in June 1703, when Max-Emmanuel moved troops into the Tyrol, while the unrest in Hungary at last flared into an open and brutal revolt led by Prince Francis Leopold Rákóczy.

In the event, tempers had calmed and Eugene's reception on arrival in Vienna was appropriately warm. He had embellished an already enviable reputation as a field commander, but his pleas, persuasions and occasional veiled threats made little impression on the Imperial War Council which appeared to be deaf to persuasion. Eugene wrote to von Starhemberg, in sentiments that soldiers down the ages will recognize as ringing true, that 'Talking to the ministers is like talking to a wall'.[25] It was, of course, not possible to make bricks without straw, or to concurrently provision and sustain operations in Italy, Germany, the Tyrol and now increasingly Hungary, as they should have been. What little was available often disappeared into the hungry pockets of nobles, placemen and bureaucrats along the line, and Leopold knew this, but he worked with the tools and with the servants he had to hand. He was outwardly sympathetic to Eugene but evasive, aware that the money demanded was simply not to hand. If the war was to be won, or at least not lost, however, then change had to come, and the composition of the Imperial War Council in particular, inefficient and slow-moving as it had become, was not adequate for the circumstances. Archduke Joseph was vocal in his own criticism of the council, as was Baden, more so perhaps than Eugene who tried without much success to be subtle and diplomatic in his approach to getting long-overdue changes made.

Leopold was loyal to his long-serving ministers, one of his most admirable traits, but this mitigated against his removing them when they were unfit and past their prime. The deadening lack of energy and aversion to new ideas hobbled everything that was attempted. 'Responsibility lay with the aging and fatalistic Leopold who clung to the servants he knew [and] closed his eyes to the realities of an expanding war.'[26] The crucial point, though, was that the government machinery was not capable of raising the money from the widely differing estates of the Austrian empire to prosecute the conflict vigorously, the German electors of the Holy Roman Empire were not inclined to provide money, and an efficient tax system such as had been devised to fund Louis XIV's wars was absent. The emperor's finances, already shaky, were brought close to complete collapse by the bankruptcy of the financial house of Samuel Oppenheimer on the old gentleman's death, in a blow felt to be 'heavier than anything the French could desire'.[27] The stricken company, now in the hands of Samuel's son, had been owed 18 million gulden at the time of his demise, and there was no way that such a vast sum could be recovered. That being so, the debt was ignored, damaging Vienna's standing with the great financial houses of Europe, and without subsidies from Vienna's allies, Leopold's war effort would soon collapse.

Eugene was surprised to find that consideration was being given to find funds for just two field armies in the coming year, something not in itself a bad idea perhaps but this would apparently entail not reaching a settlement in Hungary, but withdrawing all troops from northern Italy to campaign on the Rhine. He wrote to von Starhemberg that 'I can assure you that had I not been present myself, and seen everything with my own eyes, no one would believe how matters were'.[28] Everything that had been attempted and achieved at such cost would be abandoned to Vendôme without a further shot being fired. Furthermore, the possible junction of his army with that of the Elector of Bavaria, just then moving troops into the Tyrol, could not be discounted, and the line of the Danube, leading eventually to the road towards Vienna, would perhaps be laid even more bare. Eugene expressed his disapproval forcefully, and the proposal was dropped, but not before he had earned for himself the added resentment of those at court that he criticized so bluntly for supporting the apparently absurd notion of withdrawing from the Po valley.

Chapter 5

President of the Imperial War Council

Leopold had backed himself into a corner, but was encouraged to take decisive steps by Archduke Joseph, who wrote that 'My great task now, is to persuade the Emperor to change'.[1] He acted at last, with new and more sure hands being put to the wheel. The astute Graf Gundaker von Starhemberg was to head the Imperial Treasury, while at the end of June 1703, von Mansfeld was promoted to a nominal advisory role, and in his place, Eugene was appointed to be the President of the Imperial War Council. This was a moment of huge significance, as the future direction of Vienna's war effort, whether on the Rhine, in Italy or on the plains of Hungary, was now and would remain in his hands, and in the process he became one of the innermost circle of ministers and close to handling the most intimate reins of power at the court. How far this French-born exile had risen on his own merits, admittedly with the benefit of occasional helpful patronage, may now be judged. Eugene remained the nominal commander of the army in Italy, an unusual but not unique arrangement, and one that suited the circumstances, and he took care to maintain close contact with Guido von Starhemberg in the Po valley. A glint of fresh hope appeared that October, when Victor-Amadeus abandoned his alliance with Louis XIV and declared for the Austrian claimant to the throne in Madrid. That the duke would not have done so had Imperial troops already left Italy hardly needs stating, and this move substantially augmented the bayonet strength of the forces that could be deployed against the Duc de Vendôme. The declaration by Victor-Amadeus was all the more extraordinary as his elder daughter was married to Louis XIV's eldest grandson, and the younger daughter to Philip V in Madrid. The French king, to his credit, appeared to bear no ill-will towards the two young women on account of their father's change of heart, but Eugene's own rather cynical assessment of his cousin's behaviour was that it stemmed from him not getting everything he wanted from Versailles, although this is perhaps unjust.

Several tasks of competing urgency faced Eugene, the most pressing of which was to reorganize the Imperial field armies to be able to operate to better effect. It was also necessary to devise a strategy that would drive the French from Italy, and address the simultaneous threats posed on the upper Rhine, on the Danube to Vienna, and in the Tyrol, while Lower Austria and Moravia were threatened by unrest in Hungary. Reorganization of the army would plainly require time and care, but amongst the measures taken almost immediately was the forbidding of colonels to sell commissions in their regiments, a cherished practice that while long established led to inefficiency, favouritism and corruption. Predictable protests were thrust aside, and at Eugene's insistence Leopold stood firm in proclaiming this prohibition, and at least one senior officer was removed when he persisted with the banned practice. The laudable intention was that ability would play a greater part in the promotion of officers, men who 'Know well that it is only by their personal merit that they can secure advancement and who for that reason apply themselves to the service with the utmost zeal'.[2] That Eugene's own advancement, at least initially, was due to his own personal connections and a degree of special pleading with the emperor, well merited as it proved to be, remained a simple fact. In his case it could be argued that the result was hugely beneficial for the Habsburgs, but such happy outcomes were not always seen, and the sale of commissions continued covertly, and with so much vested interest involved this was almost inevitable. Instructions were also sent to commanders to reign in looting by soldiers, and steps were taken to prevent desertion, but both measures depended upon the soldiers being more regularly fed and paid, and these highly desirable factors remained something of a difficulty.

It was of course one thing to be appointed to be President of the Council, quite another to get things done. Responsible for the direction of war, the appointment of senior officers, and the general organization of the army, the Council's ability to dictate strategy to field commanders was limited, perhaps fortunately, as otherwise the temptation to direct campaigns from far off would have been strong. Nor could its members dictate matters of supply or finance, as these fell respectively within the remit of the Commissariat Department, the *General-Kriegs-Kommisariat-Amt*, and the Imperial Treasury. To add further complexity, at a local level and when troops were actively on campaign, the stocking and re-provisioning of the depots and magazines was under the supervision of the Supply Office, the *General-Provision-Amt*. All of these organizations had their own staffs, with lucrative appointments, practices and perquisites, not all of whom were well intentioned and hard working. It is only fair to add that all these bodies laboured under the perennial lack of sound finances in Vienna, and many did their level best in daunting circumstances. Perhaps surprisingly, and one way and another, large field armies were maintained with considerable effectiveness in far-flung theatres of war over extended periods.

For the moment Eugene, newly in post and not yet on firm ground when faced by predictable opposition, had like Emperor Leopold to work with what he had to hand, and long-overdue reorganization would require patience. He wrote wearily that 'It would take time to bring an army into being again, as so many years have been spent ruining it'.[3] The better tactical employment of cavalry and attention to modern siege techniques (something seriously lacking, as only in 1717 would formal instruction in military engineering be undertaken), would all receive his attention in time, as would improved conditions for the common soldier, who on occasions had even expected to pay for their worn-out shoes to be repaired. Smarter coats of uniform pattern, previously lacking, and made more close fitting than before, encouraged recruiting and fostered *esprit de corps*. The pike and matchlock having long fallen into disuse in the Austrian army, close attention to the effective use of the flintlock musket was given, in a version of the increasingly widely-adopted platoon firing technique, and this ability to build up a truly formidable volume of effective fire was recognized and nurtured.[4] The more effective use of the socket bayonet, the musket being thrust forward with the right hand wrapped around the butt-plate rather than grasping the stock where a sprained wrist might be incurred, was also taught. Such things were not Eugene's innovations, but had his warm approval, as was the use of light artillery pieces, the 2–3-pounder 'battalion guns', which accompanied the infantry as they moved forward. Concurrently the employment of what would become known as horse artillery, mobile and fast moving, was studied and developed. A military library for the better study and instruction of officers was established, the *Kriegsarkiv*, which proved also to be a real benefit for scholars and historians over the years. Eugene also abolished as redundant the separate War Council for the South, which was based in Graz, as it replicated needlessly the work of the Council in Vienna, so that he was accused of seeking to concentrate more power in his own hands, which was just what he was doing.

A significant threat was still posed by the renewed revolt in Hungary, added to renewed unrest in Transylvania, where the depredations suffered by the population during the outwardly successful wars with Ottomans had received little attention from Vienna. Resentment at neglectful rule and burdensome taxation was rife, and powerful local magnates such as Ráckóczy and Count Alexander Károyli, not entirely self-seeking in their activities, stirred up trouble and led the growing revolt.[5] That the hereditary right of the Habsburgs to rule in greater Hungary had been proclaimed without consulting the nobility and gentry aggravated matters, while local rights and privileges dating back to the 'Golden Bull' of 1222 had been abolished with unwise haste. The Imperial field commander, Count Schlick, was making a poor job of things, while Louis XIV was using the fresh opportunity to make trouble, and French money and military advisers were provided to assist the rebels and foster discontent. The Ottomans were quiet for the moment, but that might not last even though they tended to abide by agreed treaty terms. The moment was one of clear danger for Vienna, with the prospect of the potential loss of much of Hungary, the central Danube basin, Transylvania and Little (western) Wallachia, in essence all those hard-won gains following on from the lifting of the Ottoman siege of Vienna 30 years before, successes added to in great measure by Eugene at Zenta. A mood of near panic came to grip Vienna, as refugees from the growing turmoil in the east flooded in with tales of rapine, widespread plunder, atrocities, massacres and reprisals. The plight of the people in the ravaged region undoubtedly aroused the prince's sympathy, as policy in Vienna had been neglectful and even foolishly punitive, but he knew Ráckóczy well, as they had been neighbours in Vienna at one time, and distrusted him. In any case rebellion was rebellion and not to be tolerated.

Eugene was sent by Leopold to get a grip on the situation in December 1703, going first to Pressburg, where the opportunity was taken to quietly send the crown of Hungary to Vienna for 'safe keeping'. Once more, faced with having only too few ill-equipped troops under command, he had to appeal for more men and supplies, and his requests were met, at least in part. 'Your Majesty,' he wrote witheringly to Leopold, 'has neither an adequately equipped army in Hungary, or the means available to make it so.'[6] The point was made and by a variety of means funds were obtained, with the Imperial Riding School in Vienna persuaded to contribute 150,000 gulden, church property taxed for the first time (with the permission of the Vatican), and prominent private citizens encouraged to pay, equip and clothe newly enlisted soldiers. However, matters were so serious that consideration was given to accepting an offer by the Polish king of an army commanded by Prince Lubomirski to help suppress the rebellion. This was not necessary, as the measures Eugene took to augment his own forces proved effective enough, and he was able to stabilize matters and reinforce garrisons holding the key crossing points on the Danube before returning to Vienna in mid-January. He astutely permitted loyal Magyar nobles to negotiate with the rebels, not always in very good faith it should be said, as the aim really was to gain time, but in the meantime Johan Pálffy, a veteran of proven ability, was left in command at Pressburg as the Palatine.[7]

Eugene's presence back at the Imperial War Council was certainly necessary, as the Elector Max-Emmanuel of Bavaria, in combination with the French, posed a significant and growing threat to Vienna. On 21 September 1703, Marshal Villars had defeated a small Imperial army at Höchstädt on the Danube, just downstream from Ulm, but the elector was then hesitant to move decisively, with his attention diverted by a faltering campaign in the Tyrol, fought with great savagery by local militias who had been supported by troops sent by Eugene from his own slim resources. In the process, what was perhaps the most promising moment for an advance on Vienna had passed. In the meantime, Duke Victor-Amadeus and von Starhemberg in the valleys of the Po and the Mincio effectively tied down the French troops under the Duc de Vendôme and prevented any support being sent to the Bavarian venture, despite clear instructions from Versailles to do so. By the late autumn, Max-Emmanuel had been obliged to withdraw his troops in some disorder from around Innsbruck. The strategic situation for Austria was nonetheless fraught, as the alliance between Bavaria and Louis XIV had allowed the French to stand on the defensive in the Low Countries and make progress on the middle and upper Rhine, while effort and resources were simultaneously devoted to threatening Vienna and driving Leopold out of the war. On 15 November the Duke of Hesse-Cassel had been defeated at Speyerbach in the Palatinate by a French army commanded by the Comte de Tallard (for which success he received his marshal's baton), and the major Imperial fortress of Landau on the Rhine was lost.

In consequence, with active rebellion in Hungary, the persistently inconclusive fighting in Italy, the threat both on the middle and lower Rhine and now most urgently on the Danube, the attention and effort of Vienna was necessarily, almost fatally, divided into not just two, but four diverse and poorly co-ordinated campaigns. The indications were that this was too great to be maintained, even if Vienna itself could be saved, and the grand strategic effort by France to win the war was, to all appearances, taking firm shape and gathering pace.

It can be seen, with the wonderful benefit of hindsight, that any major move by Max-Emmanuel and his French allies to attack Vienna must take the form of a grand raid more than anything else – the distances from the depots and magazines around Munich and Augsburg were too great to allow anything more. Still, the shock and disruption that an occupation of the city would pose was immense, and potentially a war-winning strategy for Louis XIV. His grandson was steadily establishing himself in Madrid relatively untroubled by badly co-ordinated allied efforts on behalf of Archduke Charles, while the Earl of Marlborough's Anglo-Dutch campaign in the Low Countries went forward slowly, with only modest successes, none of which would outweigh the effect on the Grand Alliance of the loss of Vienna. The potential rupture of the cohesion of the allied effort was obvious, and whether the House of Habsburg could maintain its long-standing role at the head of the Holy Roman Empire, with other ambitious parties in Germany eager to take an unhelpful hand in things, was a decided question.

Eugene resisted a rather impractical suggestion that von Starhemberg's energies should be diverted to threaten Bavaria from the south, in the main because to do so would be to abandon Savoy. Vendôme could hardly be expected to stand idle while such a thing was attempted, and in any case the simple difficulty of moving troops rapidly through the Alpine passes in good time hardly needed mentioning. Also, there was the chance, however faint at the time, of Imperial successes in Italy that were not dependent upon the assistance and goodwill of England and Holland, and as such was a consideration of no small importance to the reputation and standing of Vienna as an effective ally.

A most welcome, almost unexpected, respite had been gained for Eugene, as much by a lack of co-ordination amongst his opponents as by anything else, as Vendôme was typically indolent, despite rounding up much of the Savoyard army when Victor-Amadeus' defection became known. Also, and more seriously, Marshal Villars and Max-Emmanuel failed to work well together, and collectively they managed to mishandle things. Still, the Margrave of Baden, commanding the Imperial troops on the upper Rhine, had lost the key but ill-provisioned fortress of Briesach to the French, and was left firmly on the defensive. The unfortunate garrison commander, General Arco, was made a scapegoat to save Baden's blushes, and executed for the failure.[8] That the French army operating in Bavaria could as a result be better sustained from depots and magazines in Alsace brought through the tangled country of the Black Forest, notwithstanding small Imperial garrisons in places such as Villingen, was apparent. As an unhelpful aside, Baden was also suspected of being in unwise and indiscreet correspondence with his old friend and comrade-in-arms Max-Emmanuel, and while actual treachery on his part was not thought, that the margrave might be unreliable in a real crisis was suspected in Vienna.

In mid-January 1704 Bavarian troops seized Passau on the Danube, and the threat to Vienna both from the west, and with persistent Hungarian rebellion, to the east, assumed a sharper dimension once more. There were strong doubts amongst the councils of the Grand Alliance that Leopold could remain in the war, and a Dutch diplomat in the city wrote that 'Everything here is quite desperate, the Monarchy is on its last legs, and it looks as though the enemy will soon be at the gates of Vienna, advancing from both sides. There is absolutely nothing to stop them. There is no money. There are no troops, nothing for the defence of the town.'[9] In fact, it can be seen that the best opportunity to seize Vienna had already passed, and in exasperation Villars asked to be replaced. Ferdinand Marsin, soon to be the most recently appointed of Louis XIV's marshals, was sent in his place, but the depots around Munich were still inadequate for the demands placed on them, and the whole campaign, which might if pressed resolutely have quickly decided the war in 1704, languished as the precious months of spring and early summer sped by.

In northern Italy, Vendôme made the best of things with what little could be spared him, and generally did very well while great events unfolded in southern Germany. Von Starhemberg had neatly linked up with Victor-Amadeus and the valiant rump of his army, but was unable to make much headway against the tough French commander. With so many other demands on men, money and materiel, Vienna had nothing much to send, other than Eugene's encouraging words. The two men had at one time enjoyed a firm friendship but this was now under strain, with von Starhemberg complaining bitterly of a lack of support and appreciation for his efforts, and slowly their relationship soured, so that in time he would be amongst the most vocal of Eugene's critics. Eugene had once more to implore Leopold to somehow find the funds to properly equip his armies, but his appeals were predictably unavailing. 'Most of the soldiers have not a rag to their back, and no money . . . None of the fortresses have any reserves, nor supplies for more than a few days. No one is paid, and the distress is universal; officers and men are alike despondent.'[10] The difficulty was that this was a refrain that had been sung so often before, and each time with predictably diminishing effect. This is not to suggest that these requests were unreasonable, and that the Imperial armies held together at all was quite remarkable, but there must be a suspicion of special pleading by Eugene, as the troops, for all the declared difficulties and shortages, were actually very capable when put to the test, as events later in the year would show. To say that Leopold suspected Eugene of self-serving exaggeration might be unjust, but both men knew that additional money was not to be had, until greater subsidies could be obtained from the Maritime Powers. Were those funds to be provided, then London and The Hague would reasonably require in return a greater say in how the Imperial conduct of the war was maintained, and that would be highly unwelcome to Leopold and his ministers.

The French effort at this point was enormous, putting an ultimately intolerable strain on Louis XIV's treasury, but nonetheless seemed to promise victory unless something unexpected occurred. Marshal Villeroi commanded in the Low Countries, while the Marquis de Bedmar led an army in the Moselle valley. Tallard was campaigning with success on the upper Rhine, while Vendôme remained active in northern Italy. French troops and their bayonets were supporting Philip V in Spain itself, and encouragement, advice and money was provided to the rebels in Hungary. Quiet overtures were also being made to try and bring Charles XII of Sweden into the conflict to draw away the attention of the north German electors who provide such excellent troops to the armies of the Grand Alliance. Meanwhile, Ferdinand Marsin and Max-Emmanuel apparently held the initiative in southern Germany, relatively untroubled by the ineffective efforts of the Margrave of Baden, and they threatened still to seize Vienna.

On many fronts, Versailles appeared to be pressing forward to success, so that in these straits, Leopold and his ministers called on their allies for assistance. This principally took the form of John Churchill, now made Duke of Marlborough, Captain-General of Queen Anne's army and commander of the forces of the States-General of Holland when their troops were actively in the field.[11] His campaigns in the Low Countries had so far seen success but been largely indecisive, and he was eager to find an opportunity to campaign away from the restraining hands of his staunch but understandably cautious Dutch allies. When Count Johan Wentzl Wratislaw von Mitrowitz, the jovial Austrian ambassador to London, came at the end of 1703 to Queen Anne with a request for assistance in saving Vienna, he found a ready welcome. The count was a friend and confidante of Eugene, and the approach he made to Anne and her ministers was undoubtedly with his approval, even encouragement. That his proven ability as a field commander enlisted the confidence of those in London could be seen in an offer that was made of substantial sums of money to sustain the Imperial effort in Italy, but only if he was in command. This was clearly not possible in 1703 and early 1704, as events on the Danube were too pressing, and so nothing had come of the notion, for the time being at any rate, but great events were stirring, events that would turn everything in the war for Spain, and the whole future of Europe, upside down.

Chapter 6

The Two Princes – Blenheim

Seen afterwards as a happy stroke of fortune that was bound to happen, with the combined talents of two of the greatest field commanders working together in close harmony, the joint campaign in the high summer of 1704 was nothing of the kind. The crushing defeat of one of Louis XIV's main field armies beside the Danube on a hot Wednesday afternoon was the product of careful calculation, an appreciation of what might be lost through delay, and the measured acceptance of extreme risk. The result, simply, was that everything was different after the Battle of Blenheim.

Marshal Ferdinand Marsin had replaced Villars in command of the French army operating on the Danube, and he and Elector Max-Emmanuel could between them field some 40,000 troops. In facing this threat, the slender resources of Vienna were seriously overstretched, with the risk that the poorly-defended city would soon fall. However, such things are often complex, and all was not well, with Marsin and Max-Emmanuel having to rely upon supplies brought in mid-May 1704 through the Black Forest by Marshal Tallard. The Margrave of Baden proved unable to interdict this resupply or prevent Tallard's subsequent safe return, but this did not lessen the delay that the demanding operation caused. What results a fast, dynamic advance on Vienna might have had would never be known, as with the whole of the fine summer months for campaigning before them, the French and Bavarian commanders appeared to feel unconcerned at any need to hurry.

A plan to lift the pressure on Austria had been devised between Count Wratislaw, the Duke of Marlborough, Secretary of State Sydney Godolphin and Queen Anne. The notion of combining the allied armies to better effect had first been discussed in 1703 as the threat on the Danube became evident, but there had then been neither the time nor the will to push matters along. Wratislaw had, however, been in Vienna during the latter part of that year, and would certainly have discussed the project with both Leopold and Eugene as President of the Imperial War Council, and probably also with Baden. Marlborough and Eugene had not so far met, but they had corresponded and felt an instinctive liking for each other, although it is not certain, despite some accounts that Marlborough and Eugene discussed the project between themselves in their letters, that they did so without the helpful medium of Wratislaw as intermediary.[1] It may be seen, however, that had Eugene not been available to campaign in combination with his ally, the duke would probably not have marched south.

Marlborough's intention was to free himself from the constricted nature of campaigning in the Low Countries, and take those of his troops in the pay of the queen's treasury to operate alongside Eugene and Baden to deal with the threat to Vienna. The Dutch field commander, Henry of Nassau, Veldt-Marshal Overkirk, would be left to keep things safe. The project was fraught with risk, and in conversation with the British minister in Vienna during the second week of February, Eugene was so unsure that things would proceed that he made no mention of a joint campaign on the Danube. Still, Wratislaw remained active, writing to the queen on 2 April asking that she 'Ensure that the troops which Her Majesty maintained on the continent would be used to protect Germany from a complete collapse'.[2] This was a key sentiment, setting out the simple truth that Queen Anne could direct her troops, and those she paid for, as she saw fit, although care had to be taken not to alarm the Dutch too much. Decisively, just two days after Wratislaw's letter, she instructed Marlborough to march his troops to the aid of Vienna, truly as wide-ranging a commission as could be imagined, but all would hang upon his meeting success.

That Marlborough would go as far as the Danube could not really be imagined, and the declared intention to the Dutch was indeed that he would go no further than the Moselle, to tackle the Marquis de Bedmar, that he intended to go whether or not he had their approval, and in this the attitude of Overkirk was important, as he had faith in Marlborough and his promises, but that the Veldt-Marshal was being partially misled is an inescapable conclusion. Still, this would only really matter if things went wrong, and the risk of alarming the States-General paled when compared to the danger of having Austria driven out of the war for lack of support.

One condition was insisted on, that the duke and Eugene should act in close co-operation, and Marlborough's requirement on this point was clear: 'It is absolutely necessary that I should have a supporter of his zeal and experience.'[3] Then there was Baden, resting on a fine reputation but now grown cautious, and thought to be too close to his old comrade the Elector of Bavaria. Leopold had been reluctant to release Eugene from his duties in Vienna, but at last consented, appointing him to the overall command of the Imperial armies in Germany, and writing on 15 May, 'I am sending away from myself and my supreme war council a person that I value so highly'.[4] The immediate difficulty was that Baden was at least nominally still in command, and Eugene's arrival in camp, an indication of a certain lack of faith in his abilities, would risk souring relations between the two men at a critical time, but in the end all passed off fairly well.

On 19 May 1704, Marlborough began his march southwards, gathering additional contingents of troops along the way, men all paid for with gold from

London. As predicted, Marshal Villeroi, the French commander in the Low Countries, had to march south too, in order to conform with the duke's strategic shift which did appear to be aimed at the Moselle. Meanwhile, on 25 May Eugene left Vienna to take the field, and carried with him the authority to override Baden, and even to remove him from command if necessary. This would only happen under the utmost necessity, and he wrote to Duke Victor-Amadeus that 'I have closely observed the behaviour of the Margrave *and seen absolutely nothing which would give grounds for suspicion* [author's italics]'.[5] News of Eugene's leaving Vienna carried quickly to the French and Bavarian camp, and Max-Emmanuel wrote to Louis XIV that he 'Can only have come to the seat of war to carry out some great project'.[6] On the road, Marlborough's growing army, soon to be 40,000 strong, passed Coblenz and the approaches to the Moselle valley, crossed to the right bank of the Rhine and went on to Frankfurt. The marching troops reached the river Neckar on 3 June, and arrived at Mundelheim to the south of Heilbronn a week later. The concerns of the States-General for their security were allayed, and orders were received that Dutch troops commanded by General Johan Wigand van Goor, already operating with Baden on the upper Rhine, should take part in the unfolding campaign.

On Monday 9 June 1704, Eugene went with Wratislaw to Mundelheim to meet Marlborough for the first time, and they quickly established a warm understanding that would stand the test of time. Eugene reviewed the duke's troops, and praised their good condition, aware perhaps that with the slim resources made available by Vienna, he would have been lucky to display soldiers in the same excellent trim. He declared effusively that 'Money, which you don't want in England, will buy clothes and fine horses, but it can't buy that lively air I see in every one of those troopers' faces'.[7] Marlborough in turn was at his most urbane, replying to the compliment, 'That must be attributed to their heartiness for the public cause and the particular pleasure they have in seeing your Highness'. This easy friendship was all the more remarkable because the two men were so unlike in other respects, with Marlborough ten years the elder and a devoted family man after his fashion. Eugene, although not lacking in charm when he chose to show it, was no accomplished courtier, unlike the duke, and seemed set to assume the role of a confirmed bachelor little interested in anything other than hard campaigning. Despite this difference in manner and temperament, there was undoubtedly a meeting of minds, and Eugene's private opinion of Marlborough is well expressed in a letter sent a few weeks' later to Victor-Amadeus: 'Here is a man of high quality, courageous, extremely well-disposed, and with a keen desire to achieve something.'[8]

Baden was present on 13 June when they met again at the Inn of the Golden Fleece at Gross Heppach near Stuttgart, to agree how to press their campaign forward. The margrave was already somewhat outside the cosy circle established by the other two, but the planning for the campaign proceeded well enough.

Eugene had already agreed to go to the Rhine to deter any fresh attempt by the French to reinforce Bavaria, while Baden and Marlborough combined to force decisive battle on Max-Emmanuel and Marsin.[9] It is often suggested that Baden had manoeuvred his colleagues into agreeing this division of labour, and that Marlborough would have preferred immediately to operate in close concert with Eugene. Perhaps so, in ideal circumstances, but the task of preventing any fresh reinforcement from the Rhine was important, and Eugene was as well suited to the task as Baden. At any rate, Marlborough agreed to what was proposed and to share the command of the combined army with the margrave on alternate days, but he was already tacitly acknowledged as the de facto commander-in-chief in the campaign. The duke was, however, given a word of caution from Eugene, concerning their colleague: 'He has been very free with me, in giving me the character of the Prince of Baden, by which I find I must be much more on my guard.'[10] This comment contrasts markedly with the sentiments expressed to Victor-Amadeus at the start of the campaign, but there was evidently still concern at the margrave being indiscreet.

Eugene left the following day for the elaborately constructed defensive Lines of Stollhofen, aware that with fewer than necessary troops, even after expected Prussian reinforcements arrived, his task was daunting. When Tallard's move came it was swift and capably handled, and he crossed the Rhine at Strasbourg with a 26,000-strong army, plunging into the passes of the Black Forest. Eugene left a modestly sufficient force in the Lines of Stollhofen to keep watch on Villeroi, and marched in pursuit with 18,000 men, but struggled to intercept the French, even though Tallard took with him a cumbersome convoy laden with the supplies so badly needed on the Danube, and moreover wasted several days trying to take the town of Villingen. Neither of the opposing commanders could really afford a pitched battle at this stage, as Tallard's task was to bring assistance to Marsin, while Eugene had to concentrate forces with the duke and the margrave before they, in turn, faced the newly combined and reinforced French and Bavarian armies on the Danube.

On 22 June, Baden and Marlborough achieved their own combination of forces, and they could operate with just short of 60,000 troops, for the moment outnumbering their opponents, who went into an entrenched camp at Dillingen on the north bank of the Danube, a few miles to the west of the earlier battlefield of Höchstädt. Marlborough needed a forward depot on the Danube, and he was spurred on by receiving the news from Eugene that Tallard had set off from the Rhine, and on 2 July 1704, a bitterly fought and costly success was had at the storming of the Schellenberg, routing a French and Bavarian detachment beside the small town of Donauwörth at the confluence of the Wörnitz with the Danube. Baden was amongst those wounded, shot in the foot while leading his troops on the hill, while General van Goor was killed. With this river crossing secured, they were able to move south, seizing the fortified town of Rain after a short siege, and in doing so blocked the road to Vienna. One of the strategic aims of the allied campaign had been achieved, and having lost the line of the Danube, the French and Bavarians fell back to a new entrenched position near Augsburg. Although Eugene sent word that they should be attacked there without delay, this proved to be impractical, in part because of the losses sustained on 2 July, and in an attempt to force the Elector to come to terms, Marlborough sent his cavalry to raid the Bavarian countryside, but to no avail. 'As the result of this ravaging, the fires and the forced contributions [foraging and looting] in short time there may be little of Bavaria left.'[11]

Frustration grew, and Eugene was sharp in his private criticism of what appeared to be a languishing campaign, writing to Victor-Amadeus that 'To tell the truth since the Donauwörth action, I cannot admire their performance, they have been counting on the Elector to come to terms'.[12] This concern was neatly summed in a note sent to the emperor: 'I am afraid that if we waste this opportunity, the English and Dutch will start to think of marching back.'[13] Things were complex, as Marlborough had never worked with Eugene or Baden before, yet all three were strong-willed men with decided opinions on how to proceed, even if the intention was to cooperate as fully as possible. Their troops were still gathering towards what would be regarded as full strength, the Prussian contingent under Prince Leopold of Anhalt-Dessau had only just joined Eugene, while Danish troops under the Duke of Württemberg were delayed. Overall, their campaign was in some trouble, for Tallard was close to joining Marsin and the elector, and they would soon move from Augsburg towards the Danube to meet him, so that the advantage in numbers briefly enjoyed by the allies would be gone until Eugene returned. Furthermore, they were dangerously widely separated while he was on the march, with Marlborough and Baden still in the vicinity of Rain. 'Tallard now is marching this way with all the expedition possible,' the duke wrote, 'so that he may probably join the Elector about the 2nd of the month. Prince Eugene is likewise advancing this way, and I hope will be within reach of us at the same time.'[14]

Tallard achieved his concentration with Marsin and the elector on 3 August 1704, just to the north of Augsburg, and the initiative in the whole campaign appeared to have passed to their hands. If the combined French and Bavarian armies now moved quickly against any one of the separated allied detachments, then piecemeal defeat might result. On the other hand, if matters were much delayed and no conclusion reached, Marlborough could not maintain his troops in devastated Bavaria through the coming winter and would have to move into central Germany to find quarters for his men, so that the allied campaign might yet fall to pieces. 'If he has to go home,' Eugene wrote to his cousin in Turin with acid veracity, 'he will certainly be ruined.'[15] The duke would be unlikely to get permission to return to the Danube in the following spring, so it seemed the French and Bavarian commanders could afford to play for time while avoiding being drawn into a major action.

On 6 August, 'attended by one servant',[16] Eugene rode from his army's encampment near to Münster, just to the east of the town of Höchstädt, to confer with Marlborough and Baden at Schrobenhausen to the south of Donauwörth. They faced a quandary: despite the modest numerical superiority their combined forces would soon enjoy, this advantage was not sufficient to ensure success without risk, and that was not to Baden's taste. He had proposed to take his own mostly German troops, almost 16,000 strong, to lay siege to the Bavarian garrison in Ingolstadt further down the Danube, while the other two kept their opponents under observation. Suggestions are often made that Marlborough and Eugene connived to have him out of the way, but that is to read too much into their deliberations. The next move, or as it happened the lack of movement, by the French and Bavarians could not yet be counted on or even envisaged, and in any case the capture of Ingoldstadt would have advantages, with the gaining of another crossing point over the Danube, and if Donauwörth was threatened or lost, this would be particularly valuable. Whatever the motive might have been, it was agreed that Baden should proceed immediately with the operation against Ingolstadt.

Baden marched off to begin the siege, and left Marlborough and Eugene to confer on what was to be done. It was reported that the French marshals and Max-Emmanuel were moving to cross to the left bank of the Danube at Lauingen, apparently to take up a position at their old entrenched camp to the west of Höchstädt. With this crossing of the river, it might seem prudent for Marlborough to march at once to combine with Eugene near to Münster, but for the moment he was constrained, although he edged closer to the Danube crossings around Donauwörth. Still figuratively light on his feet, he could cover Rain if necessary, and protect Baden's move against Ingolstadt, while the principal strategic aim was still the protection of Vienna, and the best way to bar that road was to remain for the moment south of the Danube. So, at least until his opponents showed their hand more clearly, he had to stand fast, while Eugene returned to his own troops encamped between Donauwörth and Höchstädt.

On 10 August, Eugene found that his outposts closest to the approaches to Höchstädt were being driven in, and wrote to Marlborough in some agitation, but with a judicious appreciation of what had happened, what was the threat and the opportunity that was presented. The letter, heavy with significance, ran:

The enemy have marched. It is almost certain that the whole army is passing the Danube. They have pushed a Lieutenant-Colonel whom I sent to reconnoitre back to Höchstädt. The plain of Dillingen is crowded with troops. I have held on all day; but with eighteen battalions I dare not risk staying the night. I quit however with much regret [the position] being good and if he takes it, it will cost us much to get it back. I am therefore marching the infantry and part of the cavalry this night to a camp I have marked out

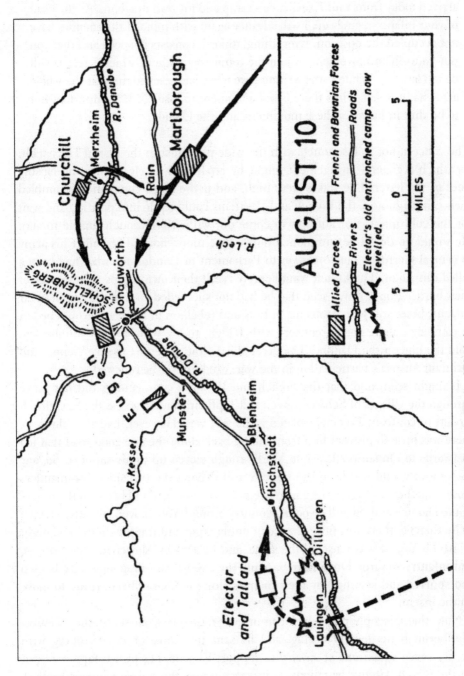

Map 4. The Movements of the Armies prior to the Battle of Blenheim.

before Donauwörth. I shall stay here as long as I can with the cavalry which arrived today from Your Excellence's camp and my own dragoons. As the head of your infantry comes up, I will advance again with mine, if the enemies have not occupied the position. Everything, milord, consists in speed and that you put yourself in movement to join me tomorrow without which I fear it will be too late. . . . While I was writing sure news has reached me that the whole army has crossed. Thus there is not a moment to lose . . . It is important not to be shut in between these mountains and the Danube.[17]

The concern not to lose touch with the wide plain just to the east of Höchstädt, on which a general engagement might be attempted, is clear from the closing lines of the letter. The stakes were high, and if the allied commanders fumbled their campaign now, the French and Bavarians could settle into position and wait for the cold months of autumn to come on, with Marlborough unable to stay. He would no doubt be summoned north once more, not only to billet his army in central Germany but to answer to Parliament in London for what had been a failed campaign. The Dutch would surely recall their own troops to help protect their borders, once it was seen that he had not succeeded, and in the coming year Eugene, beset still with problems in Italy and rebellion in Hungary, would be left to campaign alone and in concert with Baden, to try with inferior numbers to hold the line on the Danube. The great allied strategic effort to save Vienna, and maintain Austria's participation in the war, would never be renewed.

It might seem odd that the French and Bavarian commanders did not move through the villages of Schwenningen and Tapfheim and on across the Kesselbach stream to confront Eugene, isolated as he still was. However, had they done so, there was little to prevent him from falling back along the one good road that led eastwards to Donauwörth, while Marlborough closed up to his support. So, any such move would just have had the effect of driving the two allied commanders closer together, and given the constricted nature of the ground between the waters of the Danube and the hilly wooded country around Appelhoven, already referred to by Eugene, there was little chance of outflanking and trapping him. The night of 10/11 August was tense all the same, and he sent his slower-moving baggage and infantry towards Donauwörth, while the cavalry and dragoons were booted and spurred and standing by their mounts along the Kesselbach, ready to move on the instant.

Now that his opponents had committed themselves north of the Danube, Marlborough needed no urging, and he sent the Duke of Württemberg with twenty-seven squadrons of cavalry to support Eugene. His own troops were put on the march, twenty battalions of infantry under the duke's younger brother, Charles Churchill, being sent on ahead, so that Eugene, with this fresh support, brought his troops back into position along the Kesselbach. The balance of Marlborough's army, to avoid congestion, crossed the Danube at Donauwörth before swinging to the west. The combination of the allied forces was accomplished in the early afternoon of Monday, 11 August, and what might have become a crisis in less capable hands had passed, for the French and Bavarians had not come much further than Höchstädt. So, both sides in the campaign had now achieved their initial strategic aim, that of combining forces, but each had failed to prevent their opponents doing the same thing. Neither had an overwhelming superiority in numbers with Baden now gone, and with the river on the one hand and the wooded hills on the other there were no inviting exposed flanks for anyone to turn, so that something approaching a stalemate, fatal to allied hopes, seemed likely.

To Max-Emmanuel and the marshals, it surely appeared that they held the initiative, as news of Baden's departure was soon carried to their camp, and a sound defensive position was available nearby on the wide Plain of Höchstädt. This was all a fatal illusion, for their attitude was one of complacency, and the elector had already dispersed many of his best troops to guard his own states, while Marsin was concerned that Tallard's cavalry were in rather poor condition, suffering from the virulent equine glanders or 'German Sickness'. He tried to keep his own horses apart, and accordingly proper co-operation was difficult, but none of this would matter too much, unless Eugene and Marlborough sprang into action. On the Tuesday, the Marquis de Silly was sent forward with a cavalry detachment to try and assess the strength and intentions of the combined allied army, but the most that could be found was that outposts were stationed in the woods on the far side of the plain. This discovery caused no concern, as it was known that Eugene had been in the area for some time, and these troopers were likely to be a screen to warn of any impending threat.

In fact the allied cavalry were in place to enable Eugene and Marlborough to view the encampment on the Plain of Höchstädt, and it was apparent that while the French and Bavarian commanders had the shelter of the small Nebel stream running across their front, they had pitched their tents and taken no measures to entrench their position to guard against attack. Captain Robert Parker remembered that 'Here was a fine plain without a hedge or ditch, for the cavalry on both sides to show their bravery'.[18] Seeming to be quite confident, but not entirely sure yet of numerical superiority, it appeared that they were just waiting to see what the allies would do next, with the comforting thought that the strategic balance had settled in their favour, with little to fear for the time being. Such an illusion would soon fall away, and the tactical plan that Marlborough and Eugene agreed for the following day was simple in concept although demanding in execution. A major risk was certainly being run, and the Earl of Orkney, one of Marlborough's best generals, remembered that had it been left to him, he would not have chanced an attack at all. Crucially, the narrow defile at Schwenningen, allowing easy movement from the Kesselbach, was not held, and had it been, the coming battle could not have been fought as the allied commanders would have been unable to get their army in place. Marlborough was to deploy his 32,000 troops on the left, to face the bulk of the

French forces near Blindheim, while Eugene, with just under 20,000 men, was to move across to the allied right to confront the elector and Marsin near to Oberglau and Lutzingen. By attacking with enough vigour, he would hope to prevent any significant reinforcement of Tallard in position closest to the Danube. The French and Bavarians, in their camp nearby, had almost 56,000 troops, of whom only 14,000 were the elector's, so anxious had he been to protect his estates from Marlborough's raiders

That evening, troops of the allied advance guard, who with pioneers were busily clearing paths to allow the army to advance without difficulty, brushed against the French outpost screen and parties of foragers cutting fodder for their horses. The skirmishing caused no alarm, although the Comte de Merode-Westerloo, a Walloon cavalry officer, curious at the unexpected sound of firing to the east, recalled that:

I rode out beyond Blenheim [Blindheim] village into the corn-filled plain – taking good care not to get too far from my escort which I might well have needed. When I saw my troops falling back, I also returned to the camp, and sat down to a good hot plate of soup . . . I was never in better form . . . and I don't believe I ever slept sounder than on that night.[19]

Remarkably for such able and experienced men, Max-Emmanuel, Tallard and Marsin were not at all concerned at the approach of their opponents, and made no preparations to meet an attack. They had apparently received speculative reports that Marlborough was about to retire northwards towards Nordlingen, and may well have thought that this whole allied advance was just a feint intended to mislead, in preparation for such a strategic withdrawal. However, the occupation that evening of the village of Schwenningen by a brigade under Major-General Wilkes, thus giving access from the Tapfheim road to the open plain, cannot have gone entirely unnoticed, and that it raised no alarm at all is surprising.

The allied troops were raised from their brief slumbers early in the morning of Wednesday, 13 August, and the drums calling them to their feet could be plainly heard on the plain, but seemed once again to cause no concern. Eugene took the advance to form on the right of the allied deployment, moving through Schwenningen to take a position facing the Bavarians. Marlborough followed to form the centre and left, and as the mist gradually lifted with the warm morning sun, the whole march of the allied army, ready for battle, became clear. They were advancing steadily into position in full array, while their opponents were, in effect, still getting up from wherever they had spent the night.

Merode-Westerloo recalled the scene as disclosed to his astonished gaze from the comfort of his pillow that summer morning, as his groom rushed in:

This fellow, Lefranc, shook me awake and blurted out that the enemy were there. Thinking to mock him, I asked 'Where? There?' and he at once replied, 'Yes, there – there! – flinging wide as he spoke the door of the barn and drawing my bed-curtains. The door opened straight on to the fine, sunlit plain beyond – and the whole area appeared to be covered by enemy squadrons.[20]

A complete tactical surprise had been achieved by Eugene and Marlborough, but it remained to be seen whether the line of the Nebel could be forced.

The French and Bavarian commanders, caught napping as it were, reacted with commendable speed. Tallard and his French troops held Blindheim and formed the right and centre of their army as it hurried to deploy, with Marsin in the centre around Oberglau. Max-Emmanuel had his troops concentrated at Lutzingen on the left, facing Schwennenbach and the Weilheim Farm along the wooded edge of the Waldberg. For all their lack of awareness and preparation, the position they held, shielded by the marshy ground along the stream, was one from which they could expect to smartly repel their opponents. Marsin did send some of his squadrons to Tallard, despite his concern at the risk of infection in the horses, and he also detached French infantry under the Chevalier du Rozel to support the Bavarians on the left. He and the elector quickly decided to hold the line of the stream in strength, in effect making Eugene pay for every yard gained, but Tallard felt it better to allow the duke to cross relatively unhindered between Unterglau and Blindheim, intending then to drive him back into the watery obstacle, surely a battle-winning tactic but only if properly handled.

The going for Eugene and his troops as they marched across the face of the opposing army was rough, and between Wolperstetten and Schwennenbach they were also exposed to long-range cannon-shot. The uneven fields were cut through with marshy rivulets feeding down into the Nebel, and slow time was made getting into position. Marlborough had a simpler task, as the distance from Schwenningen was shorter and the open cornfields more firm underfoot. The duke moved into place fairly quickly, but Eugene found it hard work getting properly into position over ground covered with 'Brambles, hedges and other encumbrances',[21] and most of his artillery was not able to come up in good time. Marlborough's troops were also exposed to a sharp cannonade by Tallard's gunners while he waited for the prince to get into place, and he displayed an uncharacteristic (if understandable) degree of impatience. What had been gained by the march through the night might well be lost as the hot morning sped by, and Marlborough's chaplain, Francis Hare, wrote that:

Both armies continued to cannonade each other very briskly but the fire of the enemy's artillery was not so well answered by the cannon of Prince

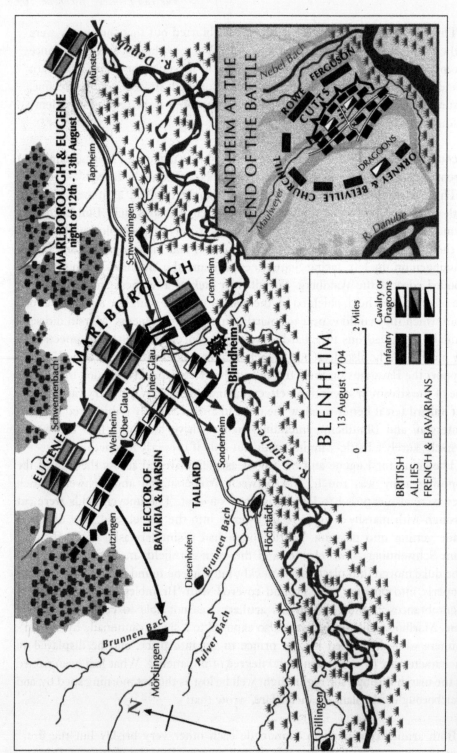

Map 5. The Battle of Blenheim, 13 August 1704.

Eugene as it was by the left wing [Marlborough's]; for his highness was obliged to sustain the fire of the enemy's artillery all the while he was drawing up his troops, but could not bring his own field pieces to bear against them on account of many ditches and other impediments from one extremity of his wing to the other.[22]

After all that the allied commanders had achieved, there was much still at risk, as their opponents were in a defensive position with much natural strength, the right flank secure on the marshy banks of the Danube and the left anchored in the wooded hills beyond Lutzingen. The villages of Blindheim, Oberglau and Lutzingen were being barricaded and prepared for defence, strong batteries were now established and in play, while the open plain, particularly between Oberglau and Blindheim, was well suited for the employment of the powerful French cavalry. To add to this, across the whole of their front, ran the Nebel, so that, for all the unpleasant surprise that had been sprung on them, Max-Emmanuel and the marshals had apparently recovered their tactical poise rather well. However, the Marquis de Montigny-Languet recalled that much of the stream had dried up with the heat of summer, and was '*un petit marais tres-déchéche à cause des grand chaleurs*', so the obstacle may not have been all that it seemed.[23]

At about midday Marlborough sent an aide to Eugene to enquire about his progress, and apply a little pressure, The reply came within half an hour that although his batteries were not all in place, the attack by the allied army could be made. Marlborough's infantry immediately began to cross the Nebel, but their initial attack was sharply repulsed, as was an early advance by the duke's cavalry. Fatally, the French commander in Blindheim, the Marquis de Clerambault, began to pull in many of the nearby infantry battalions, leaving Tallard's horsemen devoid of proper support. The marshal, distracted by events, and perplexed at an unexpected rout of the elite Gens d'Armes, inexplicably failed to prevent what the marquis was doing, and in time the consequences would be severe.

Max-Emmanuel was a brave and capable soldier, hero of the capture of Belgrade 16 years before, and his troops fought well as Eugene's infantry came across the Nebel. The elector had under command just five of his own battalions, added to the ten sent over by Marsin, which were placed in the woods to the left of the village. The prince in turn could deploy seven Danish and eleven Prussian battalions under Prince Leopold of Anhalt-Dessau (perhaps 11,000 bayonets), so opposing numbers of infantry around Lutzingen were probably only slightly in his favour, and the Bavarians had the advantage of position. Anhalt-Dessau's advance met a heavy fire, and casualties in the tightly-packed ranks mounted rapidly, so that after briefly overrunning a forward battery, the Prussians were driven back by a counter-attack by the Liebgarde Fusilier Regiment led by the redoubtable Marquis Alessandro de Maffei. The Danish infantry commanded by Count Scholten tried to flank the Bavarian position in Lutzingen, but du Rozel's

French troops in the wooded copses held their ground with great determination. As Anhalt-Dessau's troops fell back, the Danes found their flank uncovered and had no choice but to also withdraw.

Meanwhile, Eugene's cavalry, comprising ninety-two squadrons (Austrian, Prussian, Hanoverian, Palatine and Swabian), advanced to confront the elector's cavalry under Count Wolframsdorf on the fields between Lutzingen and Oberglau. The well-handled advance across the Nebel was led by Prince Maximilien of Hanover, but although the first line of Bavarian cavalry broke, the elector's second-line squadrons came forward and the attack was firmly repulsed. The Bavarian cuirassiers, free to manoeuvre for the moment, fell on the exposed flank of the Prussian infantry as they retired, and two of the battalions were scattered, regimental colours lost, and only with difficulty formed again. Although vigorously repulsed left and right, Eugene ordered Maximilien forward once more, but met a sharp crossfire from French and Bavarian artillery posted in and around both Lutzingen and Oberglau. Losses in the ranks were heavy and Marsin's French squadrons resolutely advanced in turn, so that Eugene's cavalry had to fall back, in increasing disarray, in the face of a remorseless second counter-attack.

By about 4.30pm, after two determined attacks and two sharp repulses, the fighting between Lutzingen and Oberglau had come to a weary halt. Eugene and Max-Emmanuel, on their respective sides of the Nebel, the banks littered now with the bloody wreckage of the failed attacks, re-ordered their tired troops ready for a fresh effort. Both were seen riding along their lines, rallying and encouraging their men. Marlborough wrote afterwards that 'The Elector and M. Marsin were so advantageously posted that Prince Eugene could make no impression on them'.[24] The redoubtable Prussian infantry went forward once more to try and force a way past Lutzingen, supported now by guns brought down from the Weilheim Farm to the edge of the stream. Leading his men forward on foot, Anhalt-Dessau displayed the most remarkable courage in the fresh attack: 'His valour was such that he showed no [fear of] danger, and did lead on his followers most courageously.'[25] A vicious battle at bayonet point erupted through the lanes and gardens of the village, but Eugene could not get his tired cavalry to go very far forward in support, and what they did rather half-heartedly attempt was again pushed back by the equally blown Bavarian squadrons. Leaving the re-ordering of their ranks to Prince Maximilien, Eugene rode over to encourage the Prussians and Danes in their attack, and as he did so, a dismounted Bavarian dragoon levelled his musket at close range, but was cut down before he could fire his piece. The fighting was intense and costly, the infantry on both sides showing great determination, and Eugene complimented the bravery of his soldiers in his despatch to King Frederick in Berlin a few days later, speaking of their 'Intrepid courage'.[26] Despite the losses, all that had been attempted had so far been in vain, Scholten's Danes were still unable to drive du Rozels' French infantry from the woods on the right, and Anhalt-Dessau had to withdraw his battered battalions once again in the face of such solid resistance. The intended purpose was fulfilled, however, for the attention and energy of both Max-Emmanuel and Marsin was entirely fixed on the threat to the security of their left flank. Eugene now received a message from Marlborough to assure him that all was well, and he was on the point of overwhelming Tallard on the wide fields beside Blindheim. There, the French cavalry, lacking support and desperately tired, were being driven back, while so many of their veteran infantry were bottled up in the village where they could not be used to any effect.

Marsin did turn at one point to thrust at the duke's exposed flank between Oberglau and Unterglau in the centre of the field, but the move was countered by a brigade of Imperial cuirassiers under the Swabian Count Heinrich Fugger, almost the only reserve to hand and sent down by Eugene from Weilheim Farm. Marlborough was then able to continue his assault on Tallard unhindered, and as early evening came on, his final cavalry attack broke the exhausted French squadrons who fled from the field in complete disarray. Merode-Westerloo remembered with masterly understatement that he saw 'A prompt but unauthorized movement to the rear by my men'.[27] Tallard rode towards Blindheim to try and muster some of his infantry, but too late, and he was apprehended near to Sonderheim and made a prisoner, while his army collapsed and fled the field.

Eugene in the meantime renewed his infantry attacks on Lutzingen, the Danes at last pushing du Rozel's French infantry back, and the large Bavarian battery in front of the village was overrun and taken. It was by now apparent to Marsin and Max-Emmanuel that the entire right wing of their army had gone, and with commendable skill they managed to get their own troops off the field in fairly good order. Of necessity they had to abandon some guns, but were able to reform their ranks behind the shelter of the Schwanberg and Brunnen streams before marching away. Eugene's soldiers were just too exhausted and depleted in numbers to pursue with much energy, and a few days later he told Francis Hare that he 'Much commended the conduct of the Elector of Bavaria, as well as the behaviour of his troops, and frankly told how often and how bravely he had been repulsed by them'.[28] The withdrawal from contact was noticed, but in the failing evening light Eugene's cautiously advancing troopers were mistaken for Bavarian cavalry by Graf Reynard van Hompesch, one of the duke's commanders, and he turned aside to meet the apparent threat, and what might have been a promising moment for pursuit passed. Accordingly, Marlborough's squadrons were allowed to chase Tallard's remnants, rather than intercept their retreating opponents on the other side of the field. Whether they actually had the energy to do so, can never be known: 'It being too late, and the troops too much tired to pursue them far.'[29] As night came on, the thousands of French troops in Blindheim, many of whom had not fired a shot all day, were persuaded, after a great deal of bluffing by the Earl of Orkney, to surrender.

Marlborough and Eugene had achieved an astonishing victory, destroying one of Louis XIV's main field armies in open battle and severely mauling another in the process. The tally of prisoners taken was vast, with hundreds of senior and middle-ranking officers amongst their numbers. Their total loss was no fewer than 34,000 killed, wounded and prisoners that extraordinary day, while their opponents, who had to fight a desperately hard battle to achieve such a success, suffered nearly 14,000 casualties. Amongst these were almost one in three of Eugene's soldiers who had gone into action, with Scholten's Danes losing particularly heavily. Victory was had, but truly only at a cost. Amongst the booty taken, leaving aside a number of coaches holding exotically-dressed ladies whose precise role on campaign was well understood, were fifty-seven field guns, fifty mortars, twenty-five cavalry standards and ninety infantry colours. The abandoned encampment yielded 5,400 loaded wagons, 3,600 tents, 4,000 horses and 3,000 pack mules, and uncountable piles of campaign gear, tentage and equipment. As a matter of courtesy, and also of internal politics, Marlborough shared the spoils and the prisoners with Eugene, but so great was the haul of booty that much had to be left where it lay.

The Battle of Blenheim (as it became known by reference to the village of Blindheim) was widely recognized as Marlborough's victory, but plainly only achieved due to the immense effort that Eugene made to pin Max-Emmanuel, and to a lesser degree Marsin, in position between Oberglau and Lutzingen. Only then could the duke first defeat Tallard's cavalry and then round up his hapless infantry, left abandoned as the broken French horsemen fled the field. The decisiveness of the day could not be overstated, as Louis XIV had up to then been dictating the pace of the conflict, but now he no longer had the ability to win in the short term, and would, if the Grand Alliance sprang forward to take the initiative, lose the war itself. Yet the victory was tantalizingly not complete, as Marsin and Max-Emmanuel had been able to draw off with their troops more or less intact, even taking with them two battalions of infantry who had already surrendered but had been left unguarded.[30] This incompleteness was of regret, so that Marlborough wrote rather carpingly to his wife that 'Had the success of Prince Eugene been equal to his merit, we should in that day's action have made an end of the war'.[31] Well, had his achievement been any less, then the duke would have struggled more and with less success against Tallard. One of Marlborough's illustrious descendants wrote that Eugene, 'After contending all day against heavy odds held the initiative and the offensive to the end; and who, moreover, in the midst of local disaster had not hesitated to answer Marlborough's call for the Cuirassier [Fugger's] brigade'.[32] Undeniably, while much of the glory attached itself to the duke, the victory was a joint effort and achievement, and had the one man failed, then so too would the other.

Emperor Leopold, amazed and elated at the scale of what had happened, wrote to Eugene begging him not to take risks, words that inevitably fell on deaf ears, but

'He could not conceal that his pleasure had been tinged with fear for the danger in which Eugene had put himself. He must implore him therefore to take more care of his safety in future.'[33] As it was, the allied army was exhausted and depleted after its efforts, and it was only on 21 August that they advanced to the vicinity of Ulm. There, Baden, perhaps rather resentful at having missed the day of glory, joined Marlborough and Eugene once more. That he would have performed a useful task in taking Ingolstadt was a potential bonus now lost to sight and mind once Tallard was defeated and his colleagues had fled. News of the disaster to French hopes flew quickly to the Rhine, and Marshal Villeroi came forward to shepherd the surviving troops back across the river on 2 September. He did so without authority from Versailles, clearly the right course but one fraught with risk had he not been so close to the king. Eugene reached Phillipsburg at the same time, and laid pontoon bridges, an operation that took five days to complete. Villeroi had by then taken up a defensive position behind the river Queich, where he could block any advance on Landau. He then prudently fell back behind the river Hotter, and on 10 September Baden was able to invest the fortress, defended as it was by a strong garrison. Although he could not prevent a siege of Landau taking place, Villeroi's performance at this perilous time attracted praise, as he clearly understood that to gradually give ground was a surer path to take than to risk all in another pitched battle. Some sneered at his caution, but Louis XIV wrote approvingly to him from Versailles: 'You have done your duty as a true man . . . You have been more concerned in preserving my army and my state than with your personal reputation.'[34]

Baden conducted the siege while Eugene covered the operations, but the preparations were rather hesitant: 'We are endeavouring all we can to get sixty pieces of cannon for the siege of Landau, which place would be of great advantage to our winter quarters.'[35] Meanwhile Marlborough took his own troops across the difficult country of the Hünsrück, to meet Dutch reinforcements under Veldt-Marshal Overkirk and strip out the French garrisons in the Moselle valley. Eugene did try to entice Villeroi into the open, but he was not to be caught, while a move to seize the French fortress of Alt-Briesach miscarried. Landau submitted at last, on 26 November, after a fine defence by the blinded Marquis de Laubanie, generally acknowledged as such. 'There is true glory in conquering such enemies,' wrote the emperor's eldest son, Archduke Joseph, who was present at the capitulation.[36]

Southern Germany was safely in allied hands, at least for the time being, and Vienna was not again to be put under such a direct threat. The Elector of Bavaria was made almost a vagrant, abandoning his lands (and sending his long-suffering wife, Theresa, and their five children to Munich), and went with the remnant of his army to resume his role as governor-general in the Spanish Netherlands. A generous offer was made that would restore everything if he would only abandon his alliance with France, but this was refused. The electress, stout of heart as would be expected of a daughter of John Sobieski, negotiated gamely with the victors, but with few cards to play had to agree to terms dictated by Leopold at Idlesheim on 11 November 1704. All military installations, fortresses and troops in Bavaria were handed over or disbanded, with the exception of her personal guard, together with almost all state tax revenues, except what was allowed as a pension at the continued pleasure of Vienna. To almost rub salt into the wound, Eugene was appointed to administer the sequestration of her assets and estates, and this was no simple matter, for the severity of the terms aroused indignation amongst the people of Bavaria. The garrison in Ingolstadt refused to admit Austrian troops, and only did so on 7 December 1704 on the orders of the electress to avoid a renewal of fighting. Eugene's firm and generally even-handed measures were enough, all the same, to ensure that a measure of stability was maintained throughout the Electorate at a time of considerable turmoil.

With the close of the campaign, Marlborough went to Berlin, Hanover, The Hague and then to London to receive acclaim and rewards, elevated alongside Eugene to the first rank of great captains. He had already been made Prince of Mindleheim by a grateful Leopold, with a theoretical vote in the house of electors of the Empire (yet a prince without a principality, the gift of which would have to wait for a while). Eugene's rewards were more modest, in part due to the continued poor state of finances in Vienna, but significantly he was already a noted commander whose established reputation spoke with certainty for him, while the duke's achievement on the Danube, his first great success, was seen as something quite new and astonishing. As a useful bonus, Eugene was able to recruit many of the French and Bavarian rank and file prisoners who were a part of his share in the spoils of the victory to serve in his own depleted ranks, and this was a better fate than the alternative offered, which was to be sent to labour in the mines of Moravia and Silesia. The Margrave of Baden, brave and obstinate, was inevitably cast into the shade by all that had happened that momentous summer. He suffered still with the wound to his foot received at the storm of the Schellenberg, and rather sadly, for one who as 'Turken Louis' on campaign in Hungary had been so skilful and valiant in his youth, and most helpful to Eugene in his early career, he would neither recover his health or the confidence of the court in Vienna, and died neglected by almost everyone two years later.

Chapter 7

The Two Cousins – Victory at Turin

While exciting events were unfolding in Bavaria, the campaign to quell the rebellion in Hungary stumbled on under the ineffective command of Count Sigbert von Heister. In June 1704 one of the principal rebels, Count Károyli, took his cavalry to raid the suburbs of Vienna, understandably causing great alarm. In response, Heister was urged to take firmer steps, and having achieved a modest success in an action at Raab, pressed on deeper into Hungary, looting and burning as he went, to again be successful at Tyrnau in December. The count's brutal activities further alienated those in Hungary who might have been inclined to have peace with Vienna, and so the conflict, and the debilitating drain on slim resources and finances, went on. All this was regularly reported to Eugene as he pursued his campaign with Marlborough that summer and autumn, and a meeting had been held with Francis Rákóczy's representatives at Schmnitz late in October to discuss a suspension of hostilities, at which British and Dutch envoys were present, but little of value was achieved. The Maritime Powers pressed Vienna to find a resolution when so much effort was being devoted to the East, while, as London and The Hague saw things, the main task lay in the West. Those in Vienna were well aware of this feeling, but to Leopold, it was an internal matter of the highest magnitude and incapable of being ignored. Tempers frayed, and the plain-spoken British envoy, George Stepney, was recalled at Count Wratislaw's request, and Marlborough's son-in-law, Charles, Earl of Sunderland, replaced him in Vienna as someone thought to be more agreeable and acceptable.

All the while, Guido von Starhemberg struggled to hold territory in northern Italy. The very capable French-born Prince Charles de Vaudémont, who had been his deputy, died of a fever in May and his replacement, Graf Leopold Herberstein, was less able and had to be removed. The Duc de Vendôme gained important towns such as Susa and Ivrea, while Verrua was placed under siege, only 20 or so miles north of Turin. Duke Victor-Amadeus, dangerously exposed now that he had abandoned his alliance with Versailles, was left with command only of the region immediately around his capital, and despite a well-handled defence by the Comte de la Roche d'Allery,[1] Verrua fell in the second week of April 1705, exposing Turin to direct attack. Although Austrian ambitions still outwardly centred on securing as much of previously Spanish-held territory in Italy as possible, a persistent lack of support hindered whatever von Starhemberg tried to achieve. Working with Victor-Amadeus was sometimes an uncertain business, for he might yet change his mind again, or perhaps even be forced to do so, and look to re-forge his alliance with Versailles.

The hard choice for the emperor lay with having Eugene take command in the East, where the Austrian Empire was at risk, or send him back to Italy. In the end the Italian campaign was more pressing, and having spent much of the winter in Vienna conferring with Leopold and his principal ministers, Eugene took up the command in the Po valley in late April 1705. Assured as usual of the emperor's continued confidence, Eugene was aware that such encouraging words meant little when it came to securing what was necessary to take forward a fresh campaign with any prospect of success. Some troop reinforcements were sent on ahead, but what he found on his arrival was not encouraging, and he wrote to Vienna from his camp at Rovereto on 26 April, 'I should be pressing on with all speed, but with starving and half-naked soldiers, and without money, tents, bread, transport, or artillery, this is quite impossible'.[2] Despite the sombre tone, his arrival in Italy encouraged those around Victor-Amadeus, who had faced what appeared to be impending defeat, and the British minister to Savoy, Richard Hill, wrote to London that 'We sleep quiet in Turin, in full assurance that Prince Eugene is making all haste he can to do something . . . We have that Prince's word.'[3]

At his final discussions with Eugene before he left Vienna, Leopold had clearly been ailing, and he died on 5 May 1705, to be succeeded by his eldest son, Joseph I. As he was the King of the Romans, there was no need for him to wait upon the necessity of seeking formal agreement from the electors of the Empire. There was genuine regret at Leopold's passing, for he had enjoyed popularity both at court and amongst the people, but a general feeling also that the younger man, naturally energetic and inclined to be better interested in affairs in Germany, would be more effective in helping to push forward the war against France. All the same, the campaign in 1705 proved to be one of fresh frustration for Eugene, and inevitably a lack of funds in Vienna hampered good intentions. The Duke of Marlborough, on his journey back to London the previous winter, had managed to secure the services of 8,000 Prussian troops for the campaign in Italy, paid for by Holland and Britain, but the men Eugene led were still often unpaid, and perhaps unsurprisingly poorly-disciplined and inclined either to malinger or desert as occasion presented itself. Von Starhemberg could not be blamed for this: he had been left with an almost impossible task, one that he had performed to the best of his considerable abilities, so that although the French had gained certainly ground since 1703, there was still much to play for.

Eugene moved to relieve the important town of Mirandola, and crossed the river Adige at Pescantini, before closing up again to the Mincio at the same point that he had bridged in 1701. An attempted crossing at Salionze on 11 May failed in the face of stubborn French resistance, but his cavalry circumvented Lake Garda without interference, and he managed to reunite his army at Gavardo on

21 May. Eugene learned in the meanwhile of the death of Leopold, the impending accession of Joseph, and incidentally the fall of Mirandolo to the French. Vendôme was always a dangerous opponent, but was intent not on taking Turin, which might have yielded great strategic benefits for Versailles, but narrowly on preventing Eugene from advancing from the Trentino into Lombardy and the valley of the Po. However, Eugene had no intention of moving forward too far, as with little more than 28,000 poorly-equipped troops he could not do so with much prospect of success, and his army was hardly in a fit state yet to face the French in open battle. He could, however, manoeuvre to threaten Vendôme's dispositions, and so maintain sufficient pressure that he would find it difficult to turn in full force against Victor-Amadeus in Turin, a move that Eugene for the moment would be powerless to prevent. In a curious parallel, the French were also constrained, as the attention of Louis XIV in the aftermath of defeat at Blenheim was set upon rebuilding the strength of the armies covering France's eastern border, and to Vendôme's frustration affairs in northern Italy for the moment took second, or perhaps even third, place in the attention at Versailles.

On 23 May, Vendôme came forward to examine Eugene's position at Gavardo, but it was clearly too strong to be attempted, so he began entrenching a position with his left flank secure on the river Chiese and his right in difficult country. The French commander then committed an uncharacteristic error, leaving the army and going to supervise the siege of Chivasso on the Po downstream from Turin, while his less-able brother, Philippe, the Grand Prior of Vendôme, was left to keep an eye on Eugene. The prior lacked patience and acumen, and lured by what appeared to be Eugene's lethargy, sent a detachment to a rather exposed position on the small river Naviglio between Gogliona and Gavardo, blocking the direct route towards Lombardy. Eugene saw the opportunity, and sent Duke Alexander of Württemberg to drive off the French troops, but Philippe managed to reinforce the post in good time. Foul weather slowed operations, and lacking a full bridging train Eugene was hampered in moving easily across the swollen rivers and streams in the region. However, once reinforced by troops from the Palatinate, he left his entrenched position with 25,000 men on 21 June and marched to Nave, a few miles to the north-east of Brescia. The grand prior was caught out by the sudden switch in emphasis, and kept his attention on the small number of Imperial troops left in place at Gavardo. Once alerted, however, he marched swiftly along the course of the Chiese to Montechiaro, but Eugene was already near to Brescia and had gained the road to the river Oglio, managing to get a pontoon bridge across the river after driving off the Spanish/Italian troops commanded by General Toralba, to establish a fresh entrenched camp at Calcio on 28 June.

Aware that more than a simple demonstration was required to hold his opponent's attention, Eugene quickly seized the towns of Pontoglio and Palazzuolo on the Oglio, securing stocks of much-needed supplies in the process. Meanwhile, cavalry under the command of the Marquis Visconti overwhelmed

Toralba's straggling columns as they withdrew towards Bergamo, and over 1,100 prisoners were taken together with their guns and equipment. The grand prior fell back to the river Adda, leaving a small detachment in Soncino, which fell to Eugene after a feeble resistance on 12 July. He then moved forward to Romanengo, clashing with French rearguards all the time, and in this way kept open his options to move either to pursue the grand prior to the Adda or turn to cross the river Po. Eugene moved on to Prembate at the junction of the river Brembo with the Adda, but the water was too high, so he marched upstream to Villa Paradiso where a bridging operation was begun. Vendôme had returned, however, and by 12 August moved to block the attempt at making a crossing, so that only an unproductive artillery exchange was undertaken, and a kind of stalemate reached.

Seeing that nothing could be achieved at Villa Paradiso, Eugene moved downstream towards Lodi, and on 16 August closed up to the crossing point formed by bridges at Cassano on the Adda, a position hastily occupied by the grand prior with a detachment of just 10,000 troops. The Imperial army approached in three columns, deployed in battle array and in greatly superior strength, Leopold of Anhalt-Dessau in command on the left, Baron August Bibra in the centre, and Count Leiningen on the right with the key task to storm the stone bridge over the nearby Ritorta stream. The prospect for success appeared to be good, as the grand prior, although aware of Eugene's approach, had made no arrangements to meet a determined attack. His troops were encamped on a large islet formed between the Adda and the Ritorta, in a very constricted position with the obvious risk of being trapped and driven to destruction in the river if the bridge over the Adda, that closest to Cassano, was lost. Despite the hot summer weather, the river was too deep to be crossed easily, but conversely the willow-fringed parallel Ritorta and adjacent tributaries were too muddily shallow to provide much of an obstacle, so that Philippe had neglectfully put himself into a tight spot. This mistake could have led to a severe defeat, but Vendôme had learned of Eugene's sidestep from Villa Paradiso, and with an advance guard of dragoons hurried to join his brother at Cassano, hoping to stave off disaster. Assessing the peril at a glance, he hastily deployed those troops immediately to hand in positions of defence along the minor Pandina and Cremasca streams that fed into the Ritorta, from where they could command the approaches to the crucial bridges. This was done not a moment too soon, and as Vendôme glanced to the east, long lines of grey-clad infantry could be seen rapidly coming on over the sun-lit fields of wheat on the far side of the streams.

Shortly after midday, Eugene's leading battery began to bombard the French position, and Leiningen's initial attack on the strongly-built farmhouse covering the stone bridge over the Ritorta was so well handled that the building and bridge were both taken in fine style. In a sharp counter-attack the French got back on the approaches to the bridge, and the press of struggling soldiers was frightful, plying bayonets, musket butts and fists with a will, and casualties mounted rapidly

1. Prince Eugene of Savoy, c. 1700. Imperial field commander and President of the War Council in Vienna.

2. Duke Victor-Amadeus of Savoy.

VICTOR-AMEDÉE.
21 du nom, Duc de Savoye, Prince de Piemont,
Roy de Sardaigne, &c.
Mort le 31 8bre 1732. agé de 66. Ans.

3. Eugene's mother Olympia
Mancini, Countess de Soissons,
c. 1670.

4. Emperor Leopold I
of Austria, c. 1680.

5. 'Turken Louis':
Louis-Guillaume,
Margrave of
Baden, sponsor
and supporter
of the young
Eugene.

Above left: 6. Count Ernst Rüdiger von Starhemberg, staunch defender of Vienna in 1683.

Above right: 7. Field Marshal Guido von Starhemberg, a close colleague of Eugene, who later became a severe critic.

8. The fortress of Belgrade, viewed from across the Danube.

9. Emperor Joseph I, a great supporter of Eugene.

10. Emperor Charles VI of Austria, Habsburg claimant to the throne of Spain.

Above left: 11. Nicholas de Catinat, Marshal of France.

Above right: 12. François de Neufville, Duc de Villeroi, Marshal of France.

Above left: 13. Louis-Joseph de Bourbon, Duc de Vendôme.

Above right: 14. Louis-François, Duc de Boufflers, Marshal of France.

Above left: 15. Claude-Louis-Hector de Villars, Marshal of France.

Above right: 16. Grand Vizier Kara Mustapha, Ottoman commander defeated at Vienna in 1683.

Above left: 17. Gräfin Elenore Batthyány, close friend of Eugene.

Above right: 18. An Ottoman janissary.

19. The Hôtel de Soissons, where Eugene was born.

20. Eugene's Winterhof Palace in Vienna, where he died.

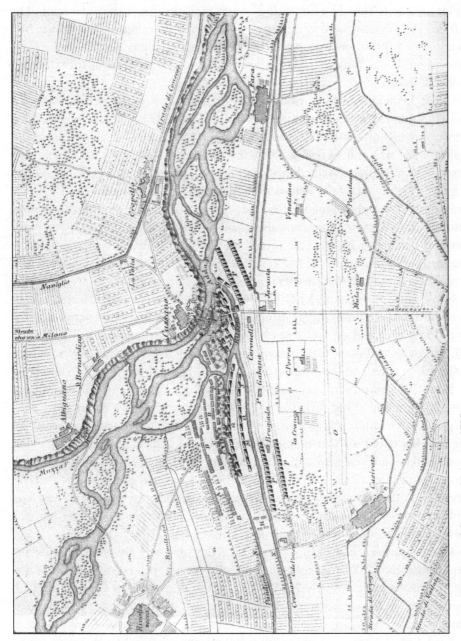

Map 6. The Battle of Cassano, 16 August 1705.

as the stone structure changed hands repeatedly. Nearby, hand-to-hand fighting erupted as Bibra and Anhalt-Dessau's troops scrambled across the streams, where sluice gates were closed by Eugene's pioneers to further lower the water levels. He hurried reinforcements to Leiningen's support and these retook the bridge, but Vendôme's dispositions were taking effect, with his artillery posted on the high ground on the far bank of the Adda firmly slowing the progress of the attacking Imperial troops.

Count Leiningen, who had been gallantly prominent in leading his men, lay gravely wounded, so Eugene came forward and led another attack onto the islet between the Ritorta and the Adda. The main body of the French and Spanish/Italian army was still hurrying along the road from Villa Paradiso to join the battle, but Vendôme directed his dragoons to form a breastwork of supply wagons which he manfully helped to drag into position, and although Eugene's grenadiers at one point stood on the barricade itself, hurling their deadly bombs into the ranks of their opponents, all was in vain. As fresh French troops arrived, hot and perspiring in the heat of the afternoon, the strength of the defence gradually grew, while Eugene had committed every man and, unable to effectively employ his cavalry due to the stream obstacles, had nothing left to feed into the fighting. His opponents had not been overwhelmed when most vulnerable, and Vendôme, in a dazzling display of improvisation in the face of fast-approaching catastrophe and making full amends for his brother's fumbling, had held him off. At this crucial point, Eugene was himself wounded in the neck by a musket ball while standing on the contested bridge, and had to hand over the command to Bibra. The baron was also wounded shortly afterwards, and with Leiningen already down and dying their troops for the moment lacked a commander able to grip the situation. As soon as his wound was dressed Eugene returned to the fray, but could see that nothing more would be gained, and so the islet and stone bridge were given up, and in the evening sunshine the tired men withdrew across the streams unmolested, and made their way wearily to the nearby town of Treviglio. An entrenched camp was prepared while the army rested and was fed, and Vendôme, with his troops equally exhausted, and perhaps counting himself lucky that night, did not try to pursue.

The two armies had been close in size that day at Cassano, with Eugene deploying some 20,000 foot soldiers and Vendôme, who had been wounded in the leg, eventually getting nearly 22,000 men on the field. Neither commander had used cavalry, as the terrain was unsuitable. The cost of the contest for the bridges was severe, a high proportion of those engaged, with almost 4,000 Imperial troops killed and wounded and another 500 prisoners left in French hands, while Vendôme could count his own casualties at well over 3,000.[4] Eugene was also obliged to abandon a battery that had been dragged forward to the edge of the Ritorta in an attempt to force the issue. The ferocity of the fighting, and the valour of the soldiers on both sides, was widely reported, yet nothing much had been achieved by either commander. Eugene had lunged forward to try and overwhelm an isolated French detachment while his opponent's army was divided, and Vendôme had valiantly prevented him from doing so, but both armies were intact, mauled and weary it is true, but still effective, and so the campaign went on. Nonetheless, it must be said that Eugene's conduct of the battle had shown much determination and energy but little finesse, and he clearly counted on defeating the grand prior before his brother could get more troops to the field. In this, he could be said to have been out-generalled for once, underestimating Vendôme's bluntly driving energy.

The removal of the wounded from the field of Cassano, under the terms of a truce agreed for the purpose, took time, but Eugene would not be content to remain on the defensive, so that Vendôme was constrained while his opponent remained active enough to cut at him. He was able, all the same, to send a rather specious message to Versailles claiming to have achieved a notable victory, but this was not so. Cassano was at most a costly and limited success when rectifying a tactical blunder, but the claim was typical of the man who combined great skill in the field, when indolence had not overtaken him, with boastfulness and mendacity. Now, the comforting thought was that Eugene might be so weakened as not able to campaign vigorously until reinforced, and so Vendôme could perhaps soon turn his thoughts to dealing with Victor-Amadeus who, after the loss of the fortress of Chivasso, was almost confined to Turin and little else. Even so, the British minister, Richard Hill, took a different view of the situation and the distracting pressure exerted on the French at this time, writing that to London that 'The French have indeed the advantage of the places, the posts, and the rivers . . . we see nothing to balance all these advantages, but the merit, the conduct and the valour of Prince Eugene'.[5] For some weeks neither commander moved, but on 10 October, Eugene broke camp at Treviglio and marched southwards towards Montodine on the river Serio, although Vendôme was able to shadow his movements and twice blocked attempts at a fresh river crossing. With the day at Cassano in mind, perhaps, Eugene prudently did not attempt to force the issue. However, a little-known ford at Mozzanica was found, and by 3 November he had his advance guard across, and closed up to the river Oglio. From there he could move over the river Brescia and threaten Castiglione, but Vendôme countered with a move towards Lonaro on the south-western shores of Lake Garda, looking to sever Imperial lines of supply and communication back towards the Tyrol. Eugene was too quick for his opponent, and occupied Lonaro himself, before the French advance guard could get there.

It seemed that neither commander could find a way to outwit the other and force a battle in the open on advantageous terms, while the cold weather months came on and Eugene had to watch as the discipline in his army deteriorated once more. That it had held up so well during a long and arduous campaign, with one particularly bloody and unproductive battle, was astonishing, and the credit must go to his leadership under difficult circumstances. Nonetheless, he wrote to Marlborough that his army was 'Ruined, the horses worn out with past fatigues, and [with] no sure footing in the country'.[6] As matters that year drew to a close, comfort could at least be taken in the fact that the shabby army was still in being, having enjoyed scant support from Vienna, and effectively diverting Vendôme's attention, whose army was now reported to be over twice as strong. 'We are carrying out here in Italy,' the prince wrote, 'not a war of conquest nor of [just] establishing winter quarters, but a war of diversion. This diversion already involves a heavy expenditure for the French in men and money. They have 80,000 men in Italy, whereas the Allies only have 40,000.'[7] Devoid of the opportunity to fight decisive actions, the terrible day at Cassano aside, and beset by all-too-familiar problems of logistics and finance, Eugene had still achieved a useful strategic success. Having sent his troops to winter quarters in neutral Venice (a neutrality that was blithely ignored more than once) he returned to Vienna, to receive the thanks of new Emperor Joseph for his efforts, while striving to arrange better supplies of money and materiel for his army in the coming year.

During that same summer, an ambitious project by Marlborough to force a way into eastern France through the Moselle valley had come to nothing, and he was obliged to take his army back to the Low Countries, so that something approaching a stalemate resulted there as well. In the meantime the oppressive and heavy-handed Austrian occupation of Bavaria caused trouble, and although eventually a weary calm returned, Eugene had to threaten two of his own senior commanders with dismissal over their levying of contributions to line their own pockets. Rebellion rumbled on in Hungary, tying down thousands of troops now under the command of Guido von Starhemberg, but the principal problem for Vienna remained a shortage of money with which to pay for the war. In the meantime, allied attempts to work up an effective campaign in Spain proceeded with glacial slowness, while the French claimant in Madrid steadily made firm his position. In short, 1705 was a year of much frustration and slender success for the Grand Alliance, even where such benefits could just about be counted, after the hopes of the breath-taking glory of the Blenheim summer.

In mid-November 1705, Marlborough had come to Vienna with the fabulous offer of £250,000 sterling (about two million gulden at the then current rate of exchange), paid for out of Queen Anne's treasury, to sustain the flagging Imperial war effort. Eugene was still away at the time, but he wrote to his friend in earnest terms, in which his own strategic vision for the conduct of the war, often cloaked from view, may be glimpsed:

The first object is money, so necessary to carry on the war with vigour and effect. You will, my lord Duke, judge on your arrival at Vienna, from your own experience, that a sovereign who is troubled with an intestine [*sic*] war [Hungary] and has large armies to maintain, cannot supply all without extreme difficulty. The loan therefore, is of the greatest consequence . . . At the same time, succours of men and money should be prepared for this army, so that it be enabled to take the field at the latest, towards the end of March.[8]

Eugene concluded with genuine regret that, being still engaged with affairs in Italy, 'I am much concerned that I cannot have the honour of joining your Highness in Vienna'. While the campaign was not immediately of strategic importance for the two Maritime Powers, other than to tie down French resources (although their ability to operate freely in the western Mediterranean would be hampered by the loss of Savoy), success in the region was still at the very heart of the Austrian aims. The paradox was, that even if Archduke Charles succeeded in Spain, if Austria did not dominate Italy then all would be regarded as a failure in Vienna.

The duke's visit to the Imperial court was an undoubted success: he was after all an accomplished courtier and flatterer, Joseph was a declared admirer of his achievements, and the vital war-loan was confirmed. Marlborough also pledged his own credit as security to raise an additional 100,000 gulden, to address the arrears of pay for the soldiers in Italy. It was notable, however, that these vital subsidies were only available if they did not pass through the hungry hands of those at court. If any insult to the emperor and his ministers was implied by this, Marlborough's urbane manners smoothed things over nicely, and the much-needed funds eventually found their way safely to Eugene through a finance house in Venice.

Marlborough did toy with the notion that he would bring his own troops south to work with Eugene once more, this time to force the issue in northern Italy, but the Dutch would have had none of it. In any case, the logistics for such an operation simply defied the imagination, and the experience of how well or how poorly Vienna had so far maintained an army in Italy was not encouraging. The duke's prospects for success in the Low Countries also appeared to be faint, but an even more pressing problem was that Duke Victor-Amadeus was in danger of defeat and being driven back into the arms of Versailles. Eugene was sure that the best way to challenge the French war effort, and divert the aid being sent to Philip V in Madrid, was to maintain firm pressure in the Po valley, concurrent with what was being done in the Low Countries, and the one was but one half of a coherent whole, with efforts both north and south meriting attention. He wrote that 'No breach can be made in the Spanish Monarchy except through Italy. This fact is evident from the efforts of the King of France to support this war, and his apparent indifference to other quarters.'[9] The plea was answered, and the army that he would command in the coming campaign was bolstered with additional German-recruited troops, for the money from London had been put to use in paying for their hire, as well as attending to the lack of pay for the patiently staunch soldiers in Italy.

Eugene found difficulty working with Joseph's new chief adviser at court, the Flemish-born Prince Charles von Salm, but fortified with the cash subsidies from London, and with the emperor's earnest support, which 'Provided decisive leadership to the talented and energetic ministers who now replaced the aged mediocrities of Leopold's reign',[10] he could certainly move forward with more confidence. On 7 April 1706, he set out once more, but matters in Italy got off to a poor start, when twelve days later Vendôme defeated the Imperial army in battle at Calcinato, just before the prince arrived to take up his duties once again. Graf von Revantlau, commanding in his absence, had been outmanoeuvred and then overwhelmed, with the French securing 1,200 prisoners in the victory, some of whom were subsequently very ill-treated.[11] Eugene was met with the sight of fleeing soldiers on the road to Roveroto, but his arrival was timely, sharp orders were issued and the disheartened men fell into their ranks once more. What had been flight became an orderly withdrawal to a new position at Gavardo, and when Vendôme approached two days later, he decided against making another attack, choosing instead to manoeuvre against the lines of communication around Lake Garda. Eugene had insufficient strength to challenge him, and withdrew from Brescia towards Riva, leaving behind a stout rearguard under the able command of Colonel Rolf Zumjungen to hold Vendôme off.

The feeling in the French camp was that after so severe a mauling of his army at Calcinato, Eugene would have to be content to hold the mountain passes leading to the Tyrol and do little along the length of the River Po. That he had not in command on the crucial day, and what conclusion might have been drawn from the fact, seemed to have gone unremarked. Von Reventlau, having proved himself lacking, was quietly transferred elsewhere, but Eugene refused to criticize him, simply commenting that not everyone could command an army in open battle. He then had to spend most of the next two months in reorganizing the army after the reverse suffered, while waiting for the German reinforcements to join the campaign. Vendôme characteristically failed to make the most of his recent success, and was content to adopt a blocking position on the river Adige, with strong defences constructed at critical points along the river sufficient enough to hold back any probe by Eugene until the French and their Spanish/Italian allies could concentrate at any threatened spot.

By mid-May Marshal Louis-François d'Aubisson, Marquis de La Feuillade, with almost 40,000 troops, had resumed operations against the garrison in Turin, commanded by the veteran general Graf Philip von Daun. The obvious prize for the French here was to effectively force Victor-Amadeus to seek what terms he could from his old ally Louis XIV, so that at one stroke both the Grand Alliance and the Imperial efforts in Italy would be ruptured. The formidable fortifications of the city, shielded on one side by the river Po, had been massively rebuilt to Vauban's design, but Victor-Amadeus astutely avoided being shut up in the city, and took himself off with some 6,000 cavalry to raid and harass the besiegers. This he did with skill, hampering the rather languid French operations and distracting La Feuillade who attempted, without success, to corner him. However, the situation in mid-1706 appeared to be grim for Victor-Amadeus, as two strong French-led armies were in the field, the one besieging Turin and the other blocking any hope of ready relief, while Eugene appeared to be confined to the edges of the Dolomites. Both French commanders, La Feuillade and Vendôme, were highly capable men (although each had a rather mixed reputation), and they had, it seemed, all the cards to play in their own hands, so that Turin and with it Savoy must surely fall. As so often when campaigning against Eugene this was an illusion, and powerful external factors were in play, not least the destruction by Marlborough in that same month of an entire French field army in the Low Countries.

Vendôme was sure that Eugene would be unable, or unwilling, to leave the security of the Trentino and try and force the line of the Adige, but he was mistaken. The prince had learned a great deal from his earlier campaigns in the Po valley, in particular the restrictions on freedom of movement imposed by other tributary rivers in the region. Used properly as silent but ever-flowing allies, these waterways could shield an exposed flank from interference, and cloak from easy observation the real intentions of a confident and fast-marching commander. Nowhere can Eugene's mix of strategic grasp and tactical skill be seen to better effect than in the campaign he now undertook, always with inferior numbers to those enjoyed by his opponent. Sustained with the additional troops paid for with the money that Marlborough had secured, at the end of June 1706 Eugene feinted firstly towards the upper reaches of the Adige. Having then turned once more to cross neutral Venetian territory, on 4 July he brought his reinforced army close to the river at Rotanova, while driving a French detachment from its position at Ravi. Eugene's engineers threw a pontoon bridge across the Adige close to Rovigo two days later, and 26,000 troops with all their baggage and guns got across without difficulty. The value of a properly-functioning pontoon bridging train, providing an army with mobility, was now amply demonstrated, and on 21 July the prince crossed the Po at Polsella, marched past Ferrara to Santa Bianca on the river Passaro, and three days later arrived unhindered at Finale.

Vendôme's dispositions along the line of Adige had been turned, and he had done nothing to prevent it, while still appearing to be unconcerned at the likelihood of any interruption to the siege of Turin. He wrote on 10 July to Michel de Chamillart, the French Minister for War, that 'You can count definitely that Prince Eugene cannot upset it; there are plenty of places where we can stop him'.[12] Such misplaced confidence was something of a hallmark in the character of Vendôme, as time and other occasions would show, but he was about to be called to take up the command and oversee the rebuilding of the French army in the Low Countries following the catastrophic defeat recently suffered at Ramillies. He would never see the results of his own miscalculations, but it was by then clear that the pace and the initiative in the campaign had passed once more to Eugene. Just as with the Duke of Marlborough two years earlier in his renowned march

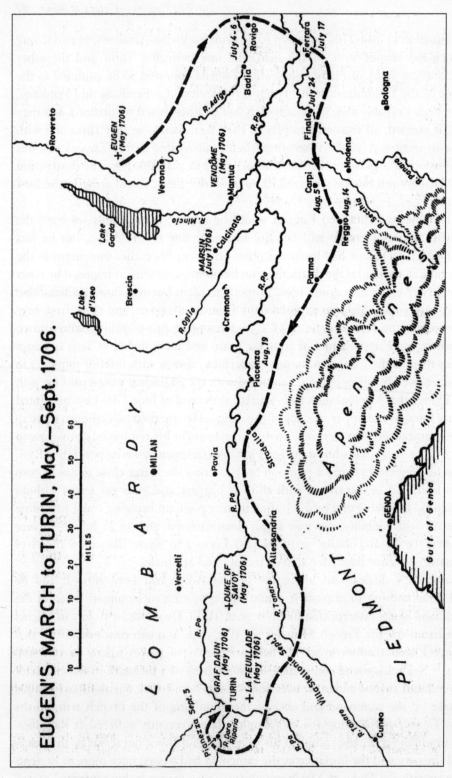

Map 7. Eugene's March to Save Turin, 1706.

south to the Danube, his opponents had to no choice but to conform to what he did, rather than the other way around.

Vendôme would be replaced in command by Philippe, Duc de Orleans, the king's nephew, aided by Marshal Ferdinand Marsin, and of course by La Feuillade who was still engaged in the siege works outside Turin. Orleans was astute enough, if not quite in the same league as his predecessor, who left strong garrisons in Modena, Ostiglia, Mantua, Reggio, Guastalla, Governolo and Mirandolo. In this clumsy way Vendôme attempted to counter Eugene's advance, but was left with a field army much reduced by these detachments, and a numerical advantage given away, so that the contending armies, when manoeuvring, were more even in numbers. When Eugene began his march to the river Po, General Wentzl had stayed on the Adige to bring forward expected Hessian reinforcements, and this neatly served to distract French attention, particularly when Wentzl took the initiative and attacked the small garrison in Goito, forcing it to surrender. Vendôme marched to save Goito, but was too late, and precious time was lost in the process. However, sending a request to La Feuillade to despatch reinforcements from the troops around Turin, he moved to occupy the pass at Stradella, looking to intercept Eugene there, but was once more too slow, for the Imperial army got across the river Secchia on 5 August to take French-held Carpi just nine miles from Modena, going on to occupy Reggio eight days' later, and then to Parma.

The confident advance of Eugene along the right bank of the river Po clearly left the French in doubt as to how to respond. The flank of the marching army was shielded by the fast-flowing river, and little resistance was met, although the soldiers suffered in the heat of the Italian summer, so that much was done at night and in the early morning. In timely fashion the weather cooled, easing the labours of the marching soldiers, so that Piacenza was passed on 19 August, and the Tanaro river bridged and crossed ten days later. The rapid passage was helped because Eugene's quartermasters and commissaries could, for once, pay for the necessary supplies from local farmers and suppliers. On 1 September 1706, his marching troops successfully effected a junction of forces with the Savoyard cavalry led by Victor-Amadeus, at Villa-Stelloni near to Carmagnola. It was undoubtedly a great moment, as the two cousins warmly greeted each other.

> With the great joy of the whole army we saw Lord Eugene arriving at about 10.00 in the evening. [The duke] went to meet him beyond Carmagnola and waited for him on foot . . . The Lord Prince saw this on arriving, and set foot on the ground and went to kiss his on the hand. H.R.H. withdrew it, and hugged him several times.[13]

A strategic move of the highest importance for the allied war effort had been skilfully accomplished, with inferior numbers and in the height of summer while marching around the outside of the curve. Eugene's French opponent, although enjoying the theoretical (but valuable) advantage of shorter 'interior lines', had looked on, seeming to be transfixed by such energy and daring, having not once moved promptly enough to intercept the vulnerable and lengthy columns. Crucially for the whole campaign, just 14 miles away from Villa Stelloni von Daun's 7,000-strong garrison in besieged Turin still held out, despite energetic French mining and counter-mining operations to try and reduce the defences.

Eugene's achievement, in conducting an uninterrupted march of some 250 miles past the Adige and along the right bank of the Po, was remarkable. He had deftly crossed numerous smaller rivers and taken possession of sizeable towns long considered to be safe, while outwitting his opponents who never once managed to divine his intentions long enough to engage him on the way. This constituted a quite unique passage of arms, arguably as great a feat as that of Marlborough's march to the Danube, and achieved without noticeable plundering of the countryside and its inhabitants, with troops who in many cases had recently been ill-disciplined and downhearted. The daring shown in the operation must also be seen in light of the fact that he could not hope, or foresee, that the French would so ineptly fail to counter his movements, to the degree that he would meet negligible opposition when on the march. French fumbling undoubtedly helped, and the Duc de St Simon wrote that 'An intercepted letter, in cipher, from Prince Eugene to the Emperor, which fell into our hands came too late; the deciphering table having been forgotten in Versailles'.[14] Even so, no matter what Eugene had already achieved and might yet achieve in Hungary, and what further successes would be had alongside Marlborough, the intrepid march of his army to relieve Turin in the summer of 1706 remains a clear testament to his standing as a great captain.

On 28 August, Orleans arrived to take up the command, and the French and their allies rather meekly achieved their own concentration of forces, but a belated attempt to force the issue and storm the defences of Turin was firmly repulsed. There was now disagreement in their camp as to the best course of action to be adopted, and as so often with Louis XIV's generals, the shared command had inherently dangerous defects, in the differing nature, reputations and ambitions of those involved. However, although many thousands of troops were unavoidably engaged in the day-to-day siege operations, they had now combined and enjoyed once more a distinct advantage in numbers. Ferdinand Marsin was cautious, and advocated waiting for Eugene and Victor-Amadeus to approach, but Orleans wanted to seize the initiative and give battle at the earliest opportunity. 'If we remain in our lines', he wrote, 'we will lose the battle.'[15] La Feuillade eventually agreed with Marsin, and so that was the course adopted, as neither were inclined to defer to Orleans any more than absolutely necessary when dealing with a prince of the blood. Such a lack of harmony would lead to unfortunate results, while at least a part of the lack of decisiveness seemed to lay with the peculiar state of mind of Marsin at that time, and he wrote to Michel de Chamillart, that 'I have not been able to clear from my mind the conviction that I shall be killed in this campaign'.[16] He hurriedly added a postscript to the letter 'At this moment the enemy are crossing the Po'. This cannot have made for the clearest judgement, and had he spent more time and attention poring over his maps and attending to the proper tactical ordering of his men, things might have gone very differently.

On 2 September 1706, Eugene and Victor-Amadeus took possession of Chieri and made a close reconnaissance from the vantage point of the Superga hill, viewing the entire French camp and siege operations. The inexplicable failure of their opponents to venture out and challenge them brought from the prince the cutting comment that 'It seems to me that these people are half-beaten'.[17] Of most interest was that La Feuillade, while busy with mining operations against the city's defences, had not fully completed the defensive lines of circumvallation on the north-western side, in the meadows between the Stura and Dora Riperia rivers, presumably because this was the angle most distant from any likely approach by a relieving army. The opportunity presented was clear, and a message was got in to von Daun that an attack was to be made, and that he should be ready to mount a sortie with the garrison troops in conjunction. The combined allied army, now some 30,000 strong and soon reinforced by a body of Piedmontese militia, left Villa Stellone two days later, just as Marsin reported in his letter, crossing the Po between the villages of Carignano and Moncalieri to the south of the city, moving on past Rivoli to take up a position opposite Pianezza on the river Dora, happily seizing on the way supplies that had been intended to sustain the siege operations. Little opposition was met, and by 6 September the advance guard had reached Veneria Reale, just three miles from Turin. They had been able to march half-way around the French army without hindrance, while Eugene sought the most advantageous spot from which to make his attack. The inactivity of his opponents was astonishing, as they had a distinct superiority in numbers, and some attempt to intercept the marching allied columns might surely have been made. Orleans did again urge on Marsin that they should challenge the allies, but was bluntly told that he had no authority over the siege that had to go on regardless of all other considerations. Any successful operations against a properly defended fortress depended upon a covering army shielding those activities from interruption, and this obvious task was neglected by the French commanders, as they waited for events to overwhelm them.

At first light on 7 September, Eugene gave his orders for the attack, while von Daun sallied out in support. The allies advanced in four double columns on a narrow front, with a first line led by the grenadiers, and a second line of similar strength in support, having flanks to either side shielded by the Stura and Dora Riperia. The Prussians under Leopold of Anhalt-Dessau were on the left, the Austrians and a detachment of Palatine grenadiers in the centre commanded by General Rehbinder, and the Saxon and Palatine main body under the Prince of Saxe-Coburg-Gotha on the right. The second line, Austrian and Hessian troops

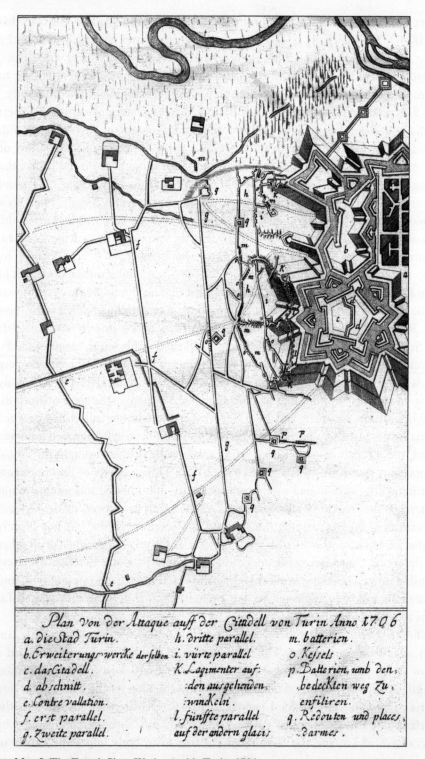

Plan von der Attaque auff der Citadell von Turin Anno 1706

a. die Stad Turin.
b. Erweiterungs wercke der selben
c. das Citadell.
d. abschnitt.
e. Contre vallation.
f. erst parallel.
g. Zweite parallel.

h. dritte parallel.
i. virte parallel
K. Lagimenter auf:
:den ausgehenden.
:winckeln.
l. fünffte parallel
auf der andern glacis

m. batterien.
o. Kessels.
p. Batterien, umb den.
.bedeckten weg zu.
enfiliren.
q. Redouten und places.
.darmes.

Map 8. The French Siege Works outside Turin, 1706.

commanded by the exuberant Marquis de Langallerie together with Prince Philip of Hesse-Darmstadt, provided support, while the bulk of the allied cavalry, Savoyard and Austrians under the immediate command of Baron Kreichbaum and the Marquis Visconti, were held in reserve, ready to move forward when the way was clear for them to do so. 'Never was a thing seen so bold and terrible as this march,' recalled Langallerie.[18]

The French commanders, alerted to the imminent approach of their opponents in full battle array, hastily formed their own troops to meet them, with their right flank under the Comte d'Estaing on the Stura, Orleans in command in the centre assisted by the taciturn Marquis Zenobe-Philippe d'Albergotti, and General Saint-Fremont commanding on the left. Marshal Marsin, still morbidly despondent and distracted by his own gloomy thoughts, accompanied Orleans as they rode out to engage the allied advance, but La Feuillade, for the moment, remained on the alert with his troops in the siege lines. That the French commanders were ill-prepared for a major action was clear, and Eugene and Victor-Amadeus had achieved a significant local superiority in numbers in the opening hour of the clash. 'I believe that there were not more than sixteen or seventeen battalions [8,000–9,000 men] on the line when the enemy attacked,' the Marquis de Chamarande remembered. 'The troops who could intervene arrived panting.'[19]

Due to the nature of the terrain there was no opportunity for the allies to turn an exposed flank, and as the range closed, the gunners in both armies began a brisk cannonade, which went on for well over a tense hour, before Eugene was satisfied with his dispositions, and at about midday he gave the signal for the army to advance. The ground to be crossed proved difficult and progress was slow, Saxe-Coburg finding the way ahead particularly tricky, but Anhalt-Dessau typically pressed hard on the left with his Prussians, and encouraged by Eugene who rode over to join him, they carried the hastily-prepared French defences to their front at the point of the bayonet:

> By the unequal [uneven] situation of the ground, our left Wing sustained alone for some time the efforts of the enemy, that stopped them a little . . . Prince Eugene came up, drew his sword, and putting himself at the head of the battalions on the left broke into the enemy's entrenchments.[20]

A large and well-placed French battery was overrun in fierce fighting, although the gunners valiantly defended their pieces, and the way was then clear for the allied cavalry under Kreichbaum to advance. Things were going too fast, though, and Eugene prudently held them back until the centre and right of the army had come up to conform with what had been achieved on the left, but in the meantime the captured French guns were turned on their previous owners. The Comte d'Estaing was nearby and valiantly rallied his shaken troops, driving back some of the Prussian infantry who, in their enthusiasm, had gone on too far and in drifting off-line were without immediate support. 'For an hour and a half some advantages were gained on either side . . . Our troops at length leaped into the entrenchments of the French, but threw themselves into disorder in the pursuit.'[21] The Stura was found to be unusually low in the summer heat, and some squadrons of Savoyard cavalry went forward to begin to try and turn the French right flank, but success was by no means certain, casualties were mounting rapidly, and Rehbinder's Austrian and Palatine troops in the centre were driven back three times as French resistance stiffened.

The two armies were locked in a deadly embrace, and the critical moment had come. Eugene had his horse shot under him, and an aide was killed while in the act of helping him back to his feet from the ditch into which he had been thrown. Victor-Amadeus, resplendent in the red coat of his own Life-Guards, rose to the occasion and led the centre of the allied army into the attack once again, gaining a fresh foothold in the French defences after a severe struggle in which Ferdinand Marsin was gravely wounded. A sharp counter-attack under d'Albergotti from the slightly higher ground on the French centre-left occupied by the Convent of the Capucines de Notre Dame threatened the flank of the advancing Saxon troops, but this effort was neatly deflected by Baron Kreichbaum who saw the threat and moved his squadrons forward. Saxe-Coburg led his troops through a withering storm of French musketry to seize the large fortified house of Lucento, and took several hundred prisoners in the process. Although now reinforced by dismounted dragoons sent across by La Feuillade, Orleans was being gradually pressed back. Eugene was mounted once more and, hitting left and right simultaneously, his cavalry were able to advance through the gradually widening gap before them.

The French commanders had lost control of the battle, and their army began to fall to pieces as Langallerie was summoned forward with his second-line infantry to bolster what had been achieved. It was enough, and d'Albergotti did not to move forward a second time to shore up the defence, perhaps seeing no value in reinforcing defeat. Orleans, although wounded in the hand, gallantly did what he could – 'Always in the thick of the battle, with cool courage'[22] – but the French and their allies had lost heart and were in increasing confusion, with some of the infantry escaping over the nearby Dora to where the heavy siege batteries were emplaced, while others fled to the crossings over the Po and away from the field entirely. Gallant attempts were made to rally, but the allied cavalry were in close pursuit, pivoting to the right on the Lucento strongpoint, and 'Our Horse counted it a scandal to cut down men that fled with so great precipitation, and this saved many lives'.[23]

While all this was going on, von Daun had come out of the Turin defences through the Palazzo Gate, leading 2,000 troops in a spirited sortie, but La Feuillade managed to hold him back, although in the process he was unable to do much to help avert the unfolding disaster that was engulfing the covering army. Not wanting to risk being trapped between the defences of the city and the advancing allies, he abandoned the siege works, heavy guns and magazines and withdrew with his troops, so that the siege was broken beyond hope of repair, and the defeated army could only hope to get away from the field. The Marquis de Langallerie, in his highly entertaining memoirs, added that 'By noon the victory was entirely ours, and the city delivered, for the enemy abandoned the Attack [on the city], and all their camp retired with the remains of their army to the other side of the Po'.[24] Having ensured that the pursuit was vigorous enough to keep their defeated opponents on the move, Eugene and Victor-Amadeus rode as victors into Turin late that afternoon, to be greeted by von Daun and Archbishop Vibò, the cheers of the troops of the garrison and the weary applause of the long-suffering citizenry.

The scale of the victory was astonishing, as the combined strength of the French army and their allies, when those in the siege lines were included in the calculation, was almost 65,000 troops, while Eugene and Victor-Amadeus together with the garrison under von Daun, had hardly more than 39,000 under command.[25] Yet the two cousins had been completely successful both in raising the siege and defeating the larger covering army, and rarely has dynamic leadership been demonstrated to better effect, while by comparison so disjointed was the exercise of French command that they failed utterly to properly deploy their full strength to meet the allied attack. The toll on that day of battle was heavy for the victors, but not out of proportion to what had been achieved, with just short of 3,000 casualties (Eugene was of course amongst them). A rather larger number of their opponents, 4,050, were reported as killed or wounded, but significantly over 5,000 more were taken as unwounded prisoners, together with 220 guns and mortars, almost all the field and siege artillery, magazines and stores, together with the French war chest containing 22,000 louis d'or, all a sure sign of their utter defeat. Ferdinand Marsin, who had belatedly thrown off his lethargy and bravely attempted to hold things together, died the following day just as he had foreseen, after the amputation of a shattered leg by one of Victor-Amadeus' surgeons.

Eugene wrote to Marlborough from the battlefield that same night, while a courier paced to and fro, ready to take the road on the instant, with news of the success:

> Your Highness will not, I am sure, be displeased to hear by the Baron de Hohendorff of the signal advantage which the arms of His Imperial Majesty and his allies have gained over the enemy. You had so great a share in it by the succours you have procured, that you must permit me to thank you again. Marshal Marsin is taken, and mortally wounded.[26]

The Duc d'Orleans' report to Versailles was appropriately sombre in tone, beginning 'I send a courier to Your Majesty to inform you that the enemy have relieved Turin'.[27] Rumours of what had taken place reached the Low Countries well before Eugene's courier could do so, and the duke wrote on 18 September: 'A trumpeter who returned last night from the French camp brings an account that they have received news yesterday of a battle in Italy, wherein the French army is said to have been defeated with the loss of their cannon and baggage.'[28] His letter of congratulation to Eugene, sent on 27 September, ran: 'It is impossible to express the joy that I have on receiving the news of the glorious victory which Your Highness has achieved over the enemy.'[29] The success must have been doubly welcome, as the achievement was in large measure due to the money and troop reinforcements secured by the duke during the preceding winter, and this fact had been acknowledged.

A few days after the battle the Comte de Medavi savaged a detachment under the Prince of Hesse-Cassel at Castiglione, but this French success meant little in the circumstances. The Marquis de Nancré reached Versailles with Orleans' despatch containing the news of the breaking of the siege, defeat and scattering of the army, and the death of Marsin, shocking tidings and so soon after the calamity at Ramillies and the loss of the Southern Netherlands. Louis XIV wrote in almost pathetic terms to Vendôme, now commanding in Flanders, asking his advice 'What would you do, what orders would you give?'[30] Orleans soon recovered from his wound, although amputation of the hand had been considered, and would have withdrawn to Lombardy to refresh and replenish his battered army, but the road was reported to be barred by Eugene's troops and he instead made for Pinerolo and the French frontier, where he and La Feuillade gratefully found sanctuary. To all intents and purposes, and for ever as it proved, the French campaign in Italy was over.

Eugene and his cousin were now free to recover and secure the whole of Piedmont and Lombardy, those French troops in the region taking their cue from Orleans and holding out in their fortresses and doing little more. The army was allowed to rest for several days, but moved on 15 September to seize Chivasso with a haul of over 1,000 French prisoners, and then marched on through the Milanese region, taking in turn Vercilli, Novaro and Crescentino. The river Ticino was crossed on 23 September, and Milan entered three days' later, the governor, Vaudémont senior, having made himself scarce. The French and Spanish/Italian troops in the garrison shut themselves up in the citadel, and defied a summons to submit, but could be safely ignored for the time being. Von Daun was sent to take Pavia, and Modena was occupied by General Wentzl. The citadel of Tortona had to be taken by storm on 28 November, and the garrison duly massacred, while Casale promptly and prudently submitted on 6 December after a two-week siege. Before long Parma, Tuscany and the Papal States were all paying handsome subsidies – 'contributions' as they were politely known – into the hungry coffers of Vienna to avoid having Eugene's troops foraging or being billeted on them, So much had been achieved that autumn, but time was lacking to press further forward, and Eugene sent his troops off to their winter quarters, before returning to Vienna. There he was acclaimed once more as the hero of the hour, presented by Joseph with a jewel-studded sword and made Field-Marshal of the Empire (rather than just of Austria), a post formerly held by the late Margrave of Baden, and now surely fitting for the victor of such an astonishing campaign.

It is appropriate to mention that Duke Victor-Amadeus, so often open to criticism for his seeming devious conduct and cynical self-interest, performed particularly well in the campaign. He had few resources, but had adroitly avoided being bottled up in Turin, and instead waged a very useful and well-handled campaign with his cavalry to hamper the French siege operations long enough for relief to arrive. The duke had also rallied the loyal Piedmontese militia to his side, ready to participate in saving Turin, and then fought gallantly and at great personal risk in the battle of 7 September, sharing in equal measure with Eugene the perils and the glory of the day.

Chapter 8

An Uncertain Business – Toulon

The final and controversial act in northern Italy came in March 1707, when a convention, largely negotiated by Eugene and generally known as the Treaty of Milan, agreed that the remaining French garrison troops could leave and their Spanish/Italian allies disband. This saved the trouble of having to clear out those now-isolated fortresses, but concern was felt in both The Hague and London that thousands of these soldiers would be free to campaign elsewhere, perhaps in Spain or the Low Countries, as no conditions for cartels of exchange or parole were imposed. The arrangement suited the interests of Emperor Joseph and his ministers, as it did to a lesser but obvious degree Eugene, although it remained suspect in terms of the effect on the Grand Alliance as a whole, and has been harshly judged by historians: 'The conduct of the Imperial court at this junction, stands forth remarkably as an example of wanton, reckless self-seeking.'[1] However, it was unlikely that Vienna, even in concert with Duke Victor-Amadeus, had the military power to drive these garrisons out against their will, other than at the expense of irretrievable time and effort. Any further projects contemplated, as they currently were at the bidding of the Maritime Powers, would have been impossible in the meantime. A careful reading of the terms of the treaty also makes it clear that the French had to leave behind a large number of their guns (each garrison only taking ten field pieces with them), stores and equipment, and that prisoners of war already held by either side were only released on strict terms of formal exchange. Nonetheless the criticism stood, but in war it is often necessary to accept what is practical, rather than what is ideal.[2]

A surprising proposal now came from the Russian tsar, Peter, that Eugene should put himself forward for election as King of Poland, but this was simple troublemaking intended to exert pressure on King Charles XII of Sweden, with whom Moscow was at war. Predictably, nothing came of this notion, and it is not at all clear that the prince would even have been able to accept the offer had it ever been formally made. As the victor of Turin, however, he was also accorded the honour by Joseph of being appointed Viceroy of Milan, with an annual stipend of 150,000 gulden, and once again he entered the city with great ceremony and pomp on 16 April 1707. His reception by the populace was genuinely warm, flowers were strewn in the streets, wine ran from the public fountains to help things along, and a *Te Deum* in celebration was sung in the cathedral. This public enthusiasm was not matched by that of Victor-Amadeus, however, as he had expected the post of viceroy for himself, but Habsburg rule over the region, which would last for 150 years, had begun in earnest, and portions of western Lombardy and Montferrat, already promised to the duke, were only belatedly handed over in 1708 after pressure from those in London and The Hague who were anxious to keep Savoy in the war. Vienna also took the quiet opportunity to annex Mantua, on the rather thin grounds that the duke there, nominally a vassal of the emperor, had allied himself to the French and therefore laid his lands open to sequestration.

Plans were simultaneously made in Vienna, with the earnest backing of Emperor Joseph, to move south and formally occupy Naples and other Spanish-held territory, but these projects were unwelcome to the Maritime Powers, who again felt that energy would be better directed against the French or in securing Spain for the Habsburg claimant, Charles. The aim of dividing the Spanish empire, a firmly-expressed intent in the creation of the Grand Alliance in the first place, was, however, addressed by such moves so it could be argued that the emperor had 'cover' for what was being done. Vienna's fixed intent on making sure of Italy was clear, to the exclusion of much else, and in May 1707 Graf Philip von Daun took 10,000 troops to occupy Naples, and quickly started raising more 'contributions', theoretically at least to better sustain the Imperial war effort. That the troops so engaged had been recently released from the duties keeping an eye on French garrisons in the north was obvious, and increased the irritation felt by the Maritime Powers. Eugene was concerned that the German troops paid for by London might now be withdrawn from his army in Italy, and with this in mind he indicated his agreement, after some hesitation, to a project that had first been suggested by the Duke of Marlborough the previous December. This was to march again into southern France, in conjunction with Victor-Amadeus, who was anxious to improve his position in the Maritime Alps and on the river Var, by co-operating with the cruising squadrons of the Royal Navy in the Mediterranean, in an attack on the great French naval base and arsenal at Toulon. The occupation of the port, together with the destruction or capture of the Mediterranean fleet there, would ease the pressure on the allied forces operating with Archduke Charles in eastern Spain and serve to divert French efforts from that crucial theatre of war. Vienna's hold on Naples would, it was argued, be strengthened in the process, while the Duc de Vendôme would almost certainly be required to send troops south, thereby easing Marlborough's troubles in Flanders. For the Maritime Powers, the strongest appeal was their warships being free to operate without interference in the Mediterranean. 'England and Holland base all their hopes on the Italian plan and are convinced that the whole future of the campaign and even of the war depends upon it.'[3]

It appears that Eugene had little real enthusiasm for the Toulon project, as despite the success at Turin he knew that working in close harmony with his cousin was an uncertain business. He was aware, however, that the Maritime Powers had to be conciliated after the wholesale release of the French troops stranded in Lombardy and the subsequent diversion of effort to occupy Naples. In the wider war, reverses in Spain such as the defeat at Almanza and renewed raiding by Marshal Villars across the Lines of Stollhofen on the Rhine, pointed to a reinvigoration of effort by Versailles and the claimant to the throne in Madrid, and accordingly a major attempt to regain the strategic initiative seemed necessary. To that end, the prince wrote rather grudgingly that 'The Provence and Toulon expedition will have to be agreed to, so as not to disgust the Maritime Powers'.[4] The fact was, though, that the occupation of Toulon, if it could be achieved, would do little towards the overall war aims of Vienna, and once occupied the port could not have been held for long, other than with enormous effort and cost, while a close naval blockade, such as the Royal Navy would become adept in years to come, would achieve the same overall result with relatively modest resources. However, the attractions of having French resources diverted from other theatres of war, particularly Spain and Flanders, were clear.

Preparations for the attempt on Toulon proceeded slowly, in part due to the occupation of Naples, but also because Victor-Amadeus was unwell and inclined to be difficult, with snow unusually late in clearing from the passes of the Maritime Alps. To add complication, the ships of the Royal Navy intended to support the operation were not available until mid-June, despite assurances to the contrary from London. Various difficulties with supply, pleas from Archduke Charles for more support in Catalonia, and contrary winds that hampered the sailing, did not impress Eugene very much. What enthusiasm had been felt in Vienna for the project faded, and Count Wratislaw wrote rather peevishly to Marlborough that 'We risk our army, in the sole view of pleasing England, and endeavouring to ruin the French Marine [fleet]'.[5] Ironically, now that Naples was secured (at least in part due to the cover given by the Royal Navy in the western Mediterranean) there was perceived to be less need in Vienna to accommodate the wishes and concerns of the Maritime Powers. In any case, Vienna's 'army' referred to so plaintively by Wratislaw was not at great risk, as the land component in the expedition would comprise only 6,000 Austrian troops, to add to some 29,000 Savoyard and German soldiers, with the latter still paid for by Queen Anne's treasury.

Certainly, appetite for the project was lukewarm, and the Earl of Manchester, British envoy in Vienna, recalled that 'He had been with the Duke of Savoy, when Prince Eugene made many difficulties about the expedition against Toulon'.[6] Despite this, it was not possible to pull back as it seemed that matters had achieved a momentum of their own, even if real enthusiasm was lacking, and everything got under way on 15 June 1707, with the troops moving forward from Cuneo in four columns along the difficult roads leading to southern France. A French pamphleteer caught the mood very well, in retrospect, writing that:

The English and the Dutch looked upon the destroying of Toulon as a matter of the greatest importance and the success thereof would procure them great advantages [but] they could never compass what they projected unless they could likewise prevail with Prince Eugene to go.[7]

Understandably, by virtue of his rank Victor-Amadeus had the nominal command of the army, but Eugene was once again the de facto field commander, and for a time things went well.

The allied army passed through the Vermegnana valley and by the first week of July had reached Sospello where a halt was called, a rendezvous with Admiral Sir Cloudsley Shovell's squadron having been achieved a few days previously. Resistance to the advance was light, with Mentone passed and Nice reached without difficulty, other than toiling along the poor roads. On 11 July, Eugene's troops closed up to the line of the fast-flowing river Var, where French troops under command of the Marquis de Seuilly were found in a strong defensive position near to San Lorenzo, and being reinforced. Acting in concert with Shovell and Admiral Sir John Norris, whose warships bombarded the French, shallow-draught boats laden with marines went up the Var to threaten their flank, so that the marquis withdrew and Eugene moved forward, now only 70 miles or so from Toulon, writing to Marlborough, optimistically but noticeably cautious, that 'We are about to march now straight for Toulon with the intention of besieging it, unless we meet such obstacles as will make the enterprise completely impracticable'.[8]

Cannes and Fréjus were passed 'along very steep paths'[9] and Antibes blockaded, so that by 26 July, La Valette, only a few miles from the French naval base, had been reached. The allied army had not had to fight a serious action during the whole 105-mile-long march into southern France, quite an achievement, but it was weary and felt growing unease both at the difficult terrain and vulnerable lines of supply and communication. Regular contact was maintained with the naval squadron under Admiral Shovell, however, and both he and Victor-Amadeus were dismissive when Eugene expressed concern at how exposed they were becoming. Of course, the problems with supply were partly addressed by gathering of forage and crops, together with outright plundering of the unfortunate locals, and for the time being, the confidence shown by Victor-Amadeus and Shovell worked a certain effect on Eugene, and his doubts seemed to be dispelled when he wrote to Marlborough with an account of the progress made and of 'Our having set aside all difficulties [and] the eagerness of my zeal for the august desires of the Queen and for the good of the common cause'.[10] He must also have been quietly aware that his concerns over the security of the allied lines of supply would have been better addressed if so many Austrian troops had not been diverted to occupy Naples, and had been instead available to join the march on Toulon.

What success had been had was an illusion, as the French commander in the region, Marshal René de Froulay de Tessé, was an experienced and wily

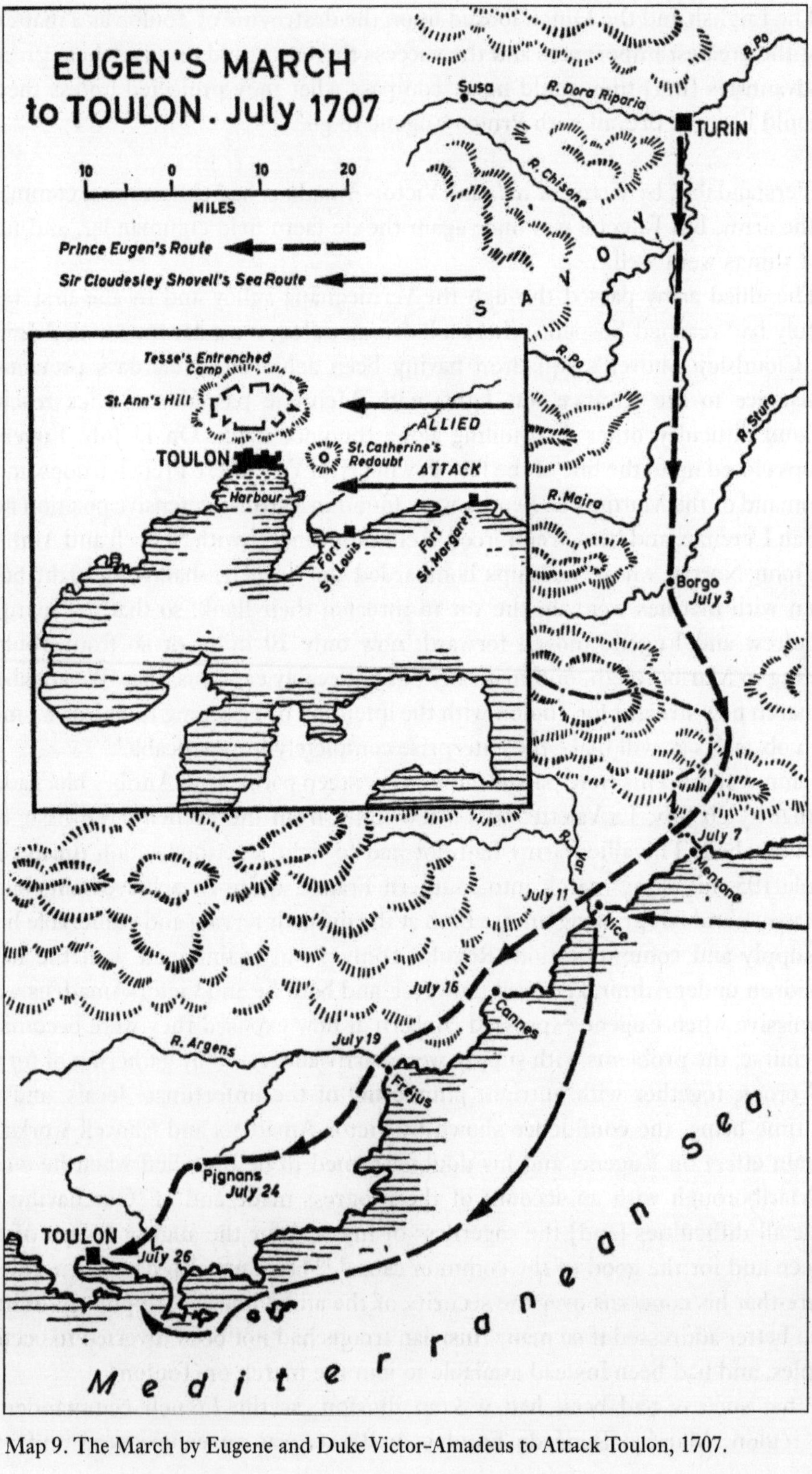

Map 9. The March by Eugene and Duke Victor-Amadeus to Attack Toulon, 1707.

campaigner, and had not been idle. Lacking numbers, he had adroitly avoided a confrontation while he was unprepared for a general action, and instead gathered his available forces to shield Toulon once it became evident that the naval base was indeed under threat. De Seuilly had joined him after falling back from the Var, so that Eugene and Victor-Amadeus found that the place was now strongly garrisoned, with previously flimsy defences hastily strengthened and improved. On 26 July 'The enemy were extremely surprised to find, upon their arrival, 40 battalions either in the place or in the fortified camp . . . and above 300 pieces of cannon, well served by officers of the Navy.'[11] Some accounts hint that this French strength was in fact a carefully constructed mirage, but a series of eight strong redoubts with emplaced artillery had certainly been erected in a half-moon arc, the flanks of which were both secured on the sea. An entrenched camp had also been constructed on an elevated site known as the Heights of St Anne, so that Tessé could easily manoeuvre with his field army to foil any attempt at a formal investment and siege. The Marquis de Goesbriand occupied that camp with 15,000 infantry, while a further 6,000 men were gathered in another camp in the valley of Faviáre, and yet another camp was being constructed further to the west and was eventually occupied by a reserve of 10,000 French troops. In this way, Tessé could draw on these camps as opportunity arose to prevent any free movement by the allied army around the port, but he was still anxious that he lacked numbers for the task. However, one boost to French hopes came from a steady trickle of deserters from the allied army, often French and Bavarians who had been taken at Blenheim and Turin and impressed into the ranks. 'Tis no wonder if they quitted a service in which they only entered because they could not do otherwise.'[12] These men were welcomed by Tessé and not questioned too closely as to how they had got there, while bringing encouraging tales of shortages, ill-discipline and low morale, so that he felt reassured and able to wait to see what his opponents would do next.

From an elevated site on Mount Croix-Pharaon Eugene carried out a careful reconnaissance of the defences on 28 July, and straightaway advised a withdrawal to rest and regroup the army, while considering the best course to take, which might perhaps even be to abandon the whole enterprise. 'I know he never had a liking for this project,' a correspondent wrote from the army's camp to Marlborough, 'but I thought when he was here he would have acted with his usual vigour.'[13] He was reassured by an outwardly confident Victor-Amadeus, while Shovell was adamant that his precise orders were to attack the naval base, and that was that. So, the allied troops settled down to begin their work of reducing the defences, and it was soon reported to Tessé that 'The Horse were encamped under the olive trees, and the Foot in the vineyards'.[14] Such bucolic comfort faded rapidly, and at Eugene's insistence a full preparatory artillery bombardment was undertaken, rather than any attempt at an outright storm of the defences, which seemed certain to fail with heavy loss. Unable to properly invest the port, with neighbouring high ground firmly occupied by the French, a formal investment and siege was not possible, and in the meantime the allied army was exposed, swinging precariously at the end of a long and vulnerable branch.

Although the prospects for success appeared to be fading, the French defences on the heights of St Catherine were stormed on 30 July by Prussian grenadiers led by Baron Rehbinder, allowing heavy guns to be dragged with difficulty into position, and the first attempt at siege trenches begun. With Shovell's assistance, another battery was established on the high ground at La Malgue close to the coast, so that French warships moored in the Inner Roads could be brought under fire. Morale in the allied camp was fragile, however, desertion increased and sickness became rife through the men having to drink from marshy streams. Tessé was plainly not without a certain sense of wry humour, and each day teasingly sent parcels of ice to the quarters of Eugene and Victor-Amadeus at La Valette to alleviate their thirst, but such comforts, of course, could not be enjoyed by the common soldiers. The bombardment appeared to be having little effect, and the mood in the allied camp grew more sombre, with a noticeable lack of common purpose amongst the senior commanders. Meanwhile, the British envoy, Sir John Chetwynd, was loudly urging that better progress should be made, so that Eugene wrote to Count Wratislaw on 4 August, describing the loss of what had at best been a fragile form of harmony:

> They are all enraged with me, and think that I wish not to risk the troops. I answer clearly that I am accustomed to act according to the rules and reasons of war, everyone knowing that I readily hazard when I have the best appearance of succeeding . . . It is the most difficult operation I have seen in my life.[15]

The simple fact was that a proper investment and siege of Toulon could not be achieved while Tessé held the high ground, and that being so the operation must fail. The battery at La Malgue kept up its work, however, and a French outpost at St Margaret had to be abandoned, allowing the ships of the allied fleet to approach close enough to begin a bombardment of the dockyard itself. In response, the French warships in harbour, commanded by the Marquis de Langeron, added their weight to the defence: 'At eleven in the morning, a deserter came over and reported that the Duke of Savoy had been in great danger, a ball from the *Tonnant* man-of-war [beached as a battery] having passed between his horse's legs.'[16] On 15 August, Tessé, having been reinforced by the Comte del Medavi a few days earlier, managed to recapture the heights of St Catherine, spiking the guns and burning the stores collected there. 'The enemy retook the post, notwithstanding the vigorous resistance of the brave Prince of Saxe-Coburg Gotha who was killed in that hot engagement.'[17] Still, on the credit side, the fort of St Marguerite, covering the harbour, was captured that evening obliging the French to evacuate nearby Fort St Louis.

Now it seemed that the previously confident Admiral Shovell was also having private doubts, with the effective strength of the allied army, taking into account the large numbers of sick, having shrunk significantly to no more than 20,0000 men, and he wrote rather despondently to Archduke Charles in Barcelona:

We have been outside Toulon now for eighteen days, but at the moment there seems little prospect of success. Owing to the large number of cannons all around the city, to the powerful garrison within, and to the numerous earthworks encircling the place. Toulon has been turned into a very strong fortress.[18]

Worrying news came in, that a strong force under Medavi had moved to threaten the lines of communication of the allied army, and Eugene was unwilling to rely upon bland assurances being given that the army could be adequately sustained by the ships lying offshore. 'The Admiralty,' he wrote to the emperor, 'do not understand land warfare, they adhere obstinately to their original point of view . . . the siege of Toulon is quite impracticable.'[19] Each came to blame the others for a lack of preparation, stores and munitions, while attempting to avoid responsibility for what was plainly a languishing enterprise. Victor-Amadeus, in particular, was uncharacteristically despondent: 'Never more concerned or out of humour in his life, no not when the French had drove him out of his country.'[20] French reinforcements continued to arrive and were seen to be entering Toulon without hindrance, and Tessé would soon be in a position to mount a major attack on the allied army, pinned still to a futile operation. Five days after the loss of the St Catherine feature, it was agreed that the campaign should be abandoned altogether. Marlborough would write with masterful understatement to Grand Pensionary Antonius Hiensius in The Hague, that 'What [news] we have from France concern Toulon is not as good as we would wish'.[21]

On 22 August the soldiers began to dismantle the batteries and break up their camp, to march off on the weary road leading back to the Var and Savoy-Piedmont. The movement, in five columns, was conducted in good order and covered by a very effective renewed bombardment laid on by the bomb ketches of the naval squadron under Admiral Sir Thomas Dilkes. Although some munitions and equipment had to be left behind, all the wounded and sick, and the heavy guns, were got safely away, many on Shovell's ships. Nothing in the whole expedition that summer was as well handed as the withdrawal, and Eugene's 4,000-strong rearguard competently held off a rather hesitant French pursuit, the troops crossing the Var on 31 August, and in the process leaving the soil of France behind. 'We have learned,' the Duke of Marlborough wrote to an acquaintance serving in Spain, 'that the Duke of Savoy has quitted the siege of Toulon, and retreated, which as you may well believe has caused much chagrin after the hopes we had

founded on the capture of this place.'[22] The duke, perhaps understandably, did
not dwell on Eugene's part in the failure. The path of a retreating army is seldom
a happy one, but despite some indiscipline, the troops overall held together. By
mid-September Eugene was able to concentrate his columns at Scalenge on the
river Lemnia just to the east of Pinerolo, while Admirals Shovell, Norris and
Dilkes, having ably covered the flank of the withdrawal as far as Nice, took their
ships to winter off Lisbon.

For Eugene to conduct such a well-ordered withdrawal in the face of two
active armies – those of Tessé and of Medavi – and to keep his troops together
in disheartening circumstances, was commendable. It was true that the French,
having achieved the primary aim to hold on to Toulon, saw no pressing need to
try and force a general action, and this perhaps speaks of a concern at crossing
swords once again with Eugene. The naval base had indeed been saved, but the
harm done to the French fleet was considerable, with the loss of major warships
sunk or burned at anchor. The *Tonnant* (100 guns) had been beached to use as a
battery alongside the wall of the Inner Roads, and was broken backed, while the
hulls of other large vessels were badly damaged, and it would be years before
French naval power could recover. In any case, Louis XIV's treasury would not
stand the strain of the expense necessary to rebuild. What more might have been
achieved at Toulon with better management and a greater degree of harmony,
cannot now be assessed with certainty, but it was reported in Versailles that
'Reckless though it was, the operation against Toulon would have succeeded if
Prince Eugene's proposals had been carried out'.[23] This is to overlook his lack of
faith in the project, but reflects a commonly-held view at the time. It should be
said, to balance the tale a little, that the pressing need to send reinforcements to
save Toulon hobbled what France achieved elsewhere that year, in particular in
Spain, where the allied position, so fragile after defeat at Almanza, was shored
up while French attention was distracted. In addition, although the initial aim of
the expedition was not achieved, French naval power in the Mediterranean was
crippled for some time, a valuable outcome deserving recognition.

Eugene's detailed explanation to Marlborough of the difficulties encountered
during the expedition to Toulon was carefully phrased, as he was aware of the
importance that the Maritime Powers placed in its success. 'By the enclosed plan,
Your Highness will see that their camp flanked on the right of the town, with
more than 100 pieces of artillery, exclusive of the fire from the two ships moved
into the [inner] harbour, and on the left covered by inaccessible rocks, while the
cannon-shot of the place reaches even to the mountains.'[24] Nonetheless, there was
acute disappointment, and cohesion within the Grand Alliance was becoming
less sure. Such things rarely bring contentment and the apparent lack of success
was keenly felt in London and The Hague. Resentment over the Treaty of Milan
and the occupation of Naples persisted, and relations between Emperor Joseph
and Victor-Amadeus were strained. The duke still longed for the Viceroyalty of

Milan, while those in Vienna who wished Eugene well had a ready scapegoat at hand in his cousin, placing the blame for the disappointing outcome unfairly on his shoulders. Count Wratislaw even wrote to Marlborough that now 'The Duke of Savoy will never act against France, except under new and advantageous conditions'.[25]

The curtain was mercifully falling on a dismal summer and autumn, both in southern France and in the north, where Marlborough had struggled to make headway in Flanders against Vendôme. Early in October, after a five-day bombardment Eugene neatly took French-held Susa some 40 miles to the west of Turin, and then saw to the dispositions of the army for the winter. The last French-held fortress in the region, Chiomonte, was taken after an attempt at relief by Tessé was frustrated by Victor-Amadeus. The Savoyard troops went to their homes or into garrisons, the sturdy Hessians and Prussians returned north to make ready for a new campaign in 1708, and the Palatinate troops were despatched to take ship to support the archduke in Catalonia. Having made the arrangements, and perhaps with a feeling of some relief, Eugene left an old comrade, the Marquis Visconti, in command in the Po valley. He had been recalled to Vienna on 28 November 1707, and never visited Italy again.

Chapter 9

The Great Campaign – Oudenarde and Lille

The year 1707 had seen frustration and disappointment for the Grand Alliance, although the French had been obliged to withdraw garrisons from northern Italy. This was of limited importance anywhere other than in Vienna, and Eugene and Victor-Amadeus had then only been partially successful at Toulon. Allied commanders in Spain had seen little success and occasional heavy defeat, while Philip V consolidated his position in Madrid and the cause of Archduke Charles languished. Marshal Villars had gone raiding that summer into central and southern Germany, while rebellion rumbled on in Hungary and then erupted in Transylvania, sapping the strength of Vienna. Louis-Guillaume, Margrave of Baden, having died during the year, was replaced as commander of the Imperial forces on the Rhine by George-Louis, the Elector of Hanover, who would in time prove to be a robust campaigner, but in the Low Countries meanwhile, the Duke of Marlborough and Veldt-Marshal Overkirk had failed to hold the Duc de Vendôme long enough to bring him to battle. The alliance which had briefly seemed so vibrant, now appeared to be growing stale.

In response to a request from Charles in Barcelona, a proposal was made to send Eugene to command the allied army in eastern Spain; only someone of his ability and reputation, it was suggested, could hope to retrieve things. This suggestion was in part a desire of the Maritime Powers to try and instil fresh spirit into things there, and such a move would be 'A very popular thing in England and very much contribute to obtain the necessary subsidies in Parliament . . . Spain cannot be supported this winter without Prince Eugene'.[1] The financial largesse that Vienna had come to depend on in the war was essential, and the reference to this is telling. Marlborough had his reservations over Eugene having to campaign there with what were bound to be inadequate resources, while at least a part of the proposal was a desire by the Imperial Court Chamberlain in Vienna, Prince von Salm, to have him replaced as the President of the Imperial War Council by Guido von Starhemberg, who might be more easily manipulated. In the end, the clumsily attempted *coup* by von Salm misfired, and instead von Starhemberg was sent to campaign in Catalonia, where against all expectations he did surprisingly well.

Eugene had never the least intention of being sent to Spain, having instead written to Marlborough with a proposal to muster an Imperial army under his command in the Moselle valley, ready to co-operate with the duke during the 1708 campaign. 'We ought to have a body [of troops] which may be withdrawn to form a second army on the Moselle, with some detachments from our other armies, to act in Germany or Flanders according as circumstances require.'[2] Although the plan was ambitious, it had a good deal of merit, as they had worked together with such success four years earlier, and the desire to recreate those circumstances was clear. On 26 March 1708, Eugene left Vienna to meet the duke and Grand Pensionary Hiensius at The Hague, arriving there on 12 April to co-ordinate plans for the summer. On the way, he stopped in Hanover to confer with George-Louis, but the meeting did not go well, and the elector resisted any lessening of forces available to join his own campaign on the Rhine. He was astute enough to see that he was, in effect, being sidelined by the other two men, whose 'Perfect comradeship and pre-eminence established a higher unity of command than had ever been seen in the war. "The Princes" as they came to be called, settled everything between themselves.'[3]

Despite the elector's concerns, the plan eventually agreed at The Hague was that French attention and resources would be drawn to the concentration of troops around Coblenz on the approaches to the Moselle valley, and those commanded by George-Louis on the middle Rhine. Eugene would then use the pretext of an unexpected emergency in the Low Countries and march his army northwards to combine forces with Marlborough before their opponents could react, and then with superior numbers force battle on the Duc de Vendôme. This project, on the face of things so promising, had several flaws, not least that Marlborough had been unable to make his opponent stand and fight the previous year, and he was no more likely to be caught out this time. Also the plan had little subtlety, while the notion of marching at best speed from the Moselle while the French failed to respond in good time was highly optimistic. In any case the whole idea was soon almost an open secret, and James FitzJames, the dangerously capable Duke of Berwick, commanding the 35,000 French troops on the Moselle, was aware of what might be attempted, and would be sure to try and intercept Eugene once he began his march to join Marlborough. Berwick wrote to a friend that he thought 'Prince Eugene, in imitation of the Duke of Marlborough's conduct in 1704, would make a sudden incursion into Flanders with a suitable force to crush the king's army, and invade France'.[4] A running battle between Berwick and Eugene was quite possible, depending upon the speed with which their troops undertook the march, and so the opposing commanders were each readying to spring into action, and it could not be foreseen what might be the outcome once they set off for the Low Countries.

Marlborough and Eugene went again to Hanover at the end of April, hoping to smooth over the ruffled feelings of the elector at being left out of things. His formidable mother, Electress Sophia Dorothea, admired them both but it was largely the work of Marlborough, urbane and courteous, that eventually brought her son around, although tellingly all the relevant details were still not disclosed to him. The duke wrote on 5 May that:

After a great deal of uneasiness the Elector has consented to the project for three armies; but we have been obliged to leave on the Rhine two Imperial regiments more than we designed, so that Prince Eugene will have 2,000 horse less on the Moselle; and as for the joining the two armies [those of Eugene and the Duke] we thought it best not to acquaint the Elector of it . . . *He will be very angry* [author's italics].[5]

George-Louis was not fully allowed into the secret, almost as if he could not be trusted with the information, and this was a snub that he never forgot – 'He will be very angry' indeed, but to his credit the elector did not sulk, and accepted what was a *fait accompli* with the appearance of good grace, doing his best to hold the attention of the French on the middle Rhine.

Events conspire to thwart the best-laid plans, and having visited the Grand Duke of Baden, the Landgrave of Hesse and the Elector of Saxony to encourage their continued efforts in the war, Eugene was detained in Vienna attending to his duties with the Council. There was an added difficulty in that promised reinforcements of Hessian and Palatine troops were delayed, over arrears of pay and terms of service, and on 4 June 1708 Marlborough wrote peevishly to Sidney Godolphin that 'I would not willingly blame Prince Eugene, but his arrival at the Moselle will be ten days after his promise'.[6] By the end of that month he had only managed to gather 15,000 troops at Coblenz, far fewer than planned, while in the meantime Marlborough had to employ patience and ready his own 90,000-strong Anglo-Dutch army for action once Eugene arrived. On 28 June 1708, Eugene left Count Rechteren in charge of the planned march and rode on ahead with a small escort of wild-looking Hungarian hussars, reaching Brussels on 6 July. There, he took the fleeting opportunity to visit his elderly mother, but posterity gives us few details of the touching moment, and even whether she appreciated very much the filial gesture by her renowned youngest son. Olympia died soon afterwards, grand in all her ways and yet having never quite lived down the notoriety of her youthful escapades.

All the while, the leading figures in the Southern Netherlands (so recently Spanish subjects, now to be regarded as Austrian) were increasingly resentful at burdensome taxation, extorted both by the Dutch, who were keen to recoup some of their expenditure of the war, and also by the new sovereign lord, Archduke Charles, who needed to finance his own campaign for the crown. This unsettling discontent was known in Versailles, and when plans were mooted to recover some of the ground lost at Ramillies in 1706, they found a ready audience in the major guilds and towns of the region. Marlborough was warned of the acute danger of such unrest by the Comte de Merode-Westerloo, who had two years earlier switched his allegiance to the archduke, but remembered that 'He treated my news as something of no account, telling me that it was impossible, and I could say nothing to make him change his mind'.[7] That the duke did not exactly trust him, is a likely conclusion.

Eugene's small army was still on the march from the Moselle, with Berwick in close pursuit, when the prince took leave of his mother on Sunday 8 July and rode to join Marlborough at his camp at Assche. There, he found his friend in low spirits, having just lost control of both Ghent and Bruges, where the prominent citizens had warmly welcomed flying columns of French cavalry, so that much of what had been gained two years' earlier was now lost or about to be so. Vendôme with almost 110,000 troops was reported to be standing secure behind the river Dender, well placed to counter any attempt by Marlborough to redress the situation. The sharply observant Duc de St Simon remembered that 'Early in July we took Ghent and Bruges by surprise, and the news of the success was received with the most unbridled joy at Fontainebleau. It appeared easy to profit by these two conquests, obtained without difficulty.'[8] Matters looked grim, and General Jaochim von Grumbkow wrote to King Frederick in Berlin that 'The blow which the enemy dealt us did not merely destroy our plans, but was sufficient to do irreparable harm to the reputation and previous good fortune of my Lord Duke, and he felt this misfortune so keenly'.[9] Vendôme moved to invest allied-held Oudenarde on the Scheldt, where the newly installed and formidable garrison commander, Brigadier-General Denis-François Chanclos, had quickly taken steps to ensure that the citizenry did not also throw open the gates to the French.

Vendôme was not without his difficulties though, as he had to share the command of the army with the young Duc de Bourgogne, Louis XIV's eldest grandson and eventual heir to the throne. The two men, very different in manner and temperament, were not on good terms, and tried to ignore each other, so that inevitably their respective staffs did the same to the detriment of efficiency. The actual command of the army lay with Vendôme, but the presence of the young prince of the blood and his elegant entourage naturally attracted much attention and sycophancy. Vendôme wanted to maintain his army's forward stance in northern Flanders, which the capture of Oudenarde and command of the line of the Scheldt would facilitate, but Bourgogne thought it best to move closer to the border with France, while leaving garrisons in place to secure the gains that had been made. Neither man was necessarily wrong, but neither could easily overrule the other, and as they could not agree, the question had to be referred to Versailles. The French campaign, hitherto so promising, lost its sparkle in the process.

Marlborough's spirits lifted on Eugene's arrival, as he pointed out the simple truth to the duke that the loss of a few towns counted for little if a resounding victory in the field could be had in exchange. 'The Prince was astounded to see such despondency in a general like Marlborough over a misfortune not relatively very important.'[10] Time was pressing, however, as Berwick was hurrying along the road from the Moselle, but the Prussian General Dubislaw Natzmer added that the allied army quickly regained its confidence, and that 'Our affairs improved through God's help and with the assistance of Prince Eugene'.[11] Count Rechteren and the Imperial troops had yet to arrive, but matters could not be delayed, so plans were swiftly laid to recover what was lost and support the garrison in Oudenarde. In spite of the reputation that Eugene enjoyed, the shabby impression he made was not good amongst those of Marlborough's senior officers who were little acquainted with him. Still, while suffering in contrast with the duke's handsome looks and elegant manner, the prince's optimism and enthusiasm was catching, and 'Just as Marlborough let himself be led by Eugen, so also did the army'.[12] Clearly Eugene's arrival acted as a tonic for all concerned.

Vendôme could only maintain his army's present posture while he held the line of the Dender, but he was too slow to prevent Marlborough's Quartermaster-General, William Cadogan, getting across the river at Lessines early on 10 July with an advance guard. Losing that line, the French were obliged to fall back the 15 miles to the Scheldt, but by the early morning of 11 July Vendôme was overtaken by Marlborough while crossing the river at Gavre, just downstream from Oudenarde. A sprawling general action, largely fought by infantry as the ground was in places poorly suited to cavalry, erupted along the far bank of the Scheldt. As the afternoon wore on, Vendôme mishandled things, getting involved in the bitter fighting through the enclosing gardens and orchards, while Bourgogne was irresolute, holding back an entire wing of the French army, unable to decide where best to use it. 'There was a multiplicity of errors, regiments went where they could, without receiving any orders.'[13] Had the young man been inclined to discuss what to do with Vendôme face to face, things might have been very different, but he did not.

Marlborough's rapidly drawn-together plan was to get Overkirk's Dutch and Danish troops onto the high ground of the Boser Couter hill, and outflank and then encircle the right of the French army as it was drawn into battle. The elderly Dutch commander was delayed, and for an anxious time Marlborough was engaged holding back desperate attacks directed by Vendôme, while concurrently arranging the veldt-marshal's troops in position. While doing so, he entrusted the command of the right of the allied army to Eugene, eventually no fewer than two-thirds of his growing strength, in an act of complete confidence in his abilities. As French pressure grew, with Vendôme struggling to free his infantry from the trap into which he had drifted, Marlborough was able to deftly send additional infantry under the Prussian Count Philip-Karl Lottum to shore up Eugene's hard-pressed battle line along the Ghent road. The ring could not quite be closed around Vendôme as darkness came on, but the French withdrew in confusion northwards to shelter behind the Ghent-Bruges canal. In pouring rain at the roadside, their squabbling continued: 'Vendôme went on declaring that the battle was not lost, and that it could be recommenced the next morning, when the rest of the army had arrived and so on, No one of consequence cared to reply.'[14] The tally of French casualties lying on the field amounted to over 5,000, while the

1. Prince Eugene of Savoy c. 1730.

2. The Austrian siege of Buda (Ofen), 1686.

3. The Second Battle of Mohacs, 12 August 1687.

4. A battle for a river crossing in Hungary, c. 1690.

5. Eugene at the battle for Belgrade, 16 August 1717.

6. Belgrade, the Ottoman 'White Castle', before its capture by Eugene.

7. Ottoman sipahi
regular cavalry,
c. 1700.

8. Louis XIV, c. 1680, about the time he refused Eugene a commission in his army.

9. John Churchill, 1st Duke of Marlborough with his Chief of Engineers Colonel John Richards.

10. Max-Emmanuel Wittelsbach,
Elector of Bavaria.

11. James FitzJames, Duke of
Berwick, Marshal of France.

12. The sack of Buda by Austrian troops, 1686.

13. Austrian field officer and soldiers,
c. 1700.

Franciscus Eugenius
Hertzog von Savoÿen
Kaÿserl: General Lieutenant

Eggelhoff. sc:

14. A contemporary cartoon portrait of Prince Eugene.

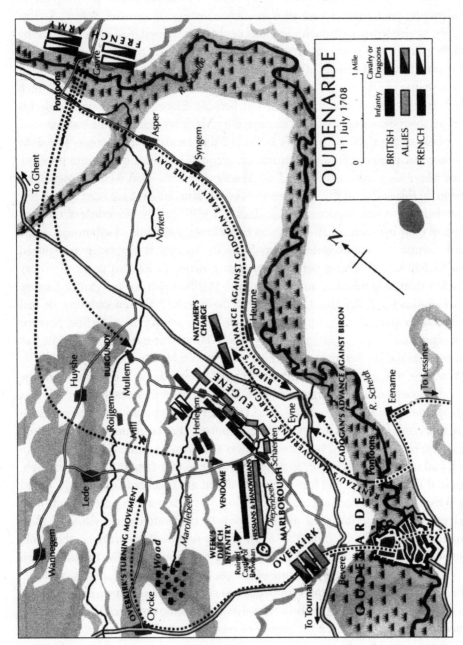

Map 10. The Battle of Oudenarde, 11 July 1708.

allied loss on the day was less than 3,000 killed or wounded. In addition, there were almost 9,000 unwounded French prisoners gathered in the town square in Oudenarde, once more a sure sign in such numbers of an utter defeat. A clear victory, as shattering to French morale as could be imagined, had been achieved by Marlborough and Eugene, acting together in complete harmony, and in an almost off-handedly casual display of competence and confidence.

The battle at Oudenarde was notable not just for the lamentable way in which the French commanders performed, but because Eugene, while having only his own personal escort present, was entrusted by Marlborough with the command of the whole of the right of the army as the fighting escalated to its crisis. The duke was in consequence able to concentrate on getting Overkirk's troops into position, from where they eventually rolled up Vendôme's flank. Had Marlborough been able to do this earlier in the day, then the French army might have been completely overwhelmed, as had happened at Ramillies two years' earlier. Nonetheless, the keen sense of trust between the two men was remarkable, and while Marlborough as the army commander was accorded the credit for the success, it was widely recognized that Eugene's enthusiastic participation was a major factor. No sense of rivalry clouded their achievement, and 'I dare say,' Marlborough wrote, 'Prince Eugene and I shall never differ about our share of the laurels.'[15] Fair enough, but he had undoubtedly arrived at the right moment, and there was a general feeling, perhaps best expressed by the not-altogether-impartial Count Wratislaw, that 'If Eugene had not come to the Netherlands, everything there would have been spoilt'.[16]

Vendôme was quick to blame the defeat at Oudenarde on the inactivity of the Duc de Bourgogne, and sent a highly misleading report to Versailles, but this was a dangerous game to play with Louis XIV, where the reputation of his grandson was concerned. It was in any case widely reported that both men had committed serious errors on the day, but Vendôme was the army commander and the main fault had to be laid at his door, and the king came to that conclusion soon enough. Marshal Berwick, who had learned of the defeat at Oudenarde on 12 July, found on arrival that consideration was only being given to manning the French-held fortresses in the region, and nothing done to confront the activities of their opponents. 'I found a great number of straggling parties of the army . . . the whole number at Tournai, Lille and Ypres amounted to upwards of nine thousand men . . . the frontier was entirely destitute of troops.'[17] The initiative clearly lay with the allies for the moment, but their immediate next course of action was not obvious. To pursue the defeated French northwards and attempt to force the line of the Ghent-Bruges canal offered the chance to recover those important towns, and the use of the valuable adjacent waterways, but also the prospect of heavy fighting for an uncertain result while an unmarked Berwick and his own newly-arrived troops were active in the rear. However, Eugene's main body of troops arrived in Brussels on 14 July and the concentration of allied forces was accomplished; the prince took the opportunity to inspect them, and briefly visited his mother for the last time. Meanwhile, as a preliminary to what might next be done, Count Lottum was sent by Marlborough to level the French defensive lines between Ypres and the Lys river, and although Berwick moved to try and prevent him he was too late. In this way, the most direct route to the French border was laid open, and in Versailles it was recalled that now 'Fear was painted on every face'.[18]

The immediate task for Eugene was to cover the movement forward from Brussels of the allied supply train, and this was accomplished without hindrance. The question of the future course of the campaign was pressing, and Marlborough put to his commanders an ambitious plan to take the war deep into northern France. Such an advance, far more than just a simple raid, would effectively mean abandoning their lines of supply and communication back to Brussels and Holland, and becoming dependant on resupply by the ships of the navies of the Maritime Powers operating off the coast of the Pas de Calais and Normandy. In this way, the massive French fortress belt, constructed with such effort and expense, would be ignored and bypassed. It was a daunting and ambitious suggestion but Eugene was not in favour, and he was not alone, as the allied generals were also almost all against the proposal, and such a decided body of opinion was not to be ignored. These officers, senior in rank and with long experience of campaigning, were the representatives of allied powers, and clearly could not be drilled as any one commander-in-chief, however gifted, saw fit. Marlborough's disappointment was expressed in a note he sent to London on 26 July 1708, containing the rather uncalled-for comment that 'Were my army all composed of the English, the project would certainly be feasible, but we have a great many among us who are more afraid of wanting provisions than of the enemy'.[19] How realistic the proposed project was is surely open to doubt, but it would never be put to the test in such an extreme form. So, it was decided instead to proceed to lay siege to the important city and fortress of Lille, the second city of France, the capture of which would lay open many fresh possibilities. Vendôme, meanwhile, was making another of his ill-judged miscalculations, by declaring that 'So wise a commander as Prince Eugene would not venture upon such an enterprise'.[20]

The huge quantity of stores, guns and munitions required for the siege had to be dragged forward from distant depots, and not surprisingly, this gathering and movement of such materiel was a time-consuming business, and one fraught with risk. Marlborough wrote on 23 July 1708, 'We are at present at a stand for want of our heavy artillery, which we are using all our diligence to bring up . . . being obliged to send as far as Maastricht for some of them'.[21] Every possible conveyance that could be found was pressed into service in a great convoy to bring forward what was needed, and the first of these left Brussels on 22 July, moving across the 70 miles to arrive at the allied encampment near to Menin three days later. The cavalry, commanded by Arnold Joost van Keppel, 1st Earl of Albemarle, covered the progress, while Eugene manoeuvred to prevent Berwick from interfering. Remarkably, no attempt was made to try and interrupt the valuable procession, without which the allied campaign would surely have fallen into disarray. A second and even larger convoy, seven miles long, came safely into the allied camp on 12 August, and once more Eugene led the covering force. The French, who could hardly have hoped for a more inviting target, failed to act yet again, indicating very well their disarray after the defeat at Oudenarde.

The investment proper of Lille was then almost complete, and the siege operations conducted by the prince could begin, while Marlborough manoeuvred with the covering army to ward off any attempt to disrupt things. 'This night the Prince of Savoy designs to open the trenches,' he wrote to London on 20 August, 'which I hope he will do with good success',[22] but the garrison commander, the veteran Marshal Louis-François de Boufflers, maintained from the outset an active defence, and establishing the allied breaching batteries in commanding positions proceeded slowly. The fortress was formidable, enlarged by Vauban and lying between the waters of the Scheldt and the river Lys, with the Deule stream close by, all providing obstacles to easy movement. It was soon apparent that both Eugene and Marlborough had underestimated the scale of the task and the resolute nature of Boufflers and his 15,000-strong garrison, while Berwick and now Vendôme hovered nearby, urged by Versailles to disrupt the siege. The French were constrained, however, by the dejection amongst their troops, resulting from their recent dismal defeat, while Berwick rather perversely indicated that he would only heed messages from the Duc de Bourgogne, and Vendôme refused to pay attention to any suggestions he made. Even so, on 1 September, Marlborough learned that the French were moving against him, and summoned Eugene to his support. The next day they rode out to see the extent of their opponents' advance, and select a good defensive location, centred on the villages of Seclin and Ennetieres, a few miles to the south of the siege lines.

The duke's troops quickly entrenched a strong position, with flanks well protected by the marshy Deule and Marque streams, and as the French approached, Vendôme urged making an immediate attack, but Berwick was reluctant. 'It is sad to see Lille taken,' he wrote 'but it would be even more sad to lose the only army which now remains to us.'[23] A rather lame message had to be sent to Louis XIV, asking for advice on how to proceed, with Vendôme indicating that if his proposal for an attack was not adopted, he would immediately resign his command. This was just bluster and it was Berwick who was permitted to resign, but he remained with the army to advise Bourgogne, and coincidentally to irritate Vendôme. Chamillart, the French Minister for War, was sent to report on the situation, and to encourage the army commanders to get on with things and raise the siege, but he agreed that the position Marlborough had taken up, with the valuable ability to call on Eugene for ready reinforcement, was too formidable to be attacked with hopes of success.

Eugene returned to the siege, and on Friday 7 September an attempt was made to storm the defences at the northern edge of Lille, at the gates of St Magdalene and St Andrew. The attackers met heavy fire, and the gallantly-pressed attempt was forced back with severe loss, while a sharp and very well handled counter-attack sent in by Boufflers the next day drove the allied troops back from what meagre gains they had made. At the same time a heavy cannonade was being directed at Marlborough's position near to Seclin, and he pondered the prospects for mounting an attack of his own on the French field army, but agreed with Eugene that the odds were too long, while concurrently having to maintain the siege operations. Still, Berwick recalled that so dismal were the spirits in the French camp that had such an attack been made it would have caused great alarm, if not something more serious. Frustrated, the French fell back towards Tournai on 15 September, and that same day another attempt was made by Eugene to storm the defences of Lille. The resulting failure was as bad as the first, although it was now possible to bring the heavy guns of the siege batteries forward to better positions. On the evening of 20 September, a third attack was made against the St Magdalene and St Mark gates, repulsed yet again, with Eugene badly concussed by a musket ball strike to his forehead just above the left eye. As army commander he should not have been so far forward, and had the stiffened brim of his tricorne hat not taken the full force of the blow he would probably have been killed. He was carried off the field, and Marlborough hurried to his side, persuading him with some difficulty to properly rest and recover. When this incident was reported in due course to Louis XIV, he commented drily that he did not want 'Prince Eugene to die, but [he] should not be sorry if his wound stopped him from taking any further part in the campaign'.[24]

It was reported at this time that an attempt had been made to assassinate Eugene, when a letter apparently impregnated with poison was received from an unknown source. The incident was macabre and certainly not trivial:

> One of the letters came from The Hague, and the Commissary imagined the other came from the same high place, but could not be positive of it. His Highness [Eugene] opening one of them, found nothing therein but a dirty greasy paper, and not knowing what might be the consequences thereof, threw it carelessly on the ground, without the least surprise. Hereupon, the Prince's Adjutant took it up, and smelt it; immediately after which he was taken with a great giddiness.[25]

The king would never have been involved in such a disgraceful thing, but the incident remained a puzzle. Eugene shrugged it off as of no account, saying that, after all, such things had not been that unusual when campaigning in Italy.

Meanwhile, Marlborough had uncovered mismanagement and theft of stores by the engineers and their quartermasters in the lines, hampering the progress of the siege. 'They did not deal well with the Prince,' he wrote to London, 'for when I told him that there did not remain powder and ball for above four days, he was very much surprised.'[26] Despite the additional burden that had to be shouldered by the duke at a time of great uncertainty, things from then on improved. As so often with ardent commanders keen to push things forward, Eugene had been too often in the siege trenches and at the batteries, and not taking enough care to ensure adequate resupply and proper accounting. Fresh munitions and stores could be called for, but lost time could not be recovered, and what would also apparent was that the engineers were not really up to the task, and they 'appreciated that they had opened the attack on too broad a front, and tried to break the fortifications at too many points'.[27] However, with hopes of better success, in early October Eugene was able to take up his duties again, so that the duke could go back to command the covering army.

Having failed to force the allies away from Lille, the French moved to sever their lines of communication and supply from Brussels, Antwerp and Ostend. Marlborough and Eugene were already short of supplies and munitions, the expenditure of both had been greatly more than expected, leaving aside the mismanagement that the duke had discovered. A severe battle was fought at Wynendael to protect a much-needed convoy of supplies coming through from Ostend, but the land all around was flooded by French engineers, and spirits flagged in the allied camp. Adam Cardonnel, Marlborough's secretary, wrote despondently that 'It were to be wished that we had quitted the siege ten days ago, and the sooner the better'.[28] However, the pressure exerted by Eugene was taking effect, and a practicable breach in the main defences was at last made by the allied gunners. On the afternoon of 22 October, after 60 days of siege, Boufflers offered to give up the city, and the battered St Magdelene gate was occupied by the allies as a token of submission. 'Eugen treated the garrison with the generosity which their brave defence so justly merited.'[29] The locally-recruited militia were released from service, prisoners exchanged, and on 25 October Boufflers withdrew with his surviving soldiers into the citadel. The agreed articles of the capitulation of the city were signed by Eugene without being read in detail, commenting that there was nothing that so fine a soldier would request that he could ever refuse. The gravely wounded Marquis de Suville-Hautfois was carried from the citadel and attended by Eugene's own surgeon before being taken to Douai to recover, a thoughtful act that brought a letter of thanks from Versailles.

In the meantime, Vendôme had secured the crossings of the Scheldt, except at Oudenarde, and in doing so severed the allied lines of supply, while Elector Max-Emmanuel, summoned from the Moselle, laid siege to Brussels. This attempt to prise the allies away from Lille failed, and in a confident counter move, Marlborough and Eugene marched to re-open the crossings over the river on 24 November, while a token force was left to watch Boufflers in the Lille citadel. The elector's clumsy effort to take Brussels failed, and the duke moved to add speed to his hasty withdrawal, while Eugene returned to resume the siege operations with hardly a missed beat. Vendôme, foiled and baffled, withdrew further into the French fortress belt, and in doing so Comte De la Motte was left holding out north of the Ghent-Bruges canal, while it was now quite clear that nothing the French did would shake the allied grip on Lille. Not daring to risk a general action, they had failed to break the lines of supply feeding the hungry army besieging the city, while their opponents, working together once more in close harmony, were dictating the pace of a highly demanding and complex campaign. That there had been mis-steps on both sides could not be denied, but the allied army was throughout in a remarkably exposed position and having to operate against superior numbers. The plain inability of the French to take advantage of all this was both dismal, and simply remarkable.

By early December, Eugene had his heavy batteries ready to begin the work of bombarding the citadel of Lille, with twenty-six 24-pounder guns and twelve large siege mortars in place. A summons was sent to Boufflers to submit, and in the evening on 9 December 1708, he signed the formal articles of capitulation, having that day received permission from Versailles to do so. He was permitted to leave unmolested with his surviving troops, without giving their parole. Private soldier John Deane remembered that 'Boufflers was admitted to march out at the head of his troops with flying colours, six pieces of cannon, and ten covered wagons, and to be safely conducted to Douai'.[30] The marshal's performance in this defence had been a considerable achievement, dragging to a standstill what had been, after a shaky start, a promising campaign for Marlborough and Eugene. Of course, the success in securing so formidable a fortress as Lille was widely applauded, but it had been had only at a significant cost in men, munitions and valuable campaign time. Louis XIV was aware of this, and wrote to Boufflers: 'I cannot sufficiently praise your vigour, and the pertinacity of the troops under your command. To the very end they have backed up your courage and zeal. I have every reason to be satisfied.'[31] The cost of the whole operation was heavy, not just in irreplaceable time, but with almost 16,000 allied casualties suffered between late July and mid-December, while it was reported some 7,000 casualties had been suffered by the stalwart garrison in Lille, almost half of all those taking part.

With the city secure at last, and desiring to get into winter quarters as bitterly cold weather came on, moves to retake Ghent and Bruges were quickly begun. De la Motte was urged to hold out, with Chamillart writing: 'The preservation of Ghent is of so great importance, that you can never take too many precautions . . . dispute the ground inch by inch, as Marshal Boufflers has done at Lille.'[32] On 19 December Ghent was invested by Count Lottum, while Eugene covered the operations between the Scheldt and the Dender, and a bombardment of the French defences was begun eleven days later. De la Motte despaired of being relieved by Vendôme and prudently submitted, being allowed to march away with his troops on 2 January 1709. The French garrisons in Bruges and the smaller forts of Leffinghem and Plas-Endael were evacuated at the same time, so that the opposing armies could at last trudge off to their billets.

The great campaign was at an end, and in the hands of Marlborough and Eugene, two commanders of consummate skill and daring, larger French armies had been outmanoeuvred, out-fought and defeated, marshals of France confounded and left at a loss, and a massively fortified city taken while they looked on. The omens for a well-negotiated and balanced end to ruinous war, longed for now by the parties on both sides, were surely there to see. Eugene remained with Marlborough at The Hague until 15 January, and then went to Vienna to confer with the emperor and the Imperial War Council. He would surely have been warmed to learn that the States-General regarded his efforts in the 1708 campaign as being of the highest order: 'After God, thanks for the successes achieved must go to the intelligence, efficiency and boldness of Prince Eugene.'[33] A commemorative medal was struck in his honour, and surprisingly Marlborough was not mentioned, the stirring inscription being 'The Duke of Vendôme being overcome in Flanders, as well as in Italy, acknowledges Prince Eugene to be his conqueror'. Whether Marlborough knew of, or cared much about, this apparent snub is not clear, but the 'Great Frost' had come, and much of France was in its grip, with the country exhausted financially and militarily, so that Louis XIV would have welcomed an equitable settlement of everything in dispute. Tentative negotiations to find mutually-acceptable terms had been taking place at The Hague for some time, and Eugene was appointed by Joseph to press for the best possible outcome for Vienna. At the core of this, unfortunately, was still the requirement that the Spanish empire, entire and undivided, should be accorded to the Habsburg claimant, Archduke Charles, and that he be installed in Madrid as Carlos III, with the young French claimant sent on his way. There was a certain absurdity about this, as Philip V was to all appearances popular and quite secure on the throne, and the Habsburg cause in Spain, by contrast, was floundering amidst a series of inept and poorly resourced military campaigns.

At the end of May 1709 a formal proposal for peace was presented to the French, containing no fewer than forty-two 'preliminaries' (in effect, demands). The most damning of these was a requirement that Louis XIV should use his own troops to remove his grandson from Madrid if the young man refused to go. In the meantime, key French fortresses were to be handed over to the allies as surety that the king would do what had been agreed. Sentiment in London was firm on this issue, although on Eugene's advice Emperor Joseph would pragmatically have given way if agreement could only otherwise have been had. 'It is certain,' wrote a British officer, 'the Imperial ministers and Prince Eugene were not for breaking upon that point.'[34] It should have been seen that such insulting conditions could not be accepted in Versailles, even with the present distressed state of France. The king was assured by Marshal Villars that he could rely upon the army, and he wrote to his provincial governors to explain why peace had not come: 'I pass in silence over the suggestion made to me that I should join my forces to those of the [Grand Alliance] and oblige the king, my grandson, to abdicate.'[35] The terms presented by the allies were rejected in their entirety on 2 June 1709, with no offer of further discussions, and in consequence the tired war had to go on.

Chapter 10

An Empire of Shadows – Malplaquet, Denain and Peace

The 1709 campaign began later than usual, largely because the allies had been sure that Louis XIV would submit, and so certain was everyone of success that arrangements had been made to disband the armies. 'The French troops as well as the country are in such a miserable condition that either the King of France must comply with what the allies shall think necessary to demand of him, or there seems nothing to hinder our army from marching to Paris.'[1] Instead, Louis XIV packed Vendôme off to campaign in Spain, and appointed in his place Marshal Villars, highly capable, aggressive and a veteran of the long-ago campaigns against the Ottomans. The troops were short of food, munitions, clothing and materiel, but he infused his threadbare men with fresh hope after the experience of the previous year. Villars was careful not to risk a battle in the open, but let the still-formidable French fortress belt take the opening blows. By mid-June the commissaries and quartermasters had been bullied into performing great feats so that the troops were re-equipped and replenished, and deployed in a defensive position between the fortress of Douai and the river Lys.

Eugene had looked forward to the renewal of campaigning with a touch of uncharacteristic gloom and a degree of weariness, writing presciently to Vienna that it was:

> True that the army is no smaller than last year and is in excellent condition. We should therefore be able to hope for a successful outcome to the season. But since nothing on earth is so variable as luck in arms the Emperor should bear in mind how much now is at stake.[2]

Both he and Marlborough were aware of the cautious stance of their opponent, and yet the necessity once more was to bring on a battle in the open where their greater strength could have most effect. Villars was unlikely to be easily caught, that was understood, but after the fall of Lille the potential loss of another major fortress might well bring him out to fight.

A careful scouting of the French dispositions, in what were known as the Lines of La Bassée, showed that an outright attack held faint prospect for success, and there was little room there in which to manoeuvre. Marlborough favoured a move against Ypres, but Eugene, more cautious for once, felt that Tournai offered greater scope for a subsequent advance towards open country. Accordingly, on 27 June 1709, having decoyed French attention away with the allied siege train moving by water towards Menin, Tournai was invested by Eugene. So neatly was this done that Villars was misled, and had drawn troops out from that same garrison to bolster the strength of his field army. 'They expected our going to another place, so that they have not half the troops in the town they should have.'[3] The marshal did what he could to mask the error in his report to Versailles, and the king was warm in congratulation: 'I count for much, that by your wise dispositions and the precautions you have taken, all the vast projects [of the enemy] are reduced to the single enterprise.'[4]

Shielded by the Scheldt, Tournai was a massively powerful Vauban-designed fortress and proved to be a rigorous test for the besiegers. The garrison under the Marquis de Surville-Hautfois, who had been 'Wounded at the siege of Lille, and has the reputation of a very good officer',[5] put up a valiant defence, and the operations proceeded slowly and at great cost. The digging of the approach trenches began on 7 July, and the breaching batteries were brought up three days later to begin their work, with Marlborough conducting the siege and Eugene covering the operations. The weather was poor and the French proved adept at counter-mining operations, which gave the allied soldiers a horror of what might, or might not, be taking place beneath their feet. The Saxon Count Matthias von Schulemburg wrote: 'This is a siege quite different from any hitherto made; the most embarrassing thing is that few officers even among the engineers have any exact knowledge of this kind of underground work.'[6] Matters were made worse when the French opened the sluice gates on the Scheldt at Condé and Valenciennes to flood out the allied siege works, but despite this by the end of the month the main defences were breached, and the garrison withdrew into the citadel to continue the defence.

This time expended was loudly criticized, as great things had been expected in London and The Hague, and yet the recently victorious allied armies, or so it seemed, were reduced to besieging just one more fortress. A letter to Lord Raby, the British ambassador in Berlin, ran that 'At our coffee houses [in London] we are very angry that the news talks of our besieging Tournai, for their opinion is that we ought not to amuse ourselves in taking towns, but march directly on Paris',[7] adding the maliciously sharp barb, 'How did Prince Eugene march his army over the mountains without such a train or money, and his march to the relief of Turin was in like manner; 'tis but to employ him, and the business is done.' Only on 31 August did the marquis asked for terms to capitulate, so that on 5 September the gates to the citadel were occupied by Marlborough's troops. The survivors of the garrison were permitted to march away with their baggage to Condé, but obliged by the terms agreed to leave behind their colours and guns.

The operations to take Tournai had once more eaten up precious months of campaign time, and so the fortress had proved its worth, but such continued losses would not be accepted in Versailles. As soon as the capitulation of the citadel was sure, Eugene and Marlborough moved swiftly to send the Prince of Hesse-Cassel with a powerful force of cavalry past St Ghislain to invest Mons. In this way he interposed himself between the fortress and the French field army, obstructing any moves that Villars might make to reinforce the garrison. On learning of this, Louis XIV was prompt in his instructions: 'Should Mons follow on the fate of Tournai, our case is undone . . . the cost is not to be considered.'[8] This was a plain call for Villars to venture out of his defensive lines and fight, and on 7 September he moved forward and arrayed his army for battle along the woods on both sides of the Gap of Aulnois, close to the small village of Malplaquet on the border of France with the Southern Netherlands.

Marlborough and Eugene could deploy some 105,000 men with 100 guns, a significant but not overwhelming advantage in numbers over Villars with the 85,000 troops and 80 guns that he had on the field. However, the marshal was using the belt of woods to his front to screen his own movements and comparative lack of numbers. He could also threaten a sudden move through the treeline to attack any exposed detachment of the allied army as it deployed to cover the siege operations against Mons. Accordingly, Eugene moved his wing of the army to cover the Gap of Bossu five miles to the north of the Gap of Aulnois, while Marlborough brought his troops into position to confront Villars. It was soon apparent that the marshal was not going to venture further forward, but was entrenching a defensive position, using the tangled wooded copses to cover his flanks. An early move by Marlborough to interrupt this work was not practical as the allied artillery was not yet up and Eugene could not march to combine forces with Marlborough until it was seen clearly what Villars was doing. This became evident by 10 September, when the combined allied army was at last in place and making ready to attack the French in position.

By then the French reserve cavalry had been detached to cover Mauberge, which was not actually under threat, so it seemed that Villars was also unsure of his opponents' intentions. He would have been unaware of an added factor, amounting almost to a cunning plan, that Lieutenant-General Henry Withers had been left at Tournai with 11,000 troops, to slight the fortifications, level the siege works and gather in the stores left behind. He was now coming to take the French army in the flank once battle was engaged, and would not be able to reach the field until 11 September. That much was expected of this novel tactical innovation, marching hot-foot to join a battle once it was in progress, can be seen in a letter Eugene wrote to the emperor, the night before the battle, and telling of 'The corps from Tournai [which] is to make a special effort, and are to be let loose upon the enemy'.[9]

The Dutch troops, under the command of Henry of Nassau, Prince of Orange, were to attack on the allied left, supported by Danish infantry under General Johan van Pallandt, while Marlborough held the British. Prussian and Hanoverian contingents in the centre of the army, opposite a strong line of French defensive earthen redans. Eugene had the command of the troops on the right, facing the copses of the Bois de Sars, and under his direction were sixty-two Imperial battalions led by Matthias von der Schulemburg, Count Philip-Karl Lottum and General August Wackerbath, as well as Temple's British brigade and the rest of the Danish contingent under Duke Charles of Württemberg. The attack went in early on 11 September, the anniversary of the victory at Zenta, which coincidence must surely have come to Eugene's mind as he took horse.

Colonel Jean-Martrin De La Colonie remembered very well the pounding his men endured, as they held the redans in the centre of the Gap of Aulnois, and that:

> At break of day, the battery of thirty cannon opened fire, and by its continuous volleys succeeded in breaching the entrenchments in the wood on our left, and the head of the enemy's infantry column made its appearance. They came

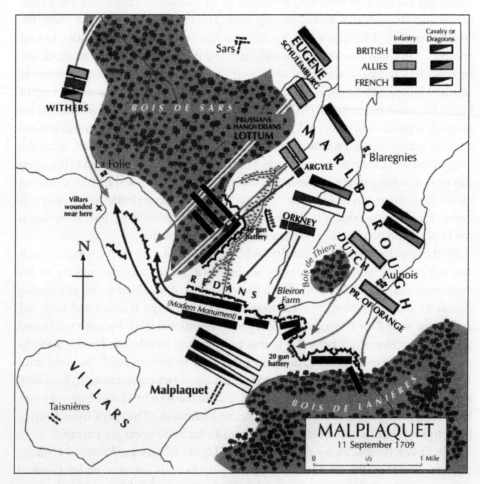

Map 11. The Battle of Malplaquet, 11 September 1709.

on at a slow pace, and by seven o'clock had arrived in line with the battery threatening our centre . . . At last the column, leaving the great battery on its left, changed its direction a quarter right and threw itself precipitately into the wood on our left, making an assault on that portion that had been breached.[10]

These were Eugene's troops, going into their first attack, driving a way at the point of the bayonet through the heavily defended thickets. Despite the punishingly effective opening artillery bombardment, they quickly ran into difficulties, due both to the constricted nature of the wooded country and to the valiant defence offered by the French infantry, commanded by the Marquis d'Albergotti, tenaciously holding their barricades in the notorious and prominent 'Triangle' feature of the woods. The French had chained large logs together, cleared fields of fire and laid dense belts of sharpened stakes to slow the advance of their opponents, and they contested every yard with dogged determination, so that what progress was made over the first line of entrenchments was only at a heavy cost. 'Although the enemy had forced their way into the woods, this success did not involve their winning the battle . . . the fighting was extremely stubborn.'[11] Von Schulemburg was driven back, and only a second effort, with a fresh British brigade sent by Marlborough, took the second and then the incomplete third line of French entrenchments. Eugene was wounded by a musket ball to the neck just behind the ear, but typically refused to have the wound dressed, declaring irritably that there was no point if he was to be killed that day, anyway 'If we live, there will be time enough in the evening'.[12] General Wackerbath, the rugged commander of the Saxon troops, was wounded at the same time, but the French position in the woods was giving way, and Villars began to draw troops from his centre to shore up that flank, so that Eugene was after all achieving his aim. Meanwhile, the Dutch and Danish troops advancing on the allied left had been savaged by heavy and concentrated French artillery fire directed by the Marquis Armand de St Hilaire, and were twice repulsed with appalling losses, so that Marlborough had to ride over and instruct Orange not to go forward again for the time being. The French right. however, was firmly fixed in position by the valiant and costly effort.

Shortly before midday, after a fierce struggle, Eugene's infantry began to emerge from the treeline. Sergeant John Wilson remembered that 'Notwithstanding the courage of our enemy, we at last made ourselves masters of the wood'.[13] The French troops on that flank fell back towards the La Folie Farm, where Henry Withers' corps of troops, straight off the line of march from Tournai, were emerging onto open ground. The small French post at St Ghislain had been stormed the previous evening, allowing direct access to the field, and Villars' position on the left was clearly turned and his army might now be rolled up. He hastened to bring more troops from his centre to restore the position, at first intending to strike back at Eugene's tired battalions at the edge of the woods, but instead having to deploy to hold off the dangerous and unexpected thrust by Withers against his exposed flank. At this crucial moment, Villars was severely wounded in the knee by a musket ball and, fainting with loss of blood, could not continue in command. Marquis Jean-Noel de Chemerault was killed at his side in the same volley, and d'Albergotti injured when thrown from his rearing horse. Marshal Boufflers, serving on the right of the army as a volunteer, promptly rode over to take up command, as Marlborough's infantry began to break through the weakened centre of the French position.

With the way cleared, the massed allied cavalry were able to move forward and engage the French squadrons drawn up to the rear of the redans on the plain of Malplaquet. Although the attacks by the Dutch and Danes on the allied left had been firmly repulsed, the structural integrity of the whole French position was compromised, and only if the remorseless and seemingly unstoppable allied advance could be held back long enough would the French army survive the day. A huge cavalry battle broke out with the French horsemen, who had stoically suffered from the 'overs' of the allied artillery bombardment all morning, putting in an admirable performance to hold their ground. However, every time the allied troopers were thrown back, they recovered their poise with the support of infantry in possession of the captured redans. The French cavalry could not do this, and lacking such support they were worn down and forced to lose touch with their infantry on either flank, so that by mid-afternoon Boufflers could do no more and began to draw the battered troops off the field of battle. Eugene and Marlborough's commands were too exhausted, and with ranks far too thinned by casualties, to pursue with much vigour. At least twenty-two French guns were left behind in the woods to be claimed as trophies, but Boufflers was able, without much interference, to reach an entrenched camp prepared between Le Quesnoy and Valenciennes, where he could look to rest and restore his army, covered by the reserve cavalry called back from covering Mauberge.

The cost of the fighting at Malplaquet that Wednesday was frightful, with some 21,000 allied and 13,000 French killed and wounded.[14] Only about 500 unwounded French prisoners were taken, a certain sign that, although driven off the position, they had retired in good order. While the allied success was notable, it could be argued (and certainly was so by the duke's opponents in London) that the cost was too heavy and should have been avoided, all seemed so different from the inexpensive glory of Ramillies. A message was sent to Boufflers to send wagons to collect the French wounded, and this was just as well, as the allied generals were too taken up with gathering the large numbers of their own casualties to be too concerned about the French. Sergeant John Wilson remembered that 'His Grace and Prince Eugene, desiring to have a suspension of arms the day ensuing, that both armies might bury their dead and search for persons of distinction that was killed'.[15]

The sorry tally of casualties told only part of the tale, for Villars had only fought at Malplaquet to save Mons, and in this he failed, for the siege went ahead with the garrison submitting to Eugene just six weeks later, while almost no effort was made by the weakened French army to interrupt the operations. However, many in the allied camp had their doubts about the whole affair, and Richard Kane, one of Marlborough's officers, felt that 'Our generals were very much blamed for throwing away so many brave men's lives when there was no occasion, it was the only rash thing the Duke of Marlborough was ever guilty of; and it was generally believed that he was pressed to it by Prince Eugene'.[16] This smacks of special pleading by one of the duke's admirers, as the decision to attack Villars at Malplaquet was taken jointly by the two commanders, and once done it was difficult to see how the assault could have been made any earlier to prevent the strengthening of the position so formidably. Crucially, the allied guns, making their ponderous way from Tournai, were not in position until the evening of 10 September, while much had been expected, perhaps too optimistically, of Withers' advance against the French left once the battle was in progress. If the siege of Mons was a worthwhile undertaking, and Louis XIV was certainly alarmed at the prospect, then to at least drive off the French field army was a necessary step. Still, with so lengthy a casualty list, for a strategically limited gain, Malplaquet should perhaps be regarded as an allied success which allowed the operations against Mons to proceed, rather than anything more. That French commentators, then and later, claimed the battle as a victory for Villars and Boufflers remains a mistake, as although their troops fought very well, they had lost.

Perhaps the allied army in the autumn of 1709 was just too large an instrument, given the means of communication of the day, to be effectively controlled by the two commanders, however gifted they might be. At Malplaquet, Eugene and Marlborough had over twice the numbers they deployed at Blenheim five years earlier, and the bloody attacks on the allied left were pressed well beyond any hope of success, and the decision to halt that effort was taken later than ideally it should have been. It is, however, pertinent to note that the main critics of Marlborough's conduct of the battle were not in The Hague, whose troops lost so severely, but to be found in London where his critics and political opponents continued to gain ground.

That autumn was notable for bad weather, and soon after the seizure of Mons, the allied troops went to winter quarters, and Eugene returned to Vienna on 9 December 1709, with standing that remained high despite a campaign that yielded slim results. The Viceroyalty of Milan had been taken from him during the summer, so that it could for diplomatic reasons be bestowed on the Duke of Modena, who just happened to be the brother-in law of the Empress Amalie; he never bothered to take up the appointment, so that Eugene remained the de facto viceroy for several more years. Amongst the fresh rewards that came to him was the promise of a confiscated estate in Hungary, valued at 300,000 gulden, an order to that effect being signed by Joseph on 17 December, but a suitable property could not be found, so Eugene was instead paid this sum by way of a pension from the Royal Hungarian Treasury. Significantly for his standing at court, his old adversary there, the principal minister Prince Charles von Salm, had been sent into retirement by Joseph, and the influence of Wratislaw and Eugene increased as a result. All the great departments of state were now in the hands of their appointees, and they in effect now formed the core of the emperor's inner circle of confidantes and advisers.

Preparations for the next year's campaigning season took a curious form, with almost 50,000 Austrian troops and local militia deployed to maintain order and guard the borders in Hungary, far more than were made available for Eugene, and it could be seen from this diversion of effort how relatively little importance was attached to the campaign in the West. Attitudes had hardened when it was learned that London had quietly agreed terms with The Hague for an enlarged Dutch Barrier, the series of fortified towns intended to ward off fresh French aggression by way of the Southern Netherlands. At least in part this was an inducement to keep Holland in the war, and extensive commercial concessions had also been granted to help offset the cost of the Dutch war effort, but all without reference to Vienna. So, each of the major parties in the Grand Alliance were clumsily guilty of self-interest, and harmony, always a thing of some fragility, was inevitably lost. Meanwhile Vienna was concerned at the growing influence of Prussia in German affairs, and Eugene went to Berlin on his way back to the Low Countries. His visit was seen as a significant diplomatic success, binding the attention and energy of King Frederick to the allied cause and keeping him engaged in the conflict with France, rather than with any wasteful distraction such as pursuing a campaign against Sweden, weakened as it was after defeat by the Rusian Tsar Peter at Poltava.

Despite these strains, the combined allied effort remained prodigious, and in the spring of 1710 an army of almost 120,000 troops could be fielded in northern France and the Low Countries. With negotiations for peace still having made no progress, in mid-April Eugene joined Marlborough at Tournai, fresh with determination to press forward and force a strategic victory. In this can be seen miscalculation, for the tough fighting of the previous year had shown that when driven into a corner, the French would fight with great tenacity. Once again, the command of this huge array was a joint enterprise, the two men working very much in harmony, although Marlborough remained the de facto commander-in-chief. The financial subsidies which Great Britain still provided to keep the Grand Alliance afloat counted for a great deal, and Eugene accepted the fact and his support for the duke, if in private he was sometimes rather critical, remained firm.

The French fortress of Douai, set on the river Scarpe, was the focus for the opening moves in the campaign for the year. 'It covered all Artois and had magnificent arsenals.'[17] The Marquis d'Albergotti could be depended on to put up a good defence with his 7,000-strong garrison, while the French field army, recovered somewhat from the trials of the previous autumn and now commanded by the newly-appointed Marshal Charles Montesquieu, fell back towards Béthune. The outpost of Mortagne was secured by the Earl of Albemarle on 18 April, but St Amand held out, although the French withdrew to Cambrai, losing some of their baggage in the process. On 5 May the siege trenches were opened before Douai, with Eugene commanding the operations. Villars, still convalescent but with Marshal Berwick in support, rejoined the army and ventured cautiously forward, but could neither find a weak spot to attack or induce the allies to turn aside from their siege. On 16 June, despite the garrison mounting two damaging sorties on the siege works, d'Albergotti sent a message to Villars that he could not resist for much longer. The marshal was constrained in what he could do, so that the garrison capitulated on good terms at the end of the month, having endured the allied siege for a creditable 63 days, and Marlborough wrote to his wife, 'I send the good news of Douai and the Fort of Scarpe being surrendered'.[18]

Despite this fresh success, the allied army was embroiled once more in an expensive and strategically unproductive campaign to break through the fortress belt that shielded France. Villars was under instructions from Versailles not to risk another battle, and he kept behind strong lines of defence, known as 'Non Plus Ultra',[19] but Béthune soon followed the fate of Douai, as did Aire-sur-la-Lys and St Venant where the allies began their siege works on 6 September. St Venant could not be held for long, but Aire only submitted on 9 November after a gruelling siege operation against a valiant French defence under the formidable Marquis de Goesbriand. Eugene covered these operations from a position on the river Lys, but the weather had turned foul, casualties were disproportionately high for what was gained, and the allied troops concluded the 1710 campaign in a mood of exhaustion and dejection. Villars had succeeding in keeping his army together, while his opponents wasted their strength away on the fortress belt, and in the meantime the will of the Grand Alliance to pursue its objectives gradually ebbed away.

In Spain, an advance on Madrid by Archduke Charles and his generals had promised much, but ended with the defeat by the Duc de Vendôme of a small British army at Brihuega. Guido von Starhemberg battered the French and Spanish army to a standstill the following day at Villa Viciosa, but had to withdraw into Catalonia. Hopes for a Habsburg success seemed to be increasingly fanciful, particularly as Philip V was making himself generally very popular with the Spanish nobility and people. The attention of Emperor Joseph was in any case not focussed on Spain, but in further consolidating the gains made in Italy. The problems in Hungary had at last been resolved, an outbreak of the plague having claimed many thousands of lives and knocked the heart out of the rebellion, so that the unrest would formally come to an end with the Treaty of Szatmár in the spring of 1711. A sordid attempt to avoid the payment of agreed sums to the principal rebel commanders, Rákóczy and Károyli, was quashed by Eugene, who insisted that the longed-for agreement for peace should not be put in jeopardy. Nonetheless, there was no significant movement of troops relieved from operations in the East towards the Low Countries or the Rhine. Marlborough anticipated this, and wrote in anxiety from The Hague to the British envoy in Vienna: 'You must do your utmost at the court that the Emperor exerts himself in proportion to the advantage he reaps by the peace of Hungary, which it is certain all the Allies will have just reason to expect, since that has hitherto been the excuse.'[20] A rather sad postscript was added to the duke's letter, giving a hint of remembrance of happier times when great plans had been laid, great things expected, and great achievements secured: 'My compliments to Comte Wratislaw.'

While in Vienna that winter, Eugene had the unusual pleasure of welcoming to his Winterhof Palace in the Himmelpfortgasse the sultan's plenipotentiary, Seifulah Aga, who had come to discuss with Joseph's ministers matters of mutual concern and interest between the two empires, for so long at loggerheads with each other. The envoy was urbane and cultured, and Eugene exerted himself as host, so that the two men got on very well, and there were hopes that the visit would presage a greater degree of understanding and harmony in the years to come. This might entail a formal extension of the 1699 Treaty of Carlowitz, and perhaps incidentally a joint approach made to address the growing power of Russia, but any overt moves to agree closer terms with Constantinople were sure to alarm the tsar, and that was to be avoided. The sultan's novel diplomatic initiative, which might have achieved much, was accordingly met with rather dismissive coolness, and brought few results, no matter what courtesy, amity and ceremony was shown to his representative in the glittering salons of Vienna.

The emperor was unwell, and declined to see Eugene before he left to resume campaigning, and the reason soon became clear, when on 17 April 1711 Joseph died of smallpox. His premature death was much regretted by the prince who had valued his support, and meanwhile Archduke Charles, who would prove a pale substitute for his older brother, had to wait for his election to the Imperial throne. In the process his already faltering claim to become the King of Spain fell away, as he could hardly have realistically expected to simultaneously occupy thrones both in Vienna and Madrid. Charles, nonetheless, never entirely forgot the idea and kept a place in his heart for Spain, where he had been warmly received in some quarters, and remained much influenced by what was known as the 'Spanish' faction at the court in Vienna. While all this was taking shape, and confirmation of his election as emperor awaited, his mother, Eleonara, acted as regent in Vienna. There was a inevitably a degree of uncertainty amongst the electors of the Empire, so that Eugene was unable to resume campaigning until things had settled down.

Marlborough was anxious for his friend's return to Flanders, but had to be patient. Nonetheless he added a postscript in a letter to Eugene '*Hâtez votre voyage autant qu'il sera possible.*'[21] Louis XIV recognized the opportunity gifted him by the unease amongst his opponents, and applied pressure upon the nerves of the Grand Alliance by moving forces under Elector Max-Emmanuel towards the Rhine frontier. This new threat caused both Marlborough and the Dutch Grand Pensionary Antonius Hiensius to urge Eugene to counter the French initiative, and in mid-June he moved to Mühlberg on the upper Rhine to assume the command of the campaign there, drawing on the 20,000 Imperial troops that had been in northern France. He even moved across the Rhine to occupy Speyerbach, but this was only a demonstration, as there was no intention or prospect of mounting a full-blooded campaign in eastern France with so slender a force at his disposal. What was done, however, was sufficient for the time being to hold Max-Emmanuel in check.

The election of Charles as emperor was at last confirmed by the Imperial Diet in Frankfurt in October 1711. Meanwhile, Marlborough had pursued a campaign without Eugene, and taken the strong French fortress of Bouchain. This tactical triumph did not save him, and he was dismissed by Queen Anne at the end of the year, so that a fine partnership of two close friends and consummate commanders, both men with a claim to be masters of the field, had come to an end. Dutch Field-Deputy Sicco van Goslinga, argumentative and contrary and whose opinion of Marlborough always wavered, was amongst those who regretted the almost complete absence of Eugene from the campaign that year, referring to his 'Genius for War . . . greatly superior to that of the Duke'.[22] Such sentiments were no doubt coloured by the revelation that ministers in London had quietly reached an outline agreement with Versailles, without consulting or notifying Vienna and The Hague. The strong suspicion, justified as it turned out, was that the British were about to make a separate peace.

Eugene was sent to London to offer support to Marlborough and to bolster the faltering British commitment to the allied cause, but his arrival was not welcomed by the powerful faction in Parliament committed to achieving a peace settlement at almost any cost. Graf Johan Wentzl von Gallas, the emperor's representative in London, had already been sent packing on trumped-up charges, presumably in order that he would not be able to combine his considerable diplomatic skills with those of Eugene in arguing the case for continued involvement in the war. The British envoy in The Hague was also under instructions to try and prevent the journey: 'To discourage as much as possible, this Prince from coming over. It is high time to put a stop to this foreign influence on British councils.'[23] Specious rumours were spread that Eugene was so unpopular that any visit would be attended by violent protests and demonstrations, but he took no notice as the firm instructions from Vienna were to do what he could to stiffen British resolve and support for the alliance.

The visit began in the third week of January 1712, but Eugene found on his arrival that Marlborough had already been dismissed, and the imminent arrival may well have accelerated the decision. Warned that it would be impolitic to publicly offer support to the duke, and in so doing implicitly to criticize the government in London, he wrote in confidence to Vienna:

> It was well known all over the world what a firm and intimate friendship I had fostered with the Duke of Marlborough, now finding him in misfortune, I could not do otherwise than uphold my friendship with him . . . lest the world should say, and I leave it as an evil echo after me, that I deserted and abandoned a friend in his hour of sorrow and distress when fortune had forsaken him.[24]

Eugene was accorded no official reception, and his first and only visitor on the day of his arrival, 16 January, was Marlborough, with whom he spent a comfortable hour in private conversation in the house recently vacated by von Gallas. In the meantime, he sent his Prussian aide, George von Hohendorff, to request an interview with government ministers. This was arranged for the next morning, and that same evening Eugene had an audience with Queen Anne at St James's Palace, it having apparently been decided that nothing would be gained, and much lost perhaps, by trying to ignore so eminent a visitor. Almost all the rather stilted conversation was carried on in French, as Eugene's command of English was limited, enabling Anne to be as reticent as she thought prudent.

It was clear that the queen had received advice as to how to answer Eugene's requests for assurance on the intentions of her government. She attempted to excuse herself by claiming ill-health (valiant and stout-heated like a true Stuart, she was in truth very unwell), but was visibly embarrassed at the almost contemptuous manner in which the prince had been treated. 'My state of health does not permit me to speak to Your Highness as often as I wish,' she murmured, adding as she indicated her principal ministers, Robert Harley and Henry St John, standing nearby, 'I have ordered these two gentlemen to receive your proposals, whenever you think proper.'[25] They were the determined prime movers in the peace party in London, and so the omens for making progress were not good. Perhaps not surprisingly, Eugene's efforts were a failure, nor could he shield Marlborough from malicious charges of embezzlement of public funds, but socially he was a great success, even if there was no official banquet to mark his presence in London. His reputation as a fine commander was widely recognized, he was hugely popular with the people, and private entertainments and invitations were provided on a lavish scale. Crowds followed his every step it seemed, and Harley even had him to dinner at his town house, when he lavished praise on the 'Greatest captain of the age'.[26] This was a thinly veiled cut at Marlborough, of course, and Eugene was not taken in.

Eugene was known to be generous to his impecunious nephews, and the time in London was marked by one personal tragedy, when his aide-de-camp, Chevalier Eugene, the younger son of his eldest brother, died of smallpox. A small consolation, perhaps, was that Eugene was able to buy books in London that were not available in Vienna, and so begin to amass what became a notable library and establish a firm reputation as a bibliophile. His diplomatic mission came to an end on 17 March 1712, when he set sail for Holland on a yacht thoughtfully provided by Queen Anne's ministers who were relieved to see him go. Eugene was now convinced that London would make a separate peace with France as soon as it could be arranged, once British interests had been secured, and in this he was right. The degree of double-dealing taking place at the time, may be judged when it is considered that the French Secretary of State, the Marquis de Torcy, was kept advised by British ministers on just how the discussions with Eugene had gone.

Marlborough's successor as commander, James Butler, 2nd Duke of Ormonde, was warned not to be led on too much by Eugene. They had met in London, gone shooting together in Richmond Park and got along very well, but this happy state did not last, for it was widely suspected that Great Britain had already reached an understanding with Louis XIV. Eugene hoped that a successful campaign in northern France might yet stir the British sufficiently to keep them active in the alliance, while the Dutch had given him the field command over their own troops, Ormonde not being trusted well enough to do so. On 21 May, Queen Anne's minsters sent what became notorious as the 'Restraining Orders', such that Ormonde was not to actively engage British troops, or those paid for by the Treasury in London, in any battle or siege, no matter what how good the chances for success. Infamously, this instruction was made known to Marshal Villars, and details were also passed on what Eugene might attempt in the campaign. 'I had almost forgot to tell you,' Henry St John blithely wrote to Ormonde, 'that communication was given of this order to the Court of France.'[27] This blatant bad faith embarrassed Ormonde, who was not lacking a sense of honour and propriety, but to his discredit he did as he was told. Accordingly, Eugene had to press on without his assistance, while 12,000 British troops stayed idle in their encampments, although a review of the combined army was held on 23 May, when both Eugene and Ormonde tried to appear to be on good terms. This was for the sake of appearances only, and when a reconnaissance of the French dispositions near to Arras showed that their right flank could be turned without great difficulty, Ormonde refused to take any active steps. His hands were, of course, tied by the orders he had from London. Eugene was now aware of this, and when he at last challenged Ormonde, it was not denied.

Pressed by Vienna to pursue a vigorous campaign, seen as the best way to secure a good peace, Eugene's response to the difficulty he faced was typically bold, although perhaps also rash. With those Dutch, Imperial and Danish troops available to him, he crossed the Scheldt at Souches, and shielded by the river Selle, moved to invest the French-held fortress of Le Quesnoy. Concurrently a brigade of cavalry was sent raiding across the rivers Somme and Oise, and on from Rheims towards Metz, a plundering expedition in effect, to distract French attention. On

8 June the siege of Le Quesnoy was begun and progressed well, but two weeks later Ormonde declared that he had instructions to withdraw his troops entirely from the campaign, to await the conclusion of peace negotiations between France and Great Britain. The Grand Alliance that might have achieved so much had it abided by its original limited aims, at last wearily fell to pieces. Ormonde may have been of lesser calibre than others around him, but he felt the difficulty of his position, and delayed putting his instructions to withdraw his troops into immediate effect. Colonel de la Colonie remembered that 'The English for their part, did not separate themselves from the allied army, but allowed the siege to progress without participating in the work'.[28] The garrison in Le Quesnoy capitulated on 4 July, but two weeks later, Ormonde announced an armistice between Great Britain and France and formally took his British troops out of the campaign. Despite protests from officers and soldiers alike, they were marched to encampments around Ghent and Bruges in preparation for eventual embarkation for England. Mean threats were made to withhold money from the contingents of Danish and German troops for any non-compliance with London's intentions, but they ignored the pressure and loyally remained in the field, stoutly declaring that 'They could not follow him nor separate from Prince Eugene without express orders from their respective princes'.[29] In fact, the numbers of troops Ormonde took away did not unduly reduce the bayonet strength of the allied army, which remained well over 100,000 strong, but the blow to confidence and morale inflicted by the British action was sharp, while the French were heartened and emboldened.

Determined to maintain the pace of the campaign, Eugene sent Prince Leopold of Anhalt-Dessau to invest Landrecies on the river Sambre to the south of the Forest of Mormal, while he took up a covering position near to Querimaing. Villars, encouraged by the knowledge that the British had left the field, drew fresh troops out of fortresses not under immediate threat, and on 18 July moved across the Scheldt near to Cambrai to threaten Eugene's dispositions. His lines of supply and communication were lengthy, as the Dutch were reluctant to pay for depots and magazines to be established close to Landrecies, so that the small town of Marchiennes on the river Scarpe was chosen instead, eight miles distant from Denain on the Scheldt which was itself all of 15 miles from Landrecies. So, the deployment of Eugene's army was widely spread out, and he was running an obvious risk, although the post at Denain was strongly entrenched with lines of defence reaching back to Marchiennes. This weakness in Eugene's extended dispositions were plain enough to so seasoned a campaigner as Villars: 'His convoys were no longer safe from attack.'[30] The centre of gravity for Eugene's whole operation against Landrecies was simply the supply base at Marchiennes. Although 4,000 troops guarded the place, should it fall into French hands, his whole advanced posture would collapse.

Villars drew his army up between Le Cateau and Cambrai, calculating that the most promising opening move would be to attack the detachment of Dutch and

German troops holding Denain before they could be supported. Success there would sever Eugene's deployment at its weakest point, and cut him off from Marchiennes. On 22 July 1712, having only taken Marshal Montesquiou into his confidence, Villars edged past Le Cateau as if to contest the siege operation against Landrecies, but the following night sent the Comte de Broglie with a strong force of cavalry to the river Selle, as if to threaten the small garrison in recently-captured Le Quesnoy. Eugene was for the moment at a loss to see clearly what was intended, as Villars might advance to relieve Landrecies, try and regain Le Quesnoy, or perhaps threaten Denain and the base at Marchiennes. In the meantime, the marshal moved quickly, his right flank on the Selle covered by de Broglie's cavalry at every crossing point, and the Marquis de Vieux Pont went ahead to lay pontoon bridges over the Scheldt near Neuville. On 24 July the fast-moving French advance guard, under the Marquis d'Albergotti, was across to the far bank. Speed was the key, but Eugene afterwards admitted to Emperor Charles that he had been under the firm impression all along that Villars' real intention in his advance was to try and directly relieve Landrecies.

The Earl of Albemarle, a highly gifted Dutch commander with just 8,000 troops, had insufficient strength to properly man the defences of Denain and those linking with Marchiennes, and if attacked in full force he must be overwhelmed. His cavalry were out foraging, and unable to give timely warning of the French approach, but they were recalled as soon as the alarm of the crossing near to Neuville was given. Pre-arranged warning signals were made to the commanders in Marchiennes, nearby Bouchain, and the small post at St Amand. The earl then disposed his troops as well as he could given their numbers, while hoping in the meantime to receive support before the French blow fell. A part of his slender force also had to be deployed to guard against any sortie from the French garrison in Valenciennes to the eastwards; this would not happen, but the risk could not be ignored.

Eugene learned of these dangerous developments early on 24 July, and all became clear, so that leaving orders that his army should follow at best speed, he rode with a small escort to Thuin, just short of Denain, and at about 10.00am, he could see for himself the advance in battle array of the French army. All that could be done immediately was to urge Albemarle to defend his position as help was on the way, but it was plain that the initiative lay entirely with their opponents. Eugene left his cavalry escort in place, and rode back towards Landrecies to spur his commanders to move faster, as if he could only combine his forces in time he would more than match the 60,000 troops Villars had brought forward. He must have known that this was a forlorn endeavour, the time and space element was just too challenging, and unless the marshal committed some highly untypical error, Albemarle could not be reinforced in good time.

Villars, of course, would commit no error, and at about 11.00am he ordered his infantry forward to overrun the allied outpost at Neuville, which was done

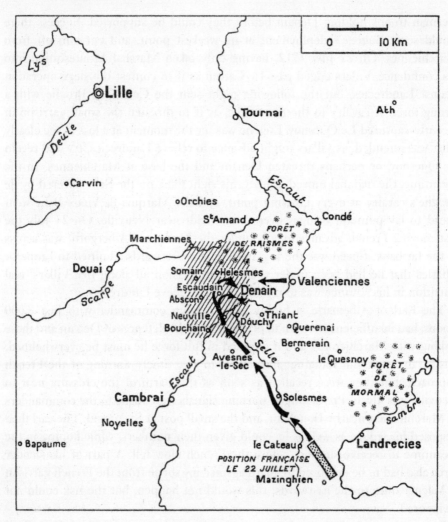

Map 12. The Manoeuvres before Denain, 1712.

efficiently, a large supply convoy being seized in the process. He then advanced on the main defences at Denain just after midday, with thirty-six full-strength infantry battalions advancing in three columns to the attack. 'In the order for the assault the front ranks of our troops were directed to sling their muskets and use their swords, so as to give greater freedom in scaling the parapets.'[31] The French soldiers at first met heavy musketry, backed up with canister from the earl's batteries, but they pressed gallantly forward, swarming over the makeshift defences to drive their outnumbered opponents back towards secondary positions and the single pontoon bridge spanning the Scheldt.[32] Only one bridge, as Ormonde had recently taken his pontoon train away with him, and a proper replacement had not yet been provided. Albemarle did his best to stem what fast became a rout, but was pulled from his horse and taken prisoner, as were the Prince of Nassau-Siegen and Count Hohenzollern. The sagging and swaying bridge was packed tight with fleeing soldiers, and as Eugene's main force came hurrying along the road from Landrecies, their progress was impeded by crowds of fugitives who had lost all order and discipline and he could do little but gather them together and withdraw towards Landrecies.

With this bold stroke, Villars achieved a notable success, mortifying for Eugene as he had clearly been outmanoeuvred, and a major detachment of his army, under the command of one of his best generals, smartly overwhelmed. The allied losses that day amounted to some 6,400, mostly taken as prisoners but also several hundred who, along with General Dohna, had drowned in the Scheldt while attempting to escape. Albemarle's twelve field guns fell into French hands, and only about 1,500 men, many having thrown away their weapons to speed themselves on their way, escaped to rejoin Eugene. The casualties suffered by Villars were reportedly fewer than 2,100 killed and wounded, a modest price for such success, and he swiftly moved to clear the line of the river Scarpe, seizing St Amand and then Mortagne a few day after the battle. Eugene, now off-balance, was unable to interfere, and on 31 July the huge allied depot at Marchiennes was overrun and looted by the French, with a remarkable 4,000 unwounded prisoners taken, arguably a more significant loss for Eugene than that at Denain, as his army's whole deployment was now undone. There was nothing for it, and the operations against Landrecies had to be abandoned, the Dutch field-deputies were in a state of alarm at the course of recent events, and the allied army withdrew to take up a hurried defensive position covering Lille.

Predictably, Albemarle was heavily criticized for the defeat at Denain, but he had an impossible task once Villars had so adroitly assessed the exposed and extended posture of Eugene's army, and subtly covered his movements and intentions. The States-General could be bleakly unforgiving of unsuccessful commanders, and Albemarle was in some peril, so that a few months later Eugene had to write to The Hague, sharply defending his subordinate's conduct in forthright terms:

It is with astonishment and grief that I hear of the injustice to which [the Earl] of Albemarle is exposed . . . It would be a dereliction of my duty as an honourable man if I did not speak out on a matter which I have witnessed at first hand . . . He did on this occasion all that a bold, intelligent and watchful general could do.[33]

Albemarle escaped punishment, but it had been a close call, and the ill-founded criticism of his conduct lingered to taint his reputation. Despite this, he remained one of the most adept and aggressive cavalry commanders of his day.

The initiative lay with Villars and he turned his attention to Douai, which was invested on 12 August. Eugene manoeuvred to challenge the French operations, but his allies were reluctant to take any risks, and Villars seemed to understand the difficulty. One promising alternative was to threaten weakly-held Mauberge on the river Sambre, the possession of which would surely draw Villars away from Douai. The field-deputies with the army would not agree, and Eugene had to watch in frustration when Douai fell on 8 September. Morale in the allied camp was fragile, but on 11 September he moved the army close to the Bois de Sars, next to the fateful battlefield of exactly three years previously, hoping to prevent Villars from moving against Le Quesnoy, but the fortress was re-taken by the marshal on 6 October, while Bouchain, the prime example of Marlborough's great skill in conducting siege operations, fell after a rather feeble defence just 15 days later. Eugene did manage to send troops to seize the minor fortress of Knokke, lying between Dunkirk and Dixmuide, but this success was small consolation after so much misfortune.

Eugene was sensitive to criticism of his handling of the army, and wrote to Count Sinzendorff in Vienna that 'The poor success of the campaign should not be blamed on the Denain affair, but to this mood of fear and irresolution which reigns in the [Dutch] Republic and which has spread among the deputies and generals'.[34] Blaming the Dutch for any lack of success had become something of a habit, and while at times the field-deputies could be over-cautious, they often saw good reason to be so. The year had undeniably been a dismal one for those allied commanders that remained active, while the French had recovered a great deal of what they had previously lost. It is only fair to say that in 1712 Eugene laboured under many disadvantages, with the British leaving the field, the Dutch increasingly cautious and German allies reluctant to risk much for what was seemed to be a fading cause, so that he struggled to regain his form. For all that this might be so, the achievement of Marshal Villars in the brilliant campaign he conducted cannot be denied.

The great matters at issue in the war were largely settled in early April 1713, at the conclusion of the range of formal agreements that were collectively known as the Treaty of Utrecht, between France and Spain on the one side, and Great Britain, Holland, Portugal, Savoy and Prussia on the other. Emperor Charles was predictably dissatisfied with the terms agreed, particularly over the position of unrepentant Bavaria and the security of the Rhine frontier, and although initially inclining to agreement, then resolved to fight on. 'The Emperor had made up his mind to continue the war, in order to exact better conditions touching certain points that concerned him in particular.'[35] This was a forlorn enterprise, and Eugene was dismayed: 'There were tears in the eyes of the good prince',[36] as Vienna had not the strength or the finances to do so for any length of time, and Louis XIV was aware of this. Furthermore, the various component parts of the Empire in Germany had grown inclined to go their own way, perhaps unsurprisingly given the long years of expensive and unproductive war in which they had been embroiled. What security their borders had enjoyed had hardly been enhanced despite the cost and effort, and they tended even more than before to pick and choose which instructions and requests from Vienna were to be heeded.

To add spice to what was an already complicated mix, the Empress Elizabeth had to leave Catalonia and go to Vienna, along with her Spanish advisers, most notably the domineering Count Rocca Stella, adding to the influence of that narrowly focussed faction at court. Count Wratislaw, so active in promoting the interests of the Empire, and coincidentally the career of Eugene, had died at his home in Vienna the previous December, and like two sides of the same coin, the count provided a firm political base on which the prince could depend when away on campaign, and he would be missed. Eugene could work with Rocca Stella, but it was clear that the emperor was much under the Spaniard's influence.

On 23 May 1713, Eugene arrived at Mühlberg on the Rhine, to the south-east of Landau, to face Marshal Villars one more. He had been assured by Charles of substantial sums with which to equip, maintain and pay his soldiers, but as usual these promises meant little. The defences known as the Lines of Ettlingen, held by General Vaubonne and covering the Duchy of Baden, were dilapidated, and Eugene had to detach a substantial portion of the 60,000 troops under his command to labour at the necessary repairs. Villars was meanwhile reinforced by troops released from other fronts, and Trier on the Moselle was threatened, while General Benoit d'Asfeld moved to Sellingen not far from Rastadt. On 4 June, Villars joined d'Asfeld, showing every intention to attack the Lines of Ettlingen, and Eugene had to move troops southwards from Phillipsburg to cover those defences. The marshal anticipated this, and doubling back, sent an advance guard under the Comte de Broglie to threaten Phillipsburg, in the process cutting communications between that fortress and the garrison in Landau. A strong detachment of French cavalry was also despatched towards Offenburg, as if clearing the way for an advance through the Black Forest, but Villars instead approached Lauterbourg with the main body of his army. The threat against Landau was always uppermost in Eugene's mind and, as he feared, the fortress was invested and a formal siege begun by 24 June, while Villars with an army some 65,000 strong covered the siege operations from a position on the Rhine from Mannheim to the river Lauter. Marshal Jacques Bezons had command in the trenches before Landau, assisted by Lieutenant General Valory, the army's highly regarded chief of engineers. The garrison commander in Landau, Duke Charles-Alexander of Württemberg, was a capable soldier, and the defences that the 11,000-strong garrison held were amongst the most formidable ever designed by Vauban, so the siege was not going to be a simple affair. Several very useful sorties were made by Württemberg, but Eugene could hardly risk another defeat, which might well rob the Empire of the only remaining army of substance that it had in the field.

The siege operations made steady progress, and on the night of 15 August, French grenadiers waded the lowered levels of water in the defensive ditch to seize the outer work of Malac, thereby breaching the main line of the defences. A sharp counter-attack was made, but after 36 hours of severe hand-to-hand combat, the position remained firmly in Valory's hands. On 18 August, French troops carried

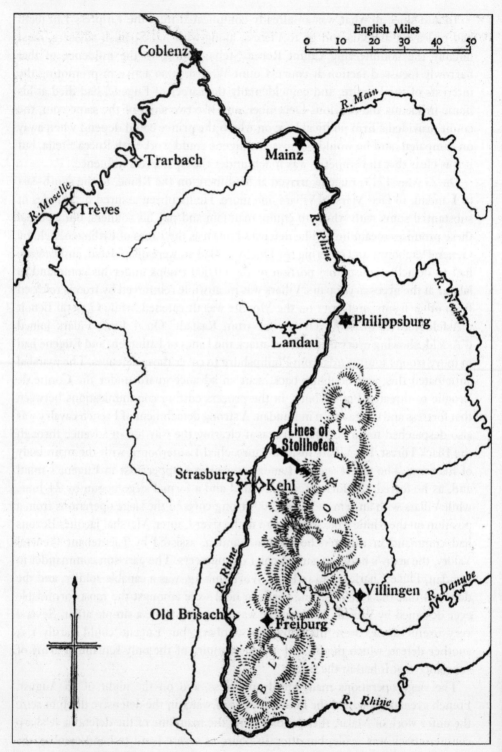

Map 13. France's Defences on the Rhine.

the main bastion and could not be dislodged, even going on to take two adjoining demi-lunes, so that the fortress submitted on 20 August, and the garrison were marched off as prisoners of war, receiving ungenerous terms as Villars had been about to mount an all-out assault. He seemed affronted that Württemberg had maintained such a lengthy defence, and did not even bother to dismount when they met to discuss the terms of the capitulation. The marshal's painfully mangled leg might have played a part in this uncivil attitude, but it was surprising nonetheless, valiant conduct by an opponent usually being properly acknowledged. The siege had certainly been an expensive endeavour, with French casualties listed at 4,804, while the garrison suffered 6,001 killed and wounded, and 5,449 taken as prisoners. All the same, Württemberg had held out for a very useful 56 days, and Villars' treatment of the defeated garrison was not to his credit. Significantly, when Valory was sent to Versailles with forty-two captured infantry colours and three cavalry standards, a sure sign of success, the shrewd old king questioned him closely on the scale of casualties suffered by his army in the siege, and the reasons behind them. Fortresses essentially played an important role in imposing cost and delay on an opponent, and Württemberg's stout defence of Landau had done just that.

While Eugene had been unable to save Landau, he had reinforced the troops holding the Lines of Ettlingen, but had to concentrate on keeping his small army intact and in the field, rather than succumb to the alluring option of dispersing his troops in garrisons which could not support each other. Now, Villars sent cavalry to threaten Mainz, and having drawn his opponent's attention there, swung south and crossed the Rhine on 16 September, to probe once more into Germany. In the process he broke through the Imperial defensive lines and forced Eugene's commander on the spot, Vaubonne, back into Villingen on the upper reaches of the Danube. Vaubonne felt too exposed there, and although not under immediate threat withdrew to entrench a position at Rottweil, much to Eugene's dismay that Villingen had not been held, while he was in the act of hurrying in support.

Villars could now thrust more deeply, and on 20 September his troops invested Freiburg 40 miles south of Strasbourg, where the 13,000-strong Imperial garrison was commanded by the Alsace-born Baron von d'Arsch, a soldier with an enviable reputation as a tough campaigner. Eugene managed to slip reinforcements into the fortress, while d'Arsch strengthened the defensive works on the nearby Roskopff and Hochgraden hills. With his superior numbers Villars was able to again jab at sensitive parts of Eugene's dispositions, and by threatening Karlsruhe and the entrance to the Hornberg valley leading towards Baden, obliged him to disperse his strength rather than in shielding Freiburg. Within ten days the French siege operations began, and the newly-prepared defences on both the Roskopff and Hochgraden features were soon lost. With the way cleared, the first parallel trenches were begun, but a sharp bombardment by the garrison's gunners slowed the work, and only on 2 October could the French siege artillery begin in earnest. Premature attempts to storm the outer defences were repulsed on three successive days in the first week, and in heavy rain on the night of 13 October, the French attempted to storm a lunette covering the main defensive wall, but a swift counter-attack by the Freiburg garrison resulted in a prolonged and costly contest with grenade and bayonet.

Two days later the baron put in a stinging sortie on a grand scale to spoil the siege works, and once again the fighting was fierce and at close quarters, with considerable damage to the trenches and the batteries, and reportedly over 2,000 casualties inflicted on the French. However, the siege went remorselessly on and four days later the heavy guns were in action once more. Breaches in the main walls were made, and on 2 November Villars summoned d'Arsch to submit on good terms. This demand was refused, so Villars was perhaps beginning to take too much for granted. Eugene's commanders might be outnumbered and weary, but they were still dangerous, and the garrison withdrew into the citadel to continue the defence. In frustration, Villars threatened to sack and burn the town if the baron did not submit, a clear indication of an awareness that time was pressing. Having obtained permission from Eugene to do so, d'Arsch capitulated the Freiburg citadel on 16 November and five days' later marched out with the honours of war, colours and arms intact on this occasion, to join Vaubonne at Rottweil. The defence of Freiburg effectively ruined Villars' hopes for a wider campaign that autumn, and had been of immense value, but the Comte de Merode-Westerloo, opinionated as ever and an ardent critic of everyone but himself, felt that Eugene had let the chance for success slip away: 'Had he risked a battle at the opening of the campaign he could under no circumstances have lost so much as he somehow managed to do by the time of its close . . . he should have been able to do something.'[37] This overlooks the lack of numbers to cover too wide a frontage when facing an opponent like Villars, and the dire results that a defeat in the open would have had. As it was, the weather had turned foul with snow flurries in the air, and the opposing armies were more than content to go to their winter quarters.

As an almost frivolous aside, an unhelpful distraction for Eugene at this critical time was a strange plan dreamt up in Vienna and irresponsibly encouraged by the vocal Spanish faction. The remarkable notion was to attack Savoy and oblige Duke Victor-Amadeus, so recently an ally of the emperor, to give up Sicily which he had received as a part of the general settlement at Utrecht. Eugene refused to discuss the release of any troops for this nonsense, and his blunt refusal, had it come from a lesser man, would surely have brought a swift rebuke. It was enough and he could not be browbeaten, so nothing more was heard. In any case, with no navy to speak of, Austria could hardly impose itself upon the island of Sicily without the active support of the Maritime Powers, which would not in any likelihood have been forthcoming.

The campaign that year had again been difficult, and outnumbered by Villars and poorly supported by a distracted Vienna, where the plague raged through the city, Eugene's footwork had not been as swift as before, and his appreciation of fast-unfolding events was sometimes less deft than usual. Still, Villars had expected to achieve a great deal, and been unable to do so while the grindingly expensive sieges of Landau and Freiburg went on. This showed why fortresses, so costly to build and maintain, had a value. In a curious reversal of fortune, the frustrating experience of Eugene and Marlborough in their later campaigns in the French fortress belt was now had by the marshal. Nonetheless, if peace had been necessary for Vienna in the spring, then it was even more so with the onset of winter, so that a wave of realism took hold, and in a move of considerable significance, and an acknowledgement of his abilities, Eugene was authorized to open negotiations with Villars. Louis XIV promptly indicated his consent to the discussions, and on 26 November 1713 they met at the castle of Rastadt, ironically enough home of the late 'Turken Louis', Margrave of Baden. They two men knew each other well, and embraced, having in bright youth fought side by side against the Ottomans, while Villars had often been in Vienna as the representative of the French king. For all the outwardly affectionate rapport between the two warriors, it soon appeared that Eugene was the more astute negotiator, although arguing from a position of comparative weakness, and he wrote: 'Villars is apprehensive, ignorant about previous negotiations, and very anxious for a treaty.'[38]

It was known that the electors of the Empire had been reluctant to participate in the recent campaign, while French military power, on the surface at least, was more formidable, with no longer a need to campaign in Flanders, and lingering matters in Spain were coming to a close. Villars set out the conditions under which Louis XIV would accept a settlement, in particular that the border in the Low Countries and on the Rhine agreed at the Treaty of Ryswick in 1697 would be re-confirmed, with the carrot offered that Vienna's hold on the Southern Netherlands and gains in Italy, including Naples, be duly acknowledged. However, Landau and Kehl were to remain permanently in French hands, and Freiburg given up only on payment to Louis XIV's treasury of the cost of the recent campaign to seize the place. Crucially, the king's allies, the Electors of Bavaria and Cologne, were to be reinstated in all their lands, titles and privileges, and fully compensated for their losses in the war. Explicit in all this, of course, was that Philip V would remain unchallenged on the throne in Madrid.

Eugene played his part well and roundly declared these terms to be unacceptable, and stalked out of the room, but a little later he returned and asked for a written copy of the French proposals, for closer consideration. The necessary formal response was given to Villars on 3 December, that Lombardy, Naples and Sicily, and the Southern Netherlands were to be acknowledged as Austrian possessions, and the fortresses of Kehl, Freiburg and Landau immediately returned by France. Also, the Catalans were to be pardoned and indemnified for their support of Charles as claimant, and in return, the two errant electors would be reinstated to the Imperial Diet and regain possession of their lands, but nothing more, and certainly no compensation paid. The respective positions of the parties were clearly not close, but Villars found that he could not outmatch Eugene in discussion, and was at a loss as to how to proceed. His most recent campaign had been one of success, and he knew the weakness in the Imperial military position, yet Versailles wanted peace and might not even sanction another campaign in 1714. Eugene certainly suspected that this was so, and any appearance of weakness in his negotiating hand was something of an illusion, as long as he held his nerve. The two old campaigners were surely astute enough to understand the fragility of their opponent's position, just as much as they knew their own.

The letters of instruction that Villars received from Versailles were unhelpful, as he was repeatedly reminded of Vienna's plight, a stern line was to be adopted, and if Eugene threatened to abandon the discussions, he should be allowed to do so. Both sides were plainly trying to bluff the other, and Villars wrote back rather despondently that he had failed in the task, and that it was he who should leave Rastadt. Eugene, however, held out an olive branch, explaining that the difficulty lay in the requirement to reinstate and recompense Max-Emmanuel. He was considered by Vienna to be little better than a turncoat, who had set himself up to become emperor at the most opportune moment, and moreover to do so with the assistance of French bayonets. Villars countered by again pointing out the Imperial military weakness, to which Eugene replied tartly that 'Your King is mistaken if he believes that the Empire is defeated by the loss of two cities [Landau and Freiburg],' adding, 'why is it that we cannot find a way to peace?'[39] He said that he would allow Villars time to request fresh instructions, but otherwise he really would have to go and rejoin his army and prepare for the next campaign.

It was almost enough, and Louis XIV agreed to recompense Max-Emmanuel from his own treasury, but otherwise the restitution of the two electors in their land, privileges and titles had to stand. The provisions of the Treaty of Ryswick would be confirmed, except that Landau would continue to be held by France, but the guarantee of an amnesty for those Spaniards who had fought for Archduke Charles was refused, and so the Catalans were to be abandoned. On 29 December, there appeared to be agreement, but the disputation went on, arguing almost for the sake of it, but over all this was the simple fact that both Vienna and Versailles wanted peace, the two old comrades and antagonists at Rastadt just had to arrange it. Villars attempted to break the deadlock by offering to give up Freiburg without any payment of compensation, and things appeared to clear, but on 22 January 1714 French Secretary of State Torcy wrote that any such agreement was only a tentative proposal, and that in effect Villars had overstepped his authority.

A confidential instruction was sent at the same time that he should prepare his now totally unprepared army to attack the Imperial Lines of Ettlingen. Villars was furious at such an absurd instruction, and asked to be recalled to Versailles, but this request was refused. All seemed to be at a standstill: Eugene and Villars wanted to reach an agreement, but ministers in far-away council chambers all thought they knew better. So, they drew up a draft treaty on the basis of what was agreed on, while quietly leaving to one side that which remained in dispute, and

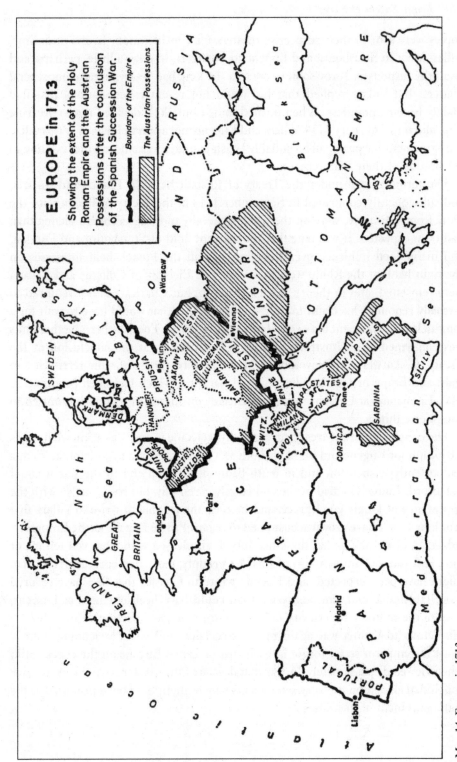

Map 14. Europe in 1713.

copies were sent to their respective masters for consideration. In the meantime, Villars went to Strasbourg and Eugene to Stuttgart, to relax a little, perhaps, and await the responses. Torcy soon wrote that the king had reservations about several matters, but Villars replied that he would not re-enter negotiations that had plainly become pointless. When pushed to it, Louis XIV decided not to overrule him, and on 7 February 1714 Villars and Eugene met again in Rastadt to formalize the agreement for peace, and a suitably lavish banquet was enjoyed that evening in celebration of their achievement.

The terms agreed under the Treaty of Rastadt between France and Austria, and subsequently confirmed in September 1714 at the Treaty of Baden with the Holy Roman Empire, were on the whole generally more agreeable to Vienna than had been expected. It was true that France kept hold of Strasbourg and Landau, and maintained influence over Lorraine, but all the French-held fortresses on the right bank of the Rhine were given up. The Electors of Cologne and Bavaria were reinstated, and in theory at least forgiven, but Charles was not required to formally renounce his claim to the Spanish throne (that would have to wait for a long-delayed agreement between Madrid and Vienna). The Southern Netherlands was confirmed as an Austrian possession (formally so at the conclusion of the Treaty of Antwerp in November 1715), as were the hard-won territories in Italy, and Emperor Charles also received Sardinia, which had been promised to Max-Emmanuel at Utrecht, but that delicate consideration was not permitted to complicate things.

The conclusion of the treaty, on generally welcome terms, was acknowledged as a triumph for Eugene and his skills both as a diplomat and a negotiator, as Vienna had ardently wished for, and in truth badly needed, an end to the war it could not afford. Louis XIV had in the end largely given way, but had done so with the appearance of kingly good grace, and he took the trouble to write to Villars that 'For long now, I have grown accustomed to regard Prince Eugene as the Emperor's subject, and as such he has done his duty. I am pleased with what you tell me of him, and you may inform him of this.'[40] Certainly, more had been achieved than might have been expected, and Eugene wrote to Charles that 'We have secured more favourable and glorious terms than could have been obtained at Utrecht, despite the military superiority of our enemy, and the defection of our allies'.[41] His return to Vienna was again to great acclaim, and when welcoming him at court the emperor so far forgot himself that he kissed Eugene on the cheek. Still, when viewed dispassionately, 'A war that desolated the greater part of Europe, was concluded almost on the very same terms which might have been procured at the commencement of hostilities'.[42]

Chapter 11

Warlord – Peterwardein and Belgrade

The hard-won Treaties of Utrecht, Rastadt and Baden brought about a kind of temporary tranquillity to Western Europe, but nothing stands still for long, particularly when there is so much unfinished business to attend to. The two contenders for the throne of Spain, King Philip V and Emperor Charles VI, remained notionally at war, at least in part because this pretence strengthened Vienna in consolidating gains in Italy. Louis XIV, who had striven for much, gained much, but also lost much, went to his grave in 1715, and left a country to his infant great-grandson weakened by long wars and close to bankruptcy. A period of regency, with the boy's uncle the Duc d'Orleans in effective charge, was required with a degree of internal turmoil in the process. Across the Rhine, the German states of the Holy Roman Empire were increasingly assertive, particularly Prussia, Saxony and Hanover, where the elector had come to the throne in London as King George I. Bavaria, with the now-restored Elector Max-Emmanuel in place, simmered uneasily while its people recovered from the war. The effective role of the Habsburgs as leaders of the Holy Roman Empire had demonstrably become less relevant, to all but themselves, while the acquisition of the Southern Netherlands held distinct but distant possibilities, if it could be wrested from Anglo-Dutch control. Above all else, the gravitational pull of the newly enlarged Austrian Empire in the East, with all its promise, was strong and incapable of being resisted for very long in Vienna.

The seemingly dormant threat from Constantinople did not mean that the Sublime Porte had given up thoughts of recovering some of its previous dominance in south-eastern Europe. That Ottoman structural weakness would not support such ambitions was not yet evident, and at first glance alluring chances for success were plainly there to see. In 1711, when most of Western Europe was engrossed still with settling matters over Spain, Grand Vizier Baltaji Muhammed sharply defeated a Russian army commanded by Tsar Peter on the river Pruth. Three years later the same treatment was meted out to the Venetians in the Morea in Greece, and Siladar Damad Ali Pasha completed that process in 1715. Sultan Ahmed III did attempt to reassure Vienna that no threat to Austrian interests was intended by all this, but in fact he was set on a reconquest of Hungary, and re-establishing sûzerainty over Wallachia and Transylvania when the moment came. Eugene, ever alert to such developments, turned aside from his discussions with Villars in January 1715 to warn the emperor of the likely threat, and at his urging a decision was taken to formally ally with the Venetian Republic and prepare to mount a pre-emptive attack. This was a bold step, as such a move would clearly break the terms of the 1699 Treaty of Carlowitz, on the face of things bad faith to a high degree, but warlike preparations undertaken by the Ottomans had already put everything at some risk. When the Sublime Porte was asked to re-confirm the terms of the treaty, no response was forthcoming, and once danger was seen it was judged better to strike first, and this was certainly Eugene's view. Additional Austrian troops began to move into Hungary in the autumn of 1715, and the following April a defensive alliance with Venice was formally concluded, while a fresh treaty with Great Britain should, it was believed, ensure security for Austria's position in the West while the Ottoman threat was dealt with. The reaction in Constantinople, when this became known, was to conveniently announce that it was forced by such openly aggressive intentions to adopt a war footing. Both Vienna and Constantinople had in effect moved towards outright hostilities, while each tried to blame the other for having to do so, and Grand Vizier Damad Ali Pasha, son-in-law to the sultan, wrote to Eugene in bitter terms, complaining that 'There is no doubt that the blood which is to flow on both sides will fall like a curse upon you'.[1]

Fresh loans were raised in Holland to finance the war, together with grants from the Vatican, and the equipping and provisioning of Eugene's army progressed well with the construction of a small fleet of heavily-armed galleys to challenge Ottoman activities along the course of the middle Danube. Hostilities broke out in earnest on 15 May 1716, with border skirmishes of increasing intensity, but Eugene only left Vienna to join his troops in the field on 2 July, delayed by having to ensure that the arrangements for finance and supply of the army were properly in place.[2] A week later he had a letter from the grand vizier declaring yet again that the war was not necessary, but it was known that a large Ottoman force was gathered in the vicinity of Belgrade, and this could not be ignored or accepted. Matters moved swiftly and the Imperial army, 65,000 strong, consisting of Austrians together with the Hungarian levies, Serbian and Croat militias and a number of German troops, concentrated at Raitzen-Stadt and Futtak just across the Danube from the massive fortress of Peterwardein. With bridges thrown over the river, the fortress and its outlying defences would provide a sally-port once Eugene crossed to confront the Ottomans should they advance. As anticipated, towards the end of July the pasha crossed the river Sava with a force said to number 120,000 troops, although only about half of these were reported to be regulars, well trained and equipped, as opposed to the Tartars and local levies who had, as was customary, been summoned to their support.[3] Damad Ali Pasha moved on to Salankament on 1 August and reached Carlowitz the following day, establishing an entrenched camp, as was the practice of Ottoman commanders as soon as anything more than a brief halt was declared.

Eugene sent Count Johan Pálffy with his cavalry towards Carlowitz to scout the Ottoman dispositions, and despite a warning not to get closely engaged he became involved in a sharp and rapidly escalating little battle. Vigorous charges by the count's troopers held their opponents off for a time, but the Tartar light horsemen swarmed around in rapidly growing numbers and he had two horses shot under him while maintaining good order, and the detachment fell back with their opponents in close pursuit. The main body of the Ottoman army came up soon afterwards, and entrenched themselves again in a fresh position on high ground within sight of Peterwardein. Both the front and the left flank of their deployment was shielded by lightly wooded country and small marshy streams running down to the Danube, while the right flank rested on the steep banks of the river itself. Apparently secure in place, again with a barricade of wagons chained together for defence, the grand vizier had by entrenching made himself secure, but once more given away the initiative in the campaign, always a dangerous thing to do when dealing with Eugene.

Ali Pasha began an artillery bombardment of the outlying Imperial posts, together with a summons to Eugene, in the face of such obviously heavy numbers, to withdraw unhindered and give up Peterwardein on good terms. This was not a trick, or meant to be impertinence, as Ottoman commanders often tried to obtain the negotiated submission of a weaker opponent, with the genuine offer of safe passage rather than staying to fight it out. Eugene ignored the message, having already moved his army across the Danube to re-occupy the old defensive camp just outside the fortress, constructed with much effort by Aeneas Caprara 20 years earlier. A number of his generals, concerned at their exposed position, advised a withdrawal across the Danube to try to manoeuvre more freely, but he was concerned that this would do no other than prolong matters unproductively, and the likely effect upon the troops of any such a move, without offering to fight, would be to lower morale.

The initiative had swung towards him for the moment, and Eugene moved to take advantage of the caution now being shown by the grand vizier. On 4 August 1716, orders were given for a march the following day, with all baggage to be left in camp, and each man carrying in his pouches fifty rounds of ammunition. Such an unusually lavish provision of expensive ammunition indicates very well the appreciation made of the value of effective musketry when dealing with the Ottomans.[4] At first light on 5 August, the Imperial troops, by now nearly 70,000 strong, left their encampment, and deployed outside the defences of Peterwardein in three lines, the first of which was commanded on the right by Count Maximilien von Starhemberg, with General Max Regal to the left. Count Harrach-Rohrau and Prince Charles Bevern led the second line, while Baron Georg von Löffelholz was in command of a brigade of infantry forming the third, reserve, line. Duke Charles-Alexander of Württemberg was placed with an enlarged German brigade as an advance guard covering Regal's main body as it moved forward.

The powerful cuirassier squadrons, under the command of Pálffy, the brigades commanded by Counts Mercy, Matigny and Nádasky and Barons von Falkenstein and Battáe, formed the left wing of the army as it advanced, while a detachment of twelve further squadrons under Baron Ladislaus von Ebérgenyl covered the right flank. This precaution was on the face of things hardly needed, as the movement of the troops was shielded to both right and left by broken ground, together with the loop of the Danube on either side, at least until the advance reached the higher ground nearer to the Pasha's encampment.

All these well-laid plans were upset by a rainstorm which came on soon after the march began. The small muddy streams in the area filled quickly, slowing progress, and the resulting delay enabled the Ottoman troops time to prepare themselves to meet the coming attack. Eugene's foot soldiers had instructions to cover the flintlock mechanisms on their muskets with strips of cloth, to prevent them getting wet and then malfunctioning, but whether their opponents took the same precaution is not known. All the same, the risk being taken by Eugene was breath-taking, as he was advancing to give battle with the wide water obstacle of the sharply bending Danube at his back and on either flank. Just two good bridges gave passage over the river, leading to Raizen Stadt and adjacent marshy meadows, and then just one more bridge led to the road to Futtak. If a serious reverse was suffered his army would in all likelihood be trapped and driven to destruction at the water's edge, cramped and hemmed in by the defensive works of the Peterwardein fortress. Everything depended on retaining the initiative, so that Damad Ali Pasha would be unable to recognize the opportunity presented, and mount an effectively sharp response in time.

At about 7.00am, Eugene directed Württemberg to advance with his brigade and silence the Ottoman battery immediately to his front, and the troops moved smartly forward through the scrub in good order, their rain-sodden uniforms steaming in the growing warmth of the morning. The guns were quickly overrun and their crews bayonetted or put to flight, but a general advance by the first line of the army in the centre was held up while clearing out a number of stubbornly defended outposts in the thickets, and the impetus behind the attack began to flag. The Janissaries in the foremost part of the position were engaged and fought with characteristic courage, so that Eugene and his commanders had anxious moments as the leading infantry, under a shower of musketry, were driven back by vigorously-mounted local counter-attacks. These, however, drew the Janissaries into an exposed position, devoid of cavalry support on either flank. A confident and well-timed attack by Pálffy's heavy cavalry on the left in support of Württemberg's infantry, reinforced now and with grenadiers bombing their way past the right flank of the Ottoman position, caused a sudden faltering in confidence amongst their adversaries. Confusion spread with the hasty giving of orders and counter-orders, and at this crucial point in the morning some of the grand vizier's ill-disciplined light cavalry suddenly took themselves off the field of battle, making for the security of Belgrade as fast as their horses could carry them.

The pasha was an experienced and highly regarded commander, and could see that matters were fast getting got out of control. He had misjudged his opponent from the outset, and he was in danger of being defeated in position, but he might yet be able to regroup and mount an orderly withdrawal with the Janissaries forming a stout rearguard to cover the movement. The guns, encampment and campaign gear would be lost, almost certainly, but he should yet save his army for another day. This was also plain to Eugene, and he brought forward his reserve under Baron Löffelholz to bolster the effort in the centre, while sending word to Württemberg that he should swing to the right and roll up the main body of the Ottoman infantry while it was still held fast in front. This difficult movement, called for at the height of a pitched battle, was carried out with great skill and panache, and the whole structure and cohesion of the Ottoman army suddenly and dramatically collapsed, as a concurrent and unexpected movement by Ebérgenyl's cavalry around the left of their position took effect. Only the sturdy Janissaries scorned the chance to flee with the rest, and so they died where they stood, cut down by the rapidly advancing Imperial troops. 'Our men wanted their blood and massacred them,' one of Eugene's officers remembered with grim satisfaction.[5]

Damad Ali Pasha was amongst the fallen, having watched the catastrophe engulfing his army from his richly decorated tent, and then rushing forward into the fray. A musket ball saved the Sublime Porte the trouble of what to do with him in his disgrace, and he died two days later. By midday on 5 August, the Ottoman batteries, wagon barricade and tented camp were in Eugene's hands, and a stunningly complete victory had been achieved. It was estimated that the casualties amongst the Pasha's army that day were over 6,000 killed, although as always such a neat round figure has to be treated with a measure of caution. The numbers of their wounded and those fortunates who managed to escape the slaughter, was not capable of being estimated in the confusion that engulfed the headlong flight of the survivors, but the Governor of Anatolia and the Aga-Bey of the Janissaries were both killed. Eugene's losses, at over 4,000 killed and wounded, were not light, for the fighting had in places been hand to hand and of the most ferocious nature, and amongst the fallen were a number of his senior officers, including Field Marshal Lieutenant Wallenstein. All the same, that hot afternoon, the Imperial troops, smoke-grimed and blood-spattered as they were, stood victorious stood on the Ottoman position, too weary to mount much of a pursuit, other than for some of Pálffy's cavalry who were sent to keep their defeated opponents on the move.

The haul of booty taken by the victors, 172 field guns, vast quantities of ammunition, tentages, wagons, bridging equipment, food and fodder, and thousands of draught animals and horses, was simply staggering; 300 carts were required to remove the more useful captured stores from the field, and even they were not sufficient, so that much had to be abandoned. Amongst this loot was the huge Ottoman war chest, partly pillaged by the soldiers before it was secured by Eugene's officers, but the remaining contents helped to defray the costs of the campaign. Less happy was the discovery of the mutilated bodies of Count Siegfried Brenner and others who had been captured in the cavalry skirmishes on 2 August, and clearly tortured to death. The knowledge that such practices were not uncommon in the fighting in Eastern Europe at the time must have gone some way to explain the ruthless reluctance of the troops to grant quarter to the defeated Janissaries in the latter stages of the battle.

The Ottoman campaign was in tatters, and their army in disarray, so Captain Zeil, of Eugene's own regiment of dragoons, in a dramatic echo of Colonel Parke's ride to London after Blenheim, was sent spurring to Vienna with the news. As might be expected, Eugene received fulsome congratulations at this remarkable success, having overwhelmed once again an opponent firmly established in a position of defence. Amongst the many letters he received, perhaps the most welcome, was that from his old adversary and friend, Marshal Villars, who wrote with warm congratulations. Emperor Charles of course could not have been more flattering in his own letter of appreciation, but solicitously urged him not to go on exposing himself to the enemy fire on a battlefield. Not so welcome, perhaps, was a violet-coloured biretta, trimmed with ermine, thoughtfully sent by the pope, which apparently made the prince look absurd, so that it was quietly packed away and forgotten.

Although victorious on the day at Peterwardein, Eugene's next options were less clear, and he was reluctant to approach Belgrade, as he had insufficient strength to properly invest the city. The Ottomans kept a substantial garrison there and could be depended upon to mount a stiff resistance to any attempt at a siege. Instead, using many of the horses and draught animals captured in the recent battle, he sent Pálffy with an advance guard north-eastwards against the key town of Temesvár. A letter from him, written in French, and addressed to the Hofkantzler, Philipp Graf von Sinzendorff, explained that 'I am preparing to march on Temesvár, Count Pálffy has already left with a part of the cavalry, I will soon follow'.[6] The place was reached on 25 August, after passing on the way the old battlefield of Zenta, with considerable exertion by the troops, amid difficulties due to the warmth of the season, swarms of gnats and poor roads, a march typically remembered as 'More tiring and arduous than that on the Rhine or in the Netherlands'.[7]

The fortress of Temesvár covered the region to the east of the river Tisza known as the Banat, with well laid out defences strengthened during construction by thousands of Wallachian labourers, who had worked as a punishment for not paying their taxes to local Ottoman beys as promptly as required. Eugene's siege operations began properly with the trenches opened on 1 September, but the 8,000-strong garrison under the command of Muhammed Aga fought with skill and bravery, and the resulting delay caused Eugene concern at the likelihood that a relieving force might come up from Belgrade. On 9 September a vigorous sally was made by the garrison to try and spoil the siege trenches, but it was handsomely beaten back, and the establishing of the breaching batteries could begin. As anticipated, on 22 September cavalry outposts reported that a large Ottoman force was making its cautious way northwards along the line of the river Themes, and a sharp and expensive action was fought at Kissoda by a detachment under Johan Pálffy who was tasked to keep any such relieving force at bay. Meanwhile, the Palanka fortified position, covering a suburb of the town, was carried by Württemberg on 30 September, after stiff fighting with Muhammed Aga's men who held on with remarkable courage. 'They defended this place with great obstinacy; the action lasted four hours, and cost upwards of 400 killed and 1,300 wounded.'[8] All the same, the position of the garrison was desperate, food and ammunition were running low, relief was clearly not at hand, and by 13 October the siege batteries had done enough damage to force a capitulation on terms. Temesvár, which had been held by Constantinople for 164 years, would from then on be a bastion for Vienna's forward stance in the East.

Muhammed Aga had held out long enough to have been seen to discharge his duty as required, and he was entertained at supper by Eugene and his senior officers and complimented on the fine performance of his troops. The Temesvár garrison was permitted to march out on 17 October, and go with their families under escort to Belgrade, Eugene having made sure they had the means to pay for supplies on the way, and the withdrawal was remarked on for the good order in which it was conducted. To his credit, as a condition of his submission Muhammed Aga stipulated that those Hungarian troops serving in his garrison should not face retribution for having remained loyal to the Sublime Porte for so long, and in recognition of the generous terms granted, he presented Eugene with his favourite horse as a gift. One hundred and twenty of the guns left behind in the fortress were found to bear the Habsburg coat of arms, having been taken as the spoils of long-past Ottoman victories, and this fresh defeat was so heavy, and came so soon after the debacle at Peterwardein, that it was not deemed wise to be announced in Constantinople for some time. The administration of the surrounding Banat was entrusted to the veteran Claude Mercy, and he was able to go on and take Pancsova and Ujpalanka, significantly strengthening the Imperial position in this border region, but the Ottoman garrison in Orsova stubbornly refused to submit and had to be left in peace for the time being. Otherwise, a generally enlightened administration was put in place, the experience of rebellion in Hungary perhaps having had a sobering effect on those in Vienna, and this policy was encouraged by Eugene. In the wider strategical sense, possession of the Banat gave Imperial commanders valuable space in which to manoeuvre in future campaigns, when the undredged marshy reaches of the major rivers of the region so often restricted what was possible other than with great effort and frustrating delay.

The year had seen a fresh triumph for Eugene, widely recognized as such, and he returned to Vienna in November, to receive another warm welcome from Charles and his court. The greater goal remained the recapture and retention of Belgrade, 'The White Castle', possession of which would effectively bar the way along the line of the central Danube basin to any future attempt at an Ottoman advance. To forestall such a move, and with the support of those ministers from Great Britain and Holland resident in Constantinople, Sultan Ahmed III proposed that an armistice be declared, with the tempting offer that recent gains made by Vienna be formally acknowledged and left in place. Eugene was unimpressed and advised Charles that this was little more than a ruse, to permit the Ottomans time and leisure to restore their strength before embarking on a fresh campaign to recover what had been lost. He was almost certainly correct, and on this occasion his advice was taken. Preparations had been made for a special levy throughout the Empire to fund the fresh campaign in 1717, and the church was persuaded to contribute substantially, as did the Jewish community, although there was an element of quiet pressure about the half-a-million gulden provided by the latter. On the credit side, after the successes at Peterwardein and Temesvár, Eugene had little difficulty fully recruiting the army and replacing campaign losses, and many volunteers stepped forward to fill any gaps in the ranks. Ten heavily-armed galleys were constructed to enable the investment of Belgrade from the Danube and the neighbouring river Sava, but almost inevitably difficulties persisted with finding the money to regularly pay the troops being gathered, and to provide for their proper sustenance in the field (the crews of the armed galleys protested that they had no money to buy beer, but then they were noted to be prodigious drinkers). Despite such inconveniences, that Eugene could still rely upon the faithfulness of his army and press onwards, says much for the trust in him shown by the troops, many of whom would be wearily familiar with having to campaign in such circumstances.

The new Ottoman commander, Grand Vizier Khálil Pasha, had reportedly not yet gathered an army strong enough to defend Belgrade, and time was therefore pressing upon Eugene to begin his campaign. His departure was made more urgent by the local defeat late in April of an Imperial detachment commanded by Baron von Petrasch while covering a convoy of supplies being sent to the Imperial garrison in Pancsova on the river Themes close to the junction with the Danube. Eugene left Vienna on 14 May 1717 (the day after the emperor's first daughter, Archduchess Maria-Theresa, was born), and one month later he crossed with the advance guard the river Tisza at Tittel, and moved on down the line of the Themes to Pancsova, approaching Ottoman-held territory from a direction downriver from Belgrade. The city was in this way cut off from ready relief by water. Despite the recent misfortune of von Petrasch's defeat, the preparations made by Mercy over the winter months paid handsome dividends in allowing Eugene to move his 62,000-strong army with relative speed and ease, and the crossing of the Danube, which took the army two days, was not contested, although it was necessary to drive off some Ottoman light cavalry who were observing the operation.

By marching in this way to invest Belgrade from the eastwards, Eugene avoided the potential difficulties of having to force a way across the Sava, while the Themes shielded his otherwise exposed flank. During the march, he received a fresh proposal for an armistice from the Sultan, courtesy of the British minister at the Sublime Porte, but he sent this on to Vienna without comment. On 18 June, the Imperial troops were close enough to Belgrade for Eugene to carry out his own close reconnaissance of the defences of the city, finding as anticipated that although they were dauntingly strong, there was no Ottoman covering army near enough to prevent the commencement of a formal siege. In his enthusiasm, he rashly went too far forward, and his escort got involved in a skirmish with a group of Ottoman horsemen, so that he had to draw his sword to defend himself, while an aide warded off a killing stroke aimed at his head, and the return to camp was appropriately hasty.

Orders were immediately given to mark out the lines necessary to cover the siege operations, with the left flank of the army resting on the Sava and the right flank on the Danube. Pontoon bridges were constructed over both rivers, protected by freshly-built redoubts, permitting Eugene ease of communication with the garrison in Peterwardein further up the Danube. Eugene's flotilla of armed galleys had now joined, having run the gauntlet of the Ottoman batteries past Belgrade, and prowled both the Danube and the Sava, on the alert for any attempt to bring reinforcements and supplies for the garrison in the city.

Belgrade sits at the sharp angle formed by the confluence of the two rivers, neatly protected by the fast flowing waters of the Danube to the east and north, and by the Sava to the west. Mustapha Pasha, the Ottoman garrison commander, was a skilful soldier, reportedly with no fewer than 30,000 well-trained troops. He could be counted on to put up a tough fight, and any slip by Eugene would be certain to be punished. The place was a notable trading centre for the whole region, and having once been recovered by the Sublime Porte would not be given up lightly, so that the prospects for ready success must have seemed slim and the preparations for the siege proceeded cautiously, with strong lines of contravallation and circumvallation being laboriously constructed. Mustapha Pasha was active in hampering the works, sending out deadly raids to stab at the gradually lengthening trenches, and making spoiling attacks upon the Imperial galleys that prowled the Danube. A detachment of Imperial troops had been sent to occupy the nearby town of Semlin, linked to the main camp by the pontoon bridge over the Sava and shielded by the redoubt on the Kleine Zigeuner island. A vigorous attempt by the pasha to recover the place was beaten off on 5 July, but only after heavy fighting in which the large armed galleys *St Stephen* and *St Francis* were hotly engaged and badly damaged, so that the hurried support of a third vessel, stirringly and appropriately named the *St Eugene*, was necessary to hold things together.

All had gone fairly well, so far, but on 13 July a powerful storm came up, damaging the long pontoon bridges over the two rivers, supply vessels foundered or drifted out of control, the galleys were further damaged, and many of the tents and stores in the Imperial camp were ruined. 'In less than an hour the damage worked by this tempest was enormous . . . Disorder, the consequence of such destruction, prevailed everywhere.'[9] Mustapha Pasha took advantage of the moment, and sent a force of 10,000 men, a full third of his strength if not more, to mount a vigorous sortie to spoil the still-incomplete siege works. After prolonged and costly fighting, in which the Irish soldier of fortune Captain O'Dwyer particularly distinguished himself, the pasha's troops were forced back into the fortress, but it had been a fine effort and came close to success, so that Eugene did well to retrieve the situation, albeit by a slim margin. The ardour of the soldiers in the Belgrade garrison was perhaps increased by a bounty paid for the decapitated head of any Imperial soldier, which inevitably added a fresh level of ferocity to the fighting, and associated brutality, when this became known to Eugene's soldiers. Two nights later a second attack was made on the camp, and due to contradictory orders issued by Count Antonio Marsigli and Count Rudolf Heister, both of whom were killed in the action, there was confusion, and the situation was only recovered by a timely counter-attack mounted by Hessian cuirassiers, led by Colonel Freiherr von Miglio. Despite this setback, the siege guns were soon hard at work with a heavy bombardment of the Belgrade defences.

A welcome contingent of veteran Bavarian troops joined the army, sent by Elector Max-Emmanuel, who was clearly once more on speaking term at least with the court in Vienna. The young Electoral Prince Charles, and his brother Prince Ferdinand, were in nominal command, and one of their number, Colonel De La Colonie, remembered that:

I went on ahead to report the arrival of our troops to Prince Eugene, and to receive his orders as to our encampment. The Prince received me in the most gracious way possible; he recognised me at once, and the same evening chatted with me regarding the capitulation of Ingolstadt, which I had arranged with him in 1704.[10]

The lines of circumvallation that Eugene constructed to shield the besieging army from interference were so strongly built that they were still in service, unchanged to any great degree, 70 years later. He had, in effect, taken up a position in a massively entrenched camp immediately before the walls of the fortress, when, as expected, a large Ottoman army, said to be well over 100,000 strong and commanded by Grand Vizier Khálil Pasha, approached from the vicinity of Adrianople, after having feinted without success towards Transylvania to try and draw Eugene away from Belgrade. On 30 July the lookouts in the garrison saw the welcome sight of his advance guard on the horizon, signal guns were fired, drums beaten and banners waved, and certain deliverance for the beleaguered fortress seemed to be at hand, together with confusion and probable defeat for their opponents. De La Colonie watched the deployment of this imposing force, and wrote that:

> A great number of their mounted men rode towards our entrenchments, apparently to reconnoitre, and to familiarize themselves gradually with them; they even came within gunshot. They let their horses go at such a speed that we could hardly believe it possible that they could check them, even right up to the brink of our ditches, but so skilful was their horsemanship that they stopped dead there.[11]

The skill of these intrepid Tartar riders, shouting insults and taunting challenges as they came, excited the admiration of the keen observers in Eugene's army, and it was only with difficulty that attempts by young officers to ride out and engage them were stopped in time.

Eugene now faced a serious dilemma, for Khálil Pasha's relieving army was apparently more numerous and able to manoeuvre freely, while his own troops were simultaneously committed to the siege operations, with an active and hostile garrison under the command of a skilful and enterprising commander at their back. Whether he was aware of the legend relating the perils of being caught between Scylla and Charybdis is not certain, but to any veteran campaigner it was surely apparent that without some careful management he and his army faced defeat if not actual disaster. The pressure was eased a little by a successful capture of an island in the Danube which had protected the Ottoman river flotilla, and threatened the bridge over which much of the army's supplies came. By the end of the first week of August, the Ottoman field army had firmly established itself to the south-east of Belgrade, in a well-chosen position on an elevated site, 'a slight eminence'[12] overlooking the Danube, and as usual began to construct strong entrenchments. A sharp crossfire bombardment of the opposing lines was begun, while Eugene's troops began to suffer, as he also did, from the debilitating effects of dysentery from having to drink brackish water, with morale understandably taking something of a blow. Day by day the trickle of casualties and the sick steadily mounted, and Comte Godfrey-Louis d'Estrades, at one time the popular Mayor of Bordeaux, was mortally wounded by a roundshot while accompanying Eugene on a reconnaissance. The Imperial army was reduced now by casualties and sickness to little more than 50,000 effective troops even after recent reinforcement, and to add to this, there was increasing difficulty in gathering fodder and forage in the surrounding countryside, so active were the swarms of Khálil Pasha's irregular cavalry that prowled around.

Delay would only make matters worse, as any hopes that the Ottoman army would itself run short of supplies and be obliged to retire seemed slim, despite it being well in advance of established depots and magazines. The sultan's commanders were not deterred by such trifles: Ottoman administration on campaign was customarily very good, and the able grand vizier was acting with well-judged care. He remained intent on the relief of the garrison in Belgrade, and a promising opportunity appeared to offer to inflict a heavy defeat upon the trapped besieging army, with the consequent chance to then regain much of what Constantinople had lost over the previous 40 years. Eugene's situation appeared perilous. Even though his flanks were secure on the Danube and the Sava and the defensive lines strongly constructed, he could be hemmed in and starved out, or forced into retreat in which event his army would have to thread a perilous way across the pontoon bridge over the Danube in order to gain the open country on the far bank. That his opponent would allow this to happen without interference was most unlikely, and the awful debacle at Zenta 20 years earlier, with an army caught in the act of crossing a wide river, might be repeated, but this time in reverse. A number of observers, among them long-time critics and those envious of the prince, predicted with ill-concealed relish that he faced either a defeat or a humiliating scrambled retreat.

Eugene remained outwardly calm and confident, visiting the men in their entrenchments every day to see the progress of the siege, and displaying remarkable *sang-froid* in the face of such difficulties. He had perhaps never faced a more troubling moment, but judged his opponents well. Mustapha Pasha he knew might attack him from the fortress, but this could only be a spoiling sortie, while the grand vizier, on the other hand, would probably be reluctant to risk all with a major assault on the formidable defensive lines that had been constructed, and prefer to starve his opponent army into submission or attempted flight. There was logic in this, and the Ottomans were not at all averse to making gains without having to fight pitched battles for them. However, such a course was to misjudge the ruthless determination and energy of Eugene, and yet to wait too long would be folly, as the army could only grow weaker as casualties and sickness took a toll. Providentially, on 14 August a mortar bomb fired by one of the siege batteries detonated the main magazine in Belgrade, causing a massive explosion and widespread damage and casualties. This happy stroke acted as a spur for Eugene, and the next day he announced to his generals that they would move out and attack the Ottoman field army in position. Not a voice was raised in opposition. The decision was a bold and desperate one, all could see that, but clearly it was the only way to break out of the bind in which they found themselves. The simple fact was that the Ottoman commanders, able and astute men, still had them in a grip, in time to be slowly strangled, so boldness had the virtue of prudence, even though it was said with more than a degree of truth that 'Eugene's hand was forced'.[13]

The army deployed for the attack late that same evening, and in the early hours before dawn on 16 August, Eugene took his troops, each man fortified with a nip of strong raki or brandy, out through gated openings made in the lines of circumvallation. They approached the sleeping Ottoman camp as stealthily as they could, and De La Colonie recalled with great clarity:

> After passing the gates the infantry were directed to turn and defile up the [defensive] ditch, those on the right of the camp to their left, and those on the left to their right, so that these two columns might meet and form up opposite the centre of the Turks, taking up their fighting order between our ditches and their trenches. It was of vital importance that our infantry should be in position before daybreak.[14]

With a bare minimum of troops, just 10,000 under Count Peter de Viard, including many of those sick and lame, tasked to watch the Belgrade garrison and guard the camp, Eugene was employing every available man in this extraordinarily bold attempt to surprise and overwhelm his opponent. The veteran Charles-Alexander of Württemberg commanded the infantry in the centre of the army together with General Maximilien von Starhemberg and Count Harrach-Rohrau, while the redoubtable Count Johan Pálffy (remarkably just recovered from suffering an apoplectic fit) led the cavalry, with Claude Mercy and Baron Ebergenyl on the right, and Counts Martigny and Montecuccoli on the left. Prince Charles Bevern led the second-line infantry, but with fewer than 38,000 effective troops in hand, Eugene had a reserve only 8,000 strong kept back under Count Frederick von Seckendorff, to either reinforce success or bolster a flagging effort as matters unfolded. Clearly, the margin for error was startlingly slim; such were the odds against Eugene and such the magnitude of the risk, that this was the one and only chance for success and if it miscarried, then surely a catastrophe awaited.

As quietly as could be managed in the darkness, thousands of armed men with all their weapons, harness, horses and gear, together with their light field guns, took up positions allotted to them after Eugene's own careful reconnaissance of the ground to be covered. At first the night was fine and clear, but a mist rose from the nearby rivers just before dawn, and was so dense that no one could see very far to their front. For a while this helped the troops to advance undetected by their opponents, but Pálffy's squadrons on the right moved off their intended line in the murky conditions, and stumbled upon working parties of Ottoman pioneers who were busily constructing some new and previously unseen entrenchments. 'The right wing fell on their march without intending it, into a branch of the trenches [of the enemy], dreadful was the confusion . . . firing began on both sides, without knowing at what.'[15] A brisk unplanned battle broke out, and the alarm was given in the grand vizier's camp that they were under attack. So dense was the mist, however, that despite the coming dawn neither army could really see the other clearly as they began their real work. Nonetheless, Pálffy soon found himself fighting a desperate action against Ottoman cavalry hurrying forward to drive back the advance along the Dedina Berg, a smart response indicating rather well the often little-reported state of readiness in an Ottoman encampment when on campaign. Pálffy soon had matters well in hand, however, and Mercy brought forward his second-line squadrons onto their opponent's flank at the right moment, so that they had to give way. While trying to reform their ranks, the Ottoman horsemen were attacked by the echeloned columns of Imperial infantry under von Starhemberg which had so far advanced without being detected, and whose long lines of levelled bayonets suddenly emerged out of the cloaking mist. Advancing in good order in this way, they stabilized things, but without realizing were also drifting off to the right of their intended deployment. Along the entire line of battle, the action proper now began in earnest across the series of small streams in front of the Ottoman position, with a rapidly growing volume of musketry rippling and flashing through the misty gloom and enveloping smoke.

Khálil Pasha and his commanders had for the moment at least lost the initiative, and such things once gone, are hard to retrieve at the height of a pitched battle. Eugene's troops quickly overran the forward entrenchments as they came on, taking a number of Ottoman guns in small and savage fights with bayonet, musket butt, scimitar and sword freely used. In the mist a strong force of the pasha's Janissary infantry advanced boldly to re-establish their front, and in doing so unexpectedly found themselves on the exposed right flank of the Imperial centre, interposing themselves between von Starhemberg's battalions and those of Harrach-Rohrau who were still forming to his left. Such was the poor visibility, however, that the chance offered was allowed to go by, and with the mist clearing in the increasingly warm early morning sun, the peril suddenly became apparent to Eugene that he was in danger of having his army split into two halves, neither of which would be able to support the other. Fatally, Khálil Pasha hesitated, his feel for the battle unsure, while Eugene rose to the occasion and ordered his second-line infantry, led by Prince Bevern, forward to wheel to their right and take the Ottoman foot soldiers in the flank. This was done with great skill and alacrity, and the immediate danger passed by as their opponents fell back a short way to gather themselves, and Eugene's army was safely re-united. Still, the grand vizier's troops stubbornly stood their ground and the fighting was savagely desperate and at close quarters for some time, and De la Colonie recalled 'It was necessary to maintain a steady unwavering advance upon them, with bayonets fixed, without regarding their terrible cries',[16] as he and his brigade formed a part of Montecuccoli's advance against the Ottoman right on the Baytina Berg, where the battle raged on at close quarters with terrible fury.

Eugene saw that the main Ottoman battery in the centre of their position, shielded by a marshy stream running down to the Sava, had not been overrun during the advance in the mist. These gunners, well trained and resolute and supported still by well-ordered ranks of Janissaries, were working their pieces well and inflicting a lot of damage on the advancing Imperial troops. Gathering a force of ten companies of grenadiers, supported by 2,000 men drawn from von Seckendorff's infantry reserve, Eugene sent them forward in a sharp assault on this key position, which was gallantly carried at the point of the bayonet, despite the heavy casualties suffered as they came on. The cannonade to which the soldiers had been subjected ceased as the guns were overrun, the Ottoman centre was clearly broken open, and Eugene seized the moment and waved his commanders forward in a general assault, even though 'They poured a terrific fire upon us, which killed a number of our people . . . they made use of a most varied sort of weapons, for javelins and arrows accompanied the bullets that fell amongst us, having to fight our way from trench to trench, so great were their numbers'.[17]

The time was not yet 9.00am, but a lack of tactical control had taken a deadly hold on the Ottoman army, so that cohesion progressively collapsed with increasing numbers of the soldiers leaving their entrenchments and making for the rear. Pulling together his troops into what semblance of order he could manage, the grand vizier was astute enough to know the day was lost, and began to withdraw his army from its position, falling back along the line of the Danube leading to Niš. The success of his daring attack was immediately clear to Eugene, and Pálffy's cavalry were once again sent in pursuit, harrying the fleeing soldiers and their camp followers to keep them on the move, so that no attempt to reform could be made. In doing this, Khálil Pasha abandoned his artillery and all campaign stores, camp gear, munitions and supplies, which fell into the eager hands of Eugene and his troops. The aftermath of Zenta and Peterwardein was repeated, and the abandoned encampment allowed to be enthusiastically looted later in the day, although the prince did his best to ensure that a fair division of the spoils was achieved so that all could share in the fruits of the army's astonishing victory. However, it was remembered rather ruefully that 'The loot from the enemy's camp did not amount to much with the exception of the Grand Vizier's tent and those of the Pashas'.[18]

The loss to Eugene's army on that day of victory was not slight, at some 5,000 killed and wounded, Eugene once again amongst their number. The troops led to defeat by Khálil Pasha had suffered an estimated 20,000 casualties, including at least 5,000 prisoners, for the ghastly butchery of Peterwardein was not repeated. As so often, there is a certain suspect neatness about the reported figure that indicates a degree of guesswork, but it is known is that 210 guns, both field and siege pieces, fifty-one standards, and nine horse-tail banners were abandoned. The Sublime Porte never obliged by confirming true losses in battle, but no one doubted the scale of the defeat the grand vizier had suffered. Attacked in position by a smaller force, his fine army had been surprised, outfought, broken and driven off in disarray, and it would take time and effort for it to be re-established as an effective fighting force.

The siege operations against Belgrade were resumed immediately, with no fear now of interference, and Mustapha Pasha, having witnessed the rout of the relieving army, could do little more, although he had adequate supplies in hand. The work of Eugene's siege artillery, bolstered by some of the captured ordnance taken in the battle, began once more battering the increasingly dilapidated defences, so that the very next day Eugene was asked to accept a capitulation. On 18 August 1717, the terms were agreed, the Constant Tor gate handed over as a token of submission, and the garrison were granted good terms. They had endured a close siege, conducted by one of the great field commanders of the age, for over 60 days and this creditable performance was acknowledged. The occupation of the city was completed on 22 August, and together with those citizens who feared to stay, the pasha and his surviving troops were permitted to march out with their weapons and standards, but not the artillery, and leave without molestation. De La Colonie recalled that 'Boats were placed at their disposal, for use in the transport of themselves, their goods, and chattels. These people were much to be pitied.'[19] A far grimmer scene was then enacted, when a number of soldiers who had absconded from Eugene's army were found hiding amongst the Ottoman garrison. By the explicit terms of the capitulation it was stipulated that 'All deserters are to be handed over'.[20] These wretched men were taken out and impaled on stakes in front of the ruined walls for their misdeeds. Such a thing would have been unthinkable in the Low Countries or northern France by now, but campaigning in the East was a much more savage affair, touching everything and everybody.

A vast gun park and store of munitions and warlike materiel was abandoned in Belgrade, along with the Ottoman Danube flotilla which was left intact at its moorings. Much of the city, noted for many years for its urbane and cultured elegance, was now in ruins, so it is only fair to guess that not a great deal was left to loot, as 'There is not a single house left undamaged in the upper or lower town'.[21] Count Hamilton travelled at speed to Vienna with the glad news of outright victories, and the emperor turned aside from the target practice in which he was engaged to graciously receive him. Charles was naturally delighted at the news but concerned that Eugene had once again been wounded, writing that 'If you had not survived, the greatest victory of all time would have been a tragedy and meant an irreplaceable loss'.[22] The success was of course widely applauded, but there was almost immediately renewed concern, and little leisure permitted in which to savour the fresh triumph. Despite the crushing defeat of their field army, a strong Ottoman detachment mounted a smart raid into Transylvania from Moldovia and moved into Upper Hungary, obliging Count Károyli to withdraw behind the river

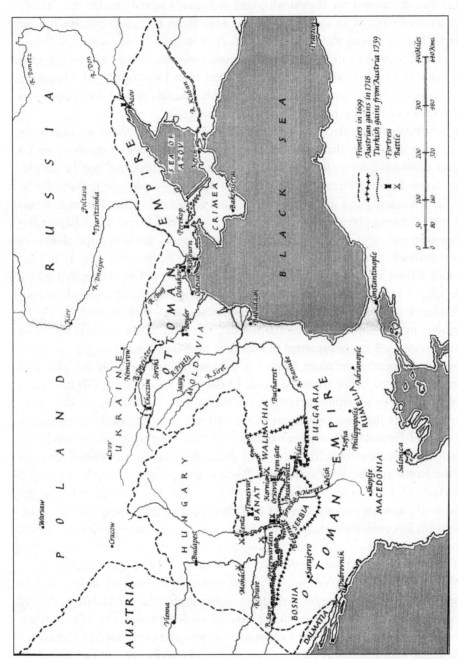

Map 15. The Ottoman Empire, and the Habsburg Empire in the East.

Tisza. This exposed the fortress of Grosswardein while the Tartar cavalry, in their usual way, devastated the region without hindrance. Eugene quickly sent Mercy with a mixed force of cavalry and infantry to the Banat to restore matters, but the raiders, having spread alarm and destruction as in days of old, withdrew before they could be intercepted. To add to Eugene's worries, troops under the joint command of Count Karl Königsegg and Count John Draskowich, who had been sent to occupy Novi, were surprised and roughly handled by local Ottoman levies and forced to withdraw in rather undignified haste.

Khálil Pasha was replaced as grand vizier by Muhammed Pasha, who shrewdly recognized that, while damaging raids and sorties might still be mounted with a degree of success, terms for a formal cessation of hostilities had best be sought. The defeat before Belgrade and the loss of that city could not realistically be overturned at any point in the near future, and time would indeed show that this was a key turning point in the history of south-eastern Europe. On 5 September a message was sent by the grand vizier to Eugene, declaring the desire in Constantinople to bring the war to a conclusion, but he had no authority to treat on such a level and referred the note to Vienna. Emperor Charles replied giving him full powers to negotiate the terms of an armistice, in a clear acknowledgment of Eugene's reputation and standing. The discussions would, unsurprisingly, be complex, for the sultan's representatives had lost none of their subtle skill, and in the meantime Eugene returned to Vienna in mid-October 1717, to be accorded a hero's welcome once more, almost a Triumph, together with the gift of a diamond-studded sword from the hands of the grateful emperor. The renowned capture of Belgrade, stemming from the victory at Peterwardein the previous year, may be seen as the most significant of the prince's successes in the East, just as the relief of Turin 11 years earlier had been the greatest of his achievements in the West. The capture of both Temesvár and Belgrade so firmly established Austrian control in the region that the Sublime Porte was never again, despite occasional successes, likely to pose a lasting threat to that rule. Pre-eminent amongst the great field commanders of Europe at that time, Eugene had, it might be thought, fought his last campaign, arguably his finest, with daring and magnificent victory in open battle.

The sultan insisted on Anglo-Dutch mediation, rather than negotiating a settlement directly with Vienna, an astute move, as it was well understood in Constantinople that the emperor relied upon the support of the Maritime Powers to counter the threat from Spain in the western Mediterranean. The talks to reach a settlement were conducted at Passarowitz, in a region devastated by the recent campaigns, with agreement only reached after weeks of dispute and persuasion on 21 July 1718. The terms were known as the Treaty (or Peace) of Passarowitz, and built on that of Carlowitz, by which Constantinople acknowledged the loss of the Banat, of both Temesvár and Belgrade, Transylvania, and substantial portions of what were Serbia, Slavonia and western Wallachia. The success recorded under the treaty could be counted as Austrian, as Venice had proved of little help in the conflict, and apart from a fairly small number of German and Bavarian troops and fortifying subsidies from the Vatican, the campaign had been waged almost entirely by Eugene and his senior commanders. On the other side of the balance sheet, the sultan regained the Morea region in Greece, while favourable trading terms were agreed for Austrian and Hungarian merchants operating throughout the respective empires, a fact that would paradoxically prove of significant benefit for both Vienna and Constantinople over the coming decades. So much of value had been achieved, but things rarely stand still for long, and a desire for the wide Hungarian plains would take time to fade in the cloisters of the Sublime Porte, so that 'Wars continued to be punctiliously waged even when the Ottoman armies journeyed, not as a glorious caravanserai to lands of booty, but to dismal and near inevitable defeats'.[23] Local opinion was, it might be noted, rather divided on what had been achieved. Leaving religious and cultural issues to one side, the hunger in Vienna for tax revenue was ever formidable, even more so than that of the Sublime Porte, and what blessings were had by these military successes were regarded by some as rather mixed. 'The new Treaty freed Hungary from Ottoman domination, a freedom for which the people owed the Imperial arms a debt; though on the whole, it would appear that Turkish occupation had not been more unbearable than Austrian dominion.'[24]

Chapter 12

The Noble Knight (*Der Erdle Ritter*)

While Eugene was striving in the East, friction between Vienna and Madrid continued, and no formal cessation of hostilities between the contending parties in the struggle for the Spanish throne had been concluded. A major point of contention was that Emperor Charles had not yet renounced his own claim, and would only do so if the Austrian hold on Italy could be strengthened as a *quid pro quo*. The expansionist tendencies of King Philip V, increasingly erratic as he grew older, were spurred on by the dynastic ambitions of his redoubtable Italian-born second wife, Elizabeth Farnese (a niece of the Duke of Parma). The declared cause for newly increased tension was the provocative detention of a senior and elderly Spanish officer when travelling through Milan, and his subsequent death while being held.[1] Sardinia had been granted to Austria by treaty, although the local nobility were in the main inclined to Spain, and when the main ports of the island were blockaded by Spanish ships in the summer of 1717, Eugene argued once again that it was not possible to fight two wars simultaneously with only one viable field army. Not only that, without the assistance of Great Britain and Holland, help that was unlikely to be forthcoming, there was little that Austria could do to recover Sardinia.

The danger of splitting scarce resources while the Ottomans had yet to agree the terms for a formal peace was obvious, but there was always the powerful Spanish-inclined faction at the court in Vienna, 'the Spanish Council', headed by Graf Johan von Althan. Eugene's shrewd and sharp advice on matters did him few favours with them, while any small hopes that the Maritime Powers might intervene and enforce peace in the Mediterranean proved illusory, particularly as the British had no wish to jeopardize hard-won trading concessions for the benefit of Vienna by picking an argument with Madrid. At the end of 1717 the emperor was formally asked by France and Great Britain to renounce his claim to the Spanish throne, in return for which he would receive Sicily while Sardinia was ceded to Savoy. This apparent moving around of diplomatic chess pieces might have been acceptable – Sicily was certainly a prize worth having – but an added condition was that the eldest son of Philip V and Elizabeth Farnese, Don Carlos, should be acknowledged as the heir to Tuscany and Parma in northern Italy. Philip's son by his first marriage, to the late Princess Marie-Louise of Savoy, was already heir to the throne in Spain.[2]

Eugene was strongly opposed to the proposal concerning Tuscany and Parma, as all the hard-won gains his armies had achieved in Italy, and confirmed in 1713 and 1714 at the Treaties of Utrecht and Rastadt, would be thrown into question. It seemed clear that those in Madrid who could not hold Italy by any passage of arms, Philip V and his chief adviser, Cardinal Guilio Alberoni (once a notoriously sycophantic admirer of the Duc de Vendôme), sought to gain it by diplomatic and dynastic sleight of hand instead. The British minister in Vienna, Baron Frederick St Saphorin, recalled that over the 20 years of their acquaintance, he had never seen Eugene in such a rage as now. However, without the naval assistance of Great Britain and to a lesser extent Holland, the Austrian stance was weak in the face of such newly-confident Spanish aggression. Philip V's position was all the stronger as he had the support of the French Regent, the Duc d'Orleans, and none of the major powers would countenance getting involved in the resumption of conflict in the western Mediterranean, so that there was to be no rerun of the ruinous War of the Spanish Succession. In April 1718, still with no resolution with the Sublime Porte confirmed, and aware of the danger of a formal Franco-Spanish alliance moving against the Austrian hold on Italy, it was reluctantly agreed in Vienna that the proposals from Madrid be accepted. Eugene had apparently been persuaded that this was the lesser evil, while it was judged that the more assertive ambitions of Philip V and his wife would be best restrained by the joint efforts of the French and British, neither of whom relished the idea that Spain should too strongly re-establish its presence in the Mediterranean. Meanwhile, Duke Victor-Amadeus in Turin proved awkward and made as much mischief as he could, attempting with some success to lay the blame for the troubles on Eugene, and tried to have him dismissed by Charles.

The emperor was not at all pleased at being expected to renounce his claim to the throne in Madrid, and delayed signing the offered treaty for two months, while his ministers hesitated to press him to do so. Nonetheless, by August 1718 a Treaty of Quadruple Alliance was agreed between Great Britain, France and Austria (Holland was supposed to join, but did not so so), and by the terms set out Sicily was indeed to come to Vienna in exchange for Sardinia being granted to Victor-Amadeus, while the eventual succession of Don Carlos to Tuscany and Parma was formally acknowledged. Eugene was back in Hungary by then, and when Spanish troops suddenly landed in Sicily and threatened Naples, renewed war seemed certain. However, Madrid had over-reached itself and the Royal Navy under Admiral Byng savaged the Spanish fleet at the Battle of Cape Passaro soon afterwards, effectively crippling Philip V's attempt at a swift coup in Sicily. The over-arching ambitions of the Spanish king (and his wife) had obliged both France and Great Britain, under the terms of the Treaty of Quadruple Alliance, to take firm action to restrain him, and French troops commanded by Marshal Berwick, Eugene's old adversary, crossed the Pyrenees into northern Spain in the spring of 1719 to apply pressure on Madrid. Effective action to expel the Spanish from Sicily limped along, and the troops, although now devoid of naval support, held on to the region around Palermo, while difficulties in Vienna with financing an effective campaign in the south came along with a certain depressing inevitability. The financial and administrative burden fell on Naples, but maladministration and corruption were rife, and the Austrian troops, when they were eventually landed in Sicily from British transports, were short of equipment, munitions and materiel, in a sad throwback to the dismal experience when Eugene had fought the French and Spanish in the Po valley many years before. All the same, French pressure in northern Spain and British attacks on Spanish shipping and dockyards obliged Philip V to come to terms and the architect of Madrid's aggressive policies, Cardinal Alberoni, was dismissed in December 1719. Spain reluctantly joined the Treaty of Quadruple Alliance, and peace came ambling back to a war-weary Europe once more. Austria formally received Sicily with Sardinia being ceded to Savoy, as originally intended by the treaty terms agreed between Vienna and Madrid, and ratified in February 1720.

To the casual observer, and on the face of things with the conclusion of the Treaty of Quadruple Alliance, and agreement reached with the Ottomans at Passarowitz, Austria and the House of Habsburg had reached an enlarged territorial extent that to a degree would not be significantly changed for many years. In fact, Sicily and Naples were always exposed and expensive to defend, and Vienna's retention of expensively-bought gains in Italy had only been maintained courtesy of British and French intervention. The Austrian Netherlands were too distant for effective administration and even adequate defence without the help of the Maritime Powers, and the eagerly looked-for tax revenue there proved elusive. Moreover, and long-term, the powerful gravitational pull on Vienna of the newly-enlarged domains in the East led to a lessening of relevance and interest in the affairs of Germany. The overriding difficulty remained, that Imperial finances were inadequate to meet the demands made on them, and while two million gulden could be found to defray the costs of the court in Vienna, the army, with multiple responsibilities stretching from Flanders to Sicily and the Balkans, had to make do with just eight million.[3]

At the court in Vienna Eugene's influence with the emperor was under strain, although their relationship had been close, with Charles writing on one occasion that he should not take so many risks as 'Generals can always be found, but not a Prince Eugene'.[4] Now, recrimination was in the air over the feeble efforts that had been made to restrain Spanish aggression, with Eugene sharply critical of the administration of events in Italy, while himself having to field charges of poor direction and leadership of the admittedly lacklustre conduct of the Imperial commanders over the recovery of Sicily. He was, of course, still President of the Imperial War Council, so it was convenient and not entirely inappropriate to lay some of the blame at his door. A powerful cabal of advisers, led by Althan and his brother-in-law the Imperial Chamberlain, Count von Nimptsch, combined to persuade the emperor of Eugene's complicity in the failure over the whole affair, and it was alleged that too much attention had been given to matters in the East, when greater efforts should have been made in the South and West. This was simple mischief-making, but Eugene's often expressed opinion that two wars could not simultaneously be fought with only one properly-resourced army went largely forgotten by those who conveniently did not wish to remember. Graf Guido von Starhemberg, once a close comrade in arms, was now openly hostile, while Charles had developed a noticeable habit of only welcoming Eugene's company and advice when active hostilities were in the offing, while conversely appearing to resent his influence in times of peace.

The emperor was also increasingly obsessed with the future succession to the Imperial throne, should he have no surviving son. His eldest daughter, Maria-Theresa, could only succeed him by virtue of the complex terms of the Pragmatic Sanction, agreed under the Treaty of Utrecht. The arcane constitution of the Holy Roman Empire did not countenance a female taking the Imperial throne, but this was set to one side. Yet all depended upon the adherence to those same complex terms by the great powers, all of whom had their own different strategic aims, and France already had a simultaneous and contradictory confidential agreement with the Elector of Bavaria over the whole matter. That Austria's neighbours would not comply with the carefully crafted agreement would be seen in time, but any more is outside the immediate scope of this book.[5] Eugene had also taken a benevolent interest in the benefits of the marriages of the late Emperor Joseph's two daughters, Maria-Amalia and Maria-Josepha respectively, to the Elector of Bavaria and the Elector of Saxony, but Charles was sensitive to the potential objection that these two nieces, or more likely their ambitious husbands, might make to the eventual succession of Maria-Theresa. As a result, Eugene was suspected of dabbling in affairs that were not his concern, while the Spanish-inclined ministers at court, together with the now-estranged von Starhemberg, schemed to have him removed and replaced with one of their own less independently-minded nominees. Quietly stirring the unrest was always Duke Victor-Amadeus, who had not forgotten the disappointment over the Viceroyalty of Milan. He also resented the requirement pressed on him to give up Sicily, as the concomitant gain of Sardinia had appeared to be a poor substitute, although one which he was arguably better able to administer and defend. His thoughts also tended to an aspiration to the Imperial throne for his own son, Charles-Emmanuel, but unless an advantageous marriage with one of the emperor's daughters could be brought about, this was an absurdity, but the duke was able to dispense substantial sums of money at the court in Vienna to suborn Eugene and further his own ambitions.

There is a strong sense at this time that many felt Eugene to have become too powerful and wilful in the warm afterglow of his acclaimed triumphs in Hungary, overly influenced by his own close circle, and in need of being reined in. Such feelings, almost amounting to simple jealousy of his achievements, were not in itself unusual (nor just to be seen in Vienna, as both Marlborough in London and Villars at Versailles had found), as power bases established by lesser men with lucrative sinecures to protect, the Schönborn family in particular, were threatened by his influence: 'The interest of the Schönborns transcends all others.'[6] Eugene courted no wide circle of powerful friends, court intrigues held little interest for him, and yet he would have been well advised to play the game rather better as it unfolded. Instead, he contemplated resignation from his official posts, to live in retirement from public life and enjoy his palaces and fine library. However, at the urging of the British minister in Vienna, Baron St Saphorin, he stayed at court and in September 1719 was able to provide the emperor with proof that Count von Nimptsch was clearly in the pay of Victor-Amadeus. The chamberlain, a sharp and vocal opponent of Eugene, was dismissed and sent in disgrace to Graz for two years, while another of the plotters, Abbot Prospero Tedeschi, was flogged in the stocks in Vienna by the public executioner and exiled. The hopes and schemes of Victor-Amadeus fell to pieces as a result, but although Eugene had pulled off something of a coup in getting rid of his most ardent critics at court, the success was dearly bought, as the whole affair had deeply embarrassed Charles, who had stood by his chamberlain and stubbornly vouched for his probity and loyalty for too long. For Eugene to be able to prove him so wrong, was something not easily forgotten by the emperor. The strain in the previously warm relationship between the two men was apparent to all, and Eugene unwisely took few steps to rebuild bridges, so that his standing at court flagged, while the influence of the 'Spanish faction' steadily grew, particularly in dealing with foreign affairs.[7]

The German states of the Holy Roman Empire figuratively flexed their muscles more, and the growing strength and independent attitude of Prussia was particularly notable, with the implication that whatever those in Vienna thought or wished had little relevance to Berlin. Furthermore, Hanover, most recent of the entrants to the Electoral College of the Empire, now had the influence of Great Britain at its call, with King George I secure on the throne in London. Although in the aftermath of the Great Northern War, Austria, Hanover and Saxony combined to persuade Moscow to withdraw its troops from Mecklenburg, a proposed coalition between Austria, Great Britain, Hanover and Prussia to edge the Russians out of the Baltic region came to nothing. Emperor Charles was understandably reluctant to engage in what might well become another war, so soon after the huge effort in Hungary and, to a lesser degree, in the Mediterranean. Relations between London and Vienna cooled as a result, and George I allied himself more closely to Prussia for the time being. Matters were not helped when the emperor refused to formally confirm in the Imperial Diet the gains that had been made at exhausted Sweden's expense in northern Germany by Prussia and Hanover. Eugene was inclined to be more accommodating, but his influence was less of a relevant force, and his advice was ignored. With such discord on the international scene clamouring for resolution, Charles perversely maintained his irrelevant claim to be acknowledged as the legitimate King of Spain, but such a declaration would surely be for form only, as there was no way of enforcing such a whimsical thing. It still stood as a key part of official policy in Vienna, but was entirely futile as London agreed a fresh treaty with Madrid and Paris in 1721, acknowledging and guaranteeing the status quo over the whole matter. Austrian foreign policy was for the time being of some irrelevance, pointlessly focussed on a redundant issue of interest only to the claustrophobic inner councils in Vienna.

One of the ways that Eugene was attacked by his opponents at court was by means of his private life, which in some ways long resembled a closed book. 'He does not get on well with women,' was one sly comment once made of him by the Duchesse d'Orleans,[8] but Eugene was in no sense a 'Mars without Venus', a man indifferent to pleasure, leisure and agreeable female company, and he formed a friendship, perhaps even an intimate understanding, with the notably charming widow, Grafin Eleonore Batthyany, to enjoy many a pleasant evening playing at cards together and it was certainly generally assumed in Vienna that they were lovers. However, it was rumoured that Eugene was too indiscreet in his conversations with the lady concerning matters of both state and the army, and that she was influencing him when making key decisions. How far this was just malicious gossip is hard to judge, but as the widow of a Hungarian officer her loyalty was oddly thought by some to be suspect, and St Saphorin wrote that 'Eugene's credit diminishes from day to day, because the Emperor has been convinced that his views on any subject have been put into his head by the Grafin Batthyany'.[9] Eugene, never that accomplished a player of the games of court intrigue, laid himself open to such insinuations and the blow struck home, but he seemed not to care all that much.

Eugene's appointment as Viceroy of Milan had ceased in June 1716, upon his being made Governor-General of the Austrian Netherlands, but he never went to Brussels during the term of his appointment, his appointed deputy being a Savoyard officer, Ercole-Louis Turmetti, Marquis de Prié. Eugene tried to keep matters in his own hands, despite the ongoing demands of campaigning in Hungary at the time, with the creation of a Council of Flanders, almost a body to rival the Spanish Council in Vienna with whom he was so often at odds. To a degree the governorship was a sinecure, worth 150,000 gulden per annum, and the new council did enable him to establish something of an alternative power base, but perhaps predictably, this again did him few favours at court.[10] He did, however, use a small coterie of gifted secretaries to conduct his day-to-day correspondence, and they proved highly effective, but were much resented by other powerful figures at court who were sidelined in the process. These secretaries were also suspected, by those who were wary of their influence, of being corrupt and venal, but this is also hard to establish with any certainty, and in any case such practices were not at all uncommon.

Apart from Italy, the Southern Netherlands were perhaps the most significant gain for Austria that resulted from the war for the throne in Madrid. Populous and wealthy, the largely Catholic southern provinces of the old Spanish Netherlands provided a significant strategic presence in north-western Europe and, potentially at least, much-needed tax revenues for Vienna. However, these proved to be disappointing, while the towns and provinces each had their own cherished rights and privileges, all jealously guarded against interference from any overbearing central authority. Furthermore, a number of the fortified towns in the region comprised the Barrier held by Dutch troops, in effect a tripwire to guard against and warn of any fresh French offensive. The States-General had achieved, at the Treaties of Utrecht and Antwerp, agreement that the cost of maintaining those garrisons should be partly met by the corporations, guilds and citizens of the region or, as a last resort, by Vienna. The same treaties had accorded favourable trading terms for Great Britain and Holland, hindering economic recovery for the distressed population after the ravages of the recent war. Resentment and evasion were the natural result, so that Austrian rule, or occupation as it seemed to many, was not welcomed, however benevolent it might be intended. So strong was local sentiment that a deputation from the provinces approached Eugene soon after his appointment to protest against what had been imposed, but he brushed them aside, as the terms of the treaties, so difficult to achieve, were not to be tampered with. He would also certainly not countenance anything that might antagonize the Maritime Powers, while the attentions of Vienna at the time were necessarily focussed on affairs in the East.

De Prié proved to be a less than ideal choice for such a sensitive role as Eugene's deputy, and had been chosen largely because the two men knew each other well, but he lacked the diplomatic skill to deal effectively with the principal magnates and nobility of the Southern Netherlands. His health was not good, with a certain natural indolence and acute sensitivity where his own personal standing and honour was concerned, so that he was difficult to deal with. While there was no intention in Vienna to seriously interfere with the long-held privileges of the region, de Prié's performance of his duties put intended goodwill in jeopardy, and Eugene made a mistake in this appointment and then in maintaining him in post for too long. Discontent inevitably led to disorder in the main towns, where tax-gathering was hindered, and once the Ottoman threat elsewhere had diminished Austrian troops had to be sent to maintain order. This was done with some severity, sanctioned by the prince, and including the controversial public execution of one of the principal troublesome guildmasters, Frans Anneesens. The fear was that with if such unrest was not quelled, then occasional whispered calls for the restoration of Spanish rule might grow to a clamour, and incline

France to again get involved. Once calm had returned, however, Eugene advised clemency, and many of the regiments were withdrawn as soon as it was thought prudent to do so, to lessen the associated financial burden on the citizenry who were required to pay for their maintenance. Significantly, Charles asked for the preparation of proper accounts from the regime in Brussels, something of an innovation, but not really meant to impinge too much upon Eugene's prerogatives as governor-general. The inference was clear however, even hinting at an oblique rebuke, that closer attention should be paid to the detail of administration than had been the case up to then. All the same, some thousands of troops had to be kept permanently in the region, to simultaneously keep an eye on the locals, watch the French on the southern border and observe the Dutch in their Barrier fortresses. The outcome of the sorry tale was that what might have been, if properly handled, a prize of great worth to Vienna, proved for too long to be a drain and distracting burden.

The commercial interests of the Southern Netherlands were hampered by a blockade of the river Scheldt by the Maritime Powers, an action permitted under treaty terms, but which effectively disabled Antwerp's recovery as a great trading entrepôt and port. Ostend could operate, of course, but was a poor substitute, although in 1722 Ercole de Prié, at the urging of the emperor, created an 'Ostend Trading Company' intended to trade with the East. The enterprise was a surprising success, with substantial dividends being paid to investors, although Eugene was careful not to be too closely involved. He was sensitive to potential charges of speculation and profiteering from his appointment as an absentee governor-general, although again that kind of thing was not in itself unusual at the time. It was also clear that the activities of the company would be unwelcome in London, where the trade with China in silk, tea, coffee and spices was seen in effect as a monopoly, and while this might not have been reasonable, or guaranteed by treaty, he was always anxious to avoid friction between Vienna and the Maritime Powers if possible. Delicate matters were made worse by the arrival in Brussels of Comte Alexander de Bonneval, another of Eugene's old campaign comrades, gravely wounded in the stomach at Peterwardein, and now intent on quickly making a fortune for himself. He enjoyed a reputation as a good soldier, if a little eccentric, and may have had the tacit support of the emperor in an attempt to get a clearer picture of the state of things in the region. Still, de Bonneval was clearly a schemer and meant trouble, so de Prié had him arrested and deported. Eventually he went to enjoy long and valued service with the Ottomans. At the same time, the Walloon nobleman, the Comte de Merode-Westerloo, made as much mischief as he could in his jealousy of the new administration, where his talents were apparently not appreciated well enough: 'I did write to Vienna more than once, though I knew it would have no effect.'[11]

Whatever credit the Marquis de Prié had enjoyed in Vienna was spent, and Eugene's own standing was weakened by the association, the two men having between them not made a great success of the administration of what was now the Austrian Netherlands. Jean Baptiste Rousseau, the noted French poet and writer, who had become a close and even fawning friend of Eugene while in Vienna, also schemed to have him removed as governor-general, a fact that deeply hurt the prince when he learned of it. At last, he accepted the inevitable and resigned the appointment in November 1724, with Charles promptly appointing him instead to the honorary position of Vicar-General in Italy, a post worth 140,000 gulden per annum, together with possession for life of a hunting estate at Siebenbrunn in Lower Austria. Without his support the ailing de Prié was soon dismissed and summoned to Vienna to give an account of himself, where he died within a year. The emperor's unmarried sister, Arch-Duchess Maria-Elizabeth, was appointed as governor-general in Eugene's place, resuming what had by long tradition been female oversight and rule, in name at least, in the Southern Netherlands, and overall she did the job very well. Stability, if not at first outright economic prosperity, returned, and the French were kept at bay for another 20 years or so, when disputes, once more over succession to a throne – in that case on behalf of Charles's robust daughter Maria-Theresa and her husband – would bring war back to the region. By then, of course, neither Eugene or Charles were any longer on the scene to worry about it.

The coolness in the relationship between Charles and Eugene ambled on, but the Spanish advisers at court were steadily dropping away, stalked by time and ill-health. The emperor's efforts to secure the succession to the Imperial throne for his eldest daughter were increasingly an obsession, and little firm direction was given to ministers and councillors who attempted, with varying degrees of success and ineptitude, to conduct Austrian domestic and foreign policy. There was a sense of drift, and Eugene, while somewhat estranged, was at least a loyal servant and wrote of the numerous councils and committees infesting the court that 'It is my duty to execute the Emperor's orders, even when I do not agree with them . . . If the others acted in the same way, at least something would get done.'[12] Foreign policy was drifting, while the relationship between Vienna and London deteriorated, with both the British and the French actively securing closer links with Spain. In part, at least, this was to foster trade, even though the continued possession of Gibraltar by Great Britain remained a sore issue in Madrid. George I also worked to foster better relations with Prussia, and the steadily strengthening link between London, Hanover and Berlin weakened yet further Vienna's standing in northern Germany.

The claims made by Philip V and Elizabeth Farnese's son, Don Carlos (who would be Carlos III of Spain in time), to succeed to the Duchies of Tuscany and Parma received the support of both Paris and London.[13] The Austrian position in Italy was, in this way, made less sure, but a proposal in the following year that the eventual succession of Maria-Theresa would be supported by Madrid in return for agreement on the future of the Italian duchies, tempted Charles to agree.

It was also suggested that his two daughters should be married to Philip's younger sons, although such a move would have alienated London in its previously expressed support for the Pragmatic Sanction. In April 1725 the 1st Treaty of Vienna was signed between the two old antagonists, Emperor Charles and King Philip, formally confirming the position of Don Carlos in Italy, acknowledgement of the Pragmatic Sanction and the continued preferential trading rights for the thriving Ostend Company. That Charles gave up any lingering hopes of the Spanish throne, already recorded by treaty, was made more explicit in the new agreement. Vienna was also to exert itself to persuade the British to relinquish both Gibraltar and the island of Minorca, although not much was done to achieve anything. The treaty, inevitably, caused offence in both France and Great Britain, as a new strategic balance had been struck in the Mediterranean, potentially threatening the commercial interests of both. A counter-treaty was agreed, the Alliance of Hanover, between the Maritime Powers, France and Prussia, but this had the predictable effect of driving Vienna and Madrid even closer together, although plainly as uncomfortable bedfellows. The danger of renewed war was there, but no-one relished the prospect, despite which the Spanish began a rather half-hearted and remarkably inept blockade of Gibraltar, almost for the sake of form. Commerce was under threat, however, and the subtly skilful and remorselessly patient French First Minister, Cardinal André Hercule Fleury, was active in smoothing things over, and what had promised at one point to become another all-out conflict eventually faded wearily away.

By the mid-1720s, given the prevailing standards of the age, Eugene was an old man, and increasingly suffered from ill-health, particularly a shortness of breath akin to bronchitis. To outward appearances he had also lost much of his earnest appetite for military matters, being absorbed in his massive library, growing zoo of exotic animals and birds of prey, and an impressive art collection. As an enthusiastic patron of artists, poets and writers, he was known as 'A generous protector and supreme lover of the fine arts'.[14] This was a period of building great houses in Vienna, an indication of growing optimism after the defeat of the Ottomans and the resulting enlargement of the Austrian Empire, although the city centre was crowded in by massive defensive walls that would survive until the mid-nineteenth century. 'The streets are very close, and so narrow, one cannot observe the fine fronts of the palaces.'[15] Despite his now cool relationship with Emperor Charles, Eugene had been well rewarded over the years for his indefatigable service, and was a wealthy man, having acquired or had built a number of fine palaces in and around the city, most notably the magnificent Belvedere (the fountains of which were reputed to have cost twenty million florins alone), the Winthof Palace in the Himmelpfortgasse close to the Hofburg, the Schlosshof and the neighbouring Engelhartstetten in the Marchfeld where hunting could be enjoyed, and the Ráckeve estate on the Danube. As it was, the pleasures of the chase never appealed to Eugene very much, as he apparently thought it rather pointless, although he relished his daily morning ride for exercise.

An earnest attempt was made in 1726 to strengthen the Austrian army, both in terms of recruitment, training, and re-equipment, while the engineer arm was improved, as was the development of artillery tactics, with Eugene remaining a firm advocate of the use of light guns close up to the line of battle. Terms of service and prospects for promotion were improved, uncomfortably baggy uniforms made smarter and *esprit de corps* encouraged. Unfortunately, no matter how good the intentions, a standing army of 90,000 troops, hardly sufficient to man the various fortresses in the enlarged Empire let alone put a viable force in the field, cost an estimated eight million gulden each year, and these funds proved hard to get. Despite this difficulty, an additional 35,000 troops were eventually recruited, mostly to serve in Italy and the enlarged Danubian provinces in the east, but equipment shortages were widespread, the cavalry poorly mounted, and, as previously seen, had Vienna to wage more than one full-blooded campaign at a time, it could hardly have done so. This was not a new problem, just that too much had been taken on with the resources available, but this structural weakness in the military sphere was only in part due to Eugene's inability to obtain the necessary funds. The past practice of maintaining a modest standing army and rapidly augmenting this with new recruits at the onset of hostilities may have worked, in a patchwork kind of way, when the remorseless demands of logistics and time and space constraints made any surprise attack unlikely, but as a model it was far from ideal. An added factor in all this was that the emperor's affection and attachment towards Eugene, so strong and vibrant in time of war, cooled with the coming of peace, and the influence he wielded inevitably faded. It must also be said that while so vigorous and vital when out on campaign, when not so engaged he appeared to devote less attention to the ordering and maintenance of the standing army than was desirable and necessary, turning his attention instead to concentrate on the seductive delights of his palaces and collections.

Vienna's tepid alliance with Madrid, intended to counter that between the Maritime Powers and France, was always on uncertain ground, and the self-interest of Philip V and his wife, particularly with regard to the eventual succession in Parma and Tuscany, was clear. The constant tension throughout Western Europe meant, in effect, that Austria had to maintain a stance that it could ill-afford, while it was commented of the emperor at the end of 1728 that he 'Desires nothing more but to enjoy what he already has, and to see his succession assured'.[16] At Versailles, Cardinal Fleury's efforts to wean Spain away from its alliance with Austria paid dividends, while he also used a declared reluctance by King Louis XV to confirm the Pragmatic Sanction as a lever to exert pressure on Charles and his ministers. Eugene remained firmly of the view that Great Britain, rather than France, would be more amenable to agreeing to a closer relationship, but he was not listened to. In the end, a diplomatic mission to Soissons by the

Court Chancellor, Count Philip Sinzendorff, undertaken in an effort to reach an understanding with Fleury, proved a complete failure and this outcome enabled Eugene to regain some of his lost ground in the emperor's regard. He could, with a certain relish, point out that he had always been sceptical of any chance of success in the excursion to Soissons, and Sinzendorff's influence was diminished by what had proved to be a thoroughly embarrassing diplomatic fiasco. Eugene cast about for an alternative strategy to bolster the Austrian strategic position, and it seems that he had the tacit support of the emperor, despite a continued preference at court for a new Spanish treaty.

Gradually, Eugene re-established much of his previous influence at court, assisted certainly by maintaining a covert intelligence-gathering network using the personal contacts he had made during his long years as an active campaigner. His confidential correspondence, mostly conducted by his principal secretary, Ignaz Koch, was prodigious, and valuable highly-placed informants were bought, bribed and blackmailed. The ability to pay for information was a key part of this network, and Eugene was given access to what was in effect a 'secret' fund by the emperor, courtesy of the renowned Vienna banking house of Palm. Just how effective this system was may be seen in the fact that the principal minister in Berlin, Frederick Grumbkow (an old comrade from the days of Blenheim), was in receipt of a confidential annual pension to provide copies of the private letters he wrote to Frederick I, and on that king's behalf to Prussian embassies abroad.

Amongst the fruits of this diplomacy, overt and covert, were alliances formed by Austria between 1726 and 1728 with both Prussia and Russia, and these were particularly gratifying for Charles as the Pragmatic Sanction's provisions for his daughter were confirmed in the process. That this was not quite so in actual practice when put to the test, he could luckily not foresee, but in the meantime the agreement with Berlin undermined the previously-agreed Treaty of Hanover. On the face of things, the potential strategic weakness for Austria in Silesia and Bohemia, regions that Vienna was ill-prepared to defend in earnest, was apparently made more secure by the agreement with Berlin. This was just as well, as the alliance with Spain collapsed late in 1729, with Elizabeth Farnese's antagonism towards the emperor being the prime, but perhaps not the only, cause as Charles' reluctance to countenance a marriage between Archduchess Maria-Theresa and Don Carlos remained a thorny matter. As an almost direct result, a fresh treaty of alliance was signed in Seville between Spain, France and Great Britain that November.[17] Under the agreed terms, Spanish garrisons were to be admitted into Parma and Tuscany, and the successful Ostend Company suppressed, while non-compliance by Vienna would, it was bluntly stated, be taken as a declaration of war. This was a clear challenge, and on 20 December 1729 Eugene denounced the new treaty in a noisy Imperial War Council meeting in Vienna, declaring that Austrian interests in Italy would be fatally undermined, and that the garrisons in the region should immediately be reinforced. Count Sinzendorff advised compromise, but he was out of favour with Charles at the time, who agreed with Eugene on this occasion, and the additional troops were hastily mustered and early in the New Year set on the road to Tuscany and Parma.

Cardinal Fleury was aware that the lasting state of near war-readiness imposed a decided strain on already fragile finances in Vienna, and that had fighting broken out in earnest, Austria would have been incapable of putting up much of a show. He had no wish to see France engage in yet another conflict, largely as it would be to further the interests of Madrid. As it was, ministers in London, made sensitive both by Fleury's subtle manoeuvring and a plainly reinvigorated French influence, sought to improve relations with Emperor Charles. He accepted the realities of the situation, and in March 1731 a 2nd Treaty of Vienna was signed between Austria, Great Britain and Holland, by which the Ostend Company ceased to trade, and Spanish garrisons were at last to be allowed into Tuscany and Parma. The pill was bitter to swallow, but in return, and crucially for the emperor and his obsessive ambitions for his daughter, the British acknowledged and guaranteed the terms of the Pragmatic Sanction. London also undertook to go to Vienna's aid if Austria were attacked. That newly-enthroned George II in London had been affronted by Charles' refusal to acknowledge his rights, as Elector of Hanover, to the Duchies of Cleves and Julich but this was quietly smoothed over, and he did receive Verden and Bremen instead.

Eugene had been active in the negotiations that resulted in the treaty, but there remains a sense that his own initial strong aversion to what was proposed had been one of several reasons for the period of mutual hostility and expensive warlike preparations that resulted. Such a state of confrontation may have suited his interests rather well, the time of tension enabling him to gradually re-establish his influence at court, while others such as Sinzendorff were wrong-footed and lost ground. Charles' understandable reluctance to give up the lucrative activities of the Ostend Company, and his intense desire to get the question of Maria-Theresa's succession settled above almost any other consideration, also played a part. Nonetheless, Eugene's role in crafting the agreement avoiding renewed war in Europe, was acknowledged by Sir Robert Walpole in London. 'I would be guilty of a gross injustice if I had delayed an instant in expressing my gratitude to you on the success of such an important and worthy task.'[18] Much had been achieved, and Austria was on the face of things made more secure, so that when Fleury approached Eugene to sound out the chance of an Austrian-French alliance, he was politely rebuffed, as that would have clearly risked antagonizing London.

In January 1732, the Imperial Diet, that strange collection of worthies who made up the governing council of the Holy Roman Empire, guaranteed the Pragmatic Sanction, so that when Charles died his daughter would take the throne in Vienna. As a female, however, that happy event would depend upon her husband being simultaneously elected as emperor, and she was as yet unmarried.

Eugene had been involved in the negotiations to achieve this remarkable acknowledgment, and the emperor knew it. The electors of both Saxony and Bavaria, however, understandably protested at the declaration, as their own wives, both daughters of the late Joseph I, were excluded in the process, and while this had long been known to be a fact, the protests were made all the same, and rather inevitably ignored. Meanwhile, Charles could look with some satisfaction at what had been achieved, not just the guarantees for the archduchess in the succession, but alliances made both with the Maritime Powers and also Prussia and Russia. Austria, with its greatly expanded territories in south-eastern Europe and bolstered by what appeared to be sound alliances, had it seemed attained a position from which to enjoy renewed influence and strength, and it was said that 'Not since [Emperor] Charles V has a prince of the House of Habsburg enjoyed such an imposing position of power as the present Emperor'.[19]

All that had been gained between the reigns of Leopold I and Joseph I, and since, could it seemed be safely counted as the enlarged Austrian Empire, but 'Never had the Habsburg domains been more extensive or more vulnerable'.[20] Vienna's hold on much of Italy was fragile and that of the Austrian Netherlands always tenuous, depending as both did upon the continued goodwill of the Maritime Powers, so any appearance of great strength was misleading and both Madrid and Versailles waited for the chance to meddle. At heart, always, lay the financial weakness of Vienna, with an inability to raise sufficient tax revenue, something that would undermine all else unless it could be properly addressed. How that could be achieved by a cumbersome but weak central government machinery dealing with vastly differing customs, taxes, dues and duties, and powerful local interests throughout the wide reaches of the enlarged Empire remained an elusive question. There would also remain questions over the security of the Rhine frontier with a reinvigorated France threatening the German principalities, duchies and electorates, all still constituent parts of the Holy Roman Empire.

As before, there was a certain inevitability about things and too many lurking unresolved questions for peace to last for very long. The flashpoint this time proved to be Poland, where King Augustus II died early in February 1733. The Polish Diet promptly moved to elect as their new monarch Stanislaus Leszczynski, who had been the previous incumbent before being deposed, and rather conveniently also just happened to be the father-in-law of Louis XV of France. A diplomatic and strategic coup of enormous significance, largely engineered by Cardinal Fleury, was about to take place, with Poland in the process becoming a pro-French satellite at the heart of Eastern Europe. Vienna's counter to this was to propose that the young son of the late king, Frederick-Augustus of Saxony, be elected as monarch instead, with the price extracted, inevitably, that he should guarantee the terms of the Pragmatic Sanction. The tsar in Moscow also favoured Frederick-Augustus for the throne, and Austrian and Russian troops moved close to the Polish borders early in 1733. Eugene again advised caution, Fleury was playing a long game skilfully and would be likely to use any fresh outbreak of war, or threat of war, over Poland to prey upon exposed parts of the Empire on the Rhine, and Austrian territory in Italy. The most obviously vulnerable of these was the Duchy of Lorraine lying on France's border, and for long rather more under the influence of Paris and Versailles than of Vienna. Eugene, still President of the Imperial War Council, was apparently not too concerned at any likely difficulties in Italy, and permitted the withdrawal of troops from Lombardy, at almost the same moment that the new ruler of Savoy, Duke Charles-Emmanuel II, chose to ally himself to the French, in the hopes of obtaining a slice of neighbouring territory for himself. This unfortunate juxtaposition of events materially weakened Austria's hold on cherished Italian territories at a time of increased uncertainty.

Leszczynski was proclaimed as king by the nobles of the Polish Diet on 11 September 1733, but Russian troops moved in to expel him and install Frederick-Augustus in his place. Leszczynski fled to Danzig, and eventually got safely back to Paris disguised as a peasant, and in the meantime Frederick-Augustus was crowned king at Cracow on 17 January 1734. France promptly declared war on both Austria and Saxony, as allies of a belligerent Russia in the dispute, and French troops moved to occupy Lorraine and the strategic fortress of Kehl on the right bank of the Rhine. At the same time, Savoyard and French troops moved further into the Po valley, where the greatly reduced Austrian garrisons were unable to resist Marshal Villars, and hastily withdrew. French troops occupied Tortona, Novara, Pizzighettone and most significantly, Milan, without much trouble. Eugene's miscalculation over the security of the region, in allowing troops to be withdrawn, was clear to all, an indication of the lessening of his mental powers and acumen. The long-held desire in Madrid to have Austria driven out of Italy, and to regain former territories, moved a step onwards.

Great Britain proved unwilling to assist Austria without Dutch support, despite the explicit terms of the 2nd Treaty of Vienna, and cited Vienna's attitude over the throne in Warsaw as the reason for such non-compliance. The eventual result would be a humiliation for Charles, embroiled in a conflict in which he had little to gain. Eugene wrote with some bitterness, and more than a degree of truth, that 'It was mainly at England's wish that the Emperor undertook to support the candidacy of the Crown Prince of Saxony for the Throne of Poland. Solely out of consideration for England did he agree to allow Spanish troops into Italy.'[21] The French would make no move against the Austrian Netherlands, so the Dutch would not be alarmed, and The Hague had in any case already declared a neutrality over the whole matter. That Eugene's diplomatic efforts in forging robust alliances had come apart was clear, but the conduct of Vienna's erstwhile allies at this time was hardly to be admired. An aggravating factor, however, was the insistence of the emperor on gaining still wider approval for the Pragmatic Sanction, at almost no matter what cost; allied to this was his desire that Maria-Theresa should marry Francis-Stephen, the Duke of Lorraine, who had grown up at the court in Vienna.

Such a match would pose a potential risk to French interests and the security of eastern France, and was accordingly a highly convenient *causus belli* for Cardinal Fleury to flaunt when the moment came.

The poor performance of Austrian commanders in Italy, striving as they were with far too few troops, brought criticism from the emperor, to which Eugene responded rather lamely that the problem arose from 'The natural consequence of a long unbroken peace, during which much disorder and abuse has crept into the regiments, while many officers have also forgotten part of their duties'.[22] The simple fact that, as de facto commander-in chief, he should have allowed such a state of affairs to arise, can hardly have been missed by those inclined to notice. The never-ending shortage of funds and reluctance by a poorly organized central administration to ensure adequate supply could, of course, also be partly blamed. Still, the ailing Eugene, unable any more to provide the same dynamic mainspring in a war effort as he had done during the war for Spain or the conquest of Hungary, must bear much of the responsibility for such unpreparedness, and had he no longer been up to the task, he should have stepped aside or been replaced. 'The greatest military genius in Austrian history proved to be an indifferent Hofkreigsrat President.'[23] Of course, the fact that he was not replaced, or required by the emperor to step aside, indicates that there was no obvious suitable alternative candidate for the job waiting in the wings, and that this lack of a talented alternative would become starkly evident on Eugene's death, makes the point very well.

As so often, miscalculation meant that war had come again to Europe. The Archbishop of Cologne and the Elector of Bavaria declared their neutrality in the renewed conflict, in effect tacitly supporting France against Vienna. The Imperial Diet was persuaded reluctantly to vote a war subsidy of over two million gulden, but little of this was real money, or would actually be provided to finance the troops when on campaign. Suffering increasingly from bronchitis and at the age of 70, Eugene was required to take the field for the last time in the spring of 1734, in highly unpropitious circumstances. However, his arrival with the army was undoubtedly something of a tonic, with one observer remarking rather macabrely, and in an echo of the fabled El Cid of Spanish folklore, that if Eugene died then his stuffed body, securely tied to his horse and with sword strapped to a lifeless hand, would be more than enough to encourage the troops. In April he moved to Ettlingen to gather his forces, but lacking sufficient numbers and short of provisions, there was no choice but to once more to pursue a cautious campaign on the Rhine, observing the French army, reportedly some 100,000 strong and commanded by dangerously capable Marshal James FitzJames, Duke of Berwick.

Difficulties in gathering and supplying such a large force caused Berwick much concern – 'To his great annoyance, he found that nothing was ready'[24] – but the Comte de Bellisle was sent to threaten Trier and Trarbach in the Moselle valley, while the Duc d'Noailles marched against Kaiserslauten on the Rhine.

Berwick, with the remaining 50,000 troops, sought to drive Eugene away from the Lines of Ettlingen, but although having fewer than half that number, he adroitly manoeuvred to take up a fresh position at Waghäusel, from where it was hoped to cover Phillipsburg. Judging that Berwick could just mask his small force and proceed unhindered, Eugene marched to strengthen the garrison, arriving on 4 May. There he learned that the Marquis d'Asfeld had crossed the Rhine and moved with 15,000 troops into the Neckar Valley, threatening his lines of communication and supply, and that even an encirclement of his army was possible. Acting with commendable swiftness, Eugene moved to concentrate his forces in a fresh position at Bruchsal. Despite gathering reinforcements on the way, he arrived there with only some 20,000 troops after leaving a barely adequate garrison in Phillipsburg under the command of the Freiherr Gotfried von Wuttgenau. Berwick was reported to be approaching in greatly superior numbers, while the detachment under d'Asfeld still manoeuvred against Eugene's lines of communication. The position at Bruchsal was clearly untenable, and so, on 9 May 1734 he fell back to Heilbronn, being joined by a small but very welcome reinforcement of Hessian troops under the able command of Prince George of Hesse.

On 11 May Berwick was joined at Bruchsal by d'Asfeld, from where he ruthlessly devastated much of the surrounding countryside to make it impractical for Eugene to re-occupy the region. Although used to the brutality attached to campaigning in south-eastern Europe, he moved to protest to Berwick that there were limits even to the horrors of war, and that the laws of humanity should not be overlooked. To his credit, the marshal stopped his commanders in their campaign of destruction, and on 13 May d'Asfeld was sent to begin the siege of Phillipsburg. In this curious but suddenly hesitant way for such an intrepid campaigner, Berwick took the immediate pressure off Eugene, who had been faced by odds of nearly three to one at the time of his arrival at Heilbronn. He wrote to the emperor on 20 May:

> Despite all my preparations, I do not know how I should have warded off the enemy's attack, if he had done what he ought to have done. As little do I understand why, during the last twelve days, he has remained inactive, contenting himself with ravaging the country. He has given me time to refresh my tired troops, to send away my heavy baggage, to draw troops to myself, so that in a few days I shall have thirty thousand able fighting men.[25]

Eugene had command of an army that, for all its shortages, he felt confident enough to cautiously put into the field. Two days' after penning the letter to Charles, he learned that Berwick had moved to cover the siege of Phillipsburg, and would not try and confront him in the open. The operations against such a strong fortress would certainly be demanding, and Eugene had once more been allowed time and space in which to manoeuvre. Berwick's conduct remains a puzzle, but it is an intriguing and not intentionally ungenerous thought that both army commanders, each so fine and daring in their prime, were now aged and weary men rather past their best when out on campaign with all its attendant rigours.

The French defensive lines of circumvallation and contravallation were in place around Phillipsburg, between the outlying villages of Oberhausen and Waghäusel and the Rhine, by the end of May. The Comte de Bellisle commanded the siege from the left bank of the river, while Berwick covered the operation from Weisloch. On 2 June the French attacked an Imperial bridgehead over the Rhine, and after some ferocious fighting were driven back by von Wuttgenau's troops, but the position could not be held any longer, and he withdrew his men into the fortress. The investment of Phillipsburg was accordingly complete, and the place would fall in time unless Eugene could do something to prevent it. Berwick was aware of the difficulties his engineers faced; the defences were strong and the ground sodden and swampy after heavy rain. He wrote to the young King Louis XV in Versailles that 'We will endeavour to remove the obstacle of the waters, either by making drains to reduce them as we can, or by employing a quantity of fascines for carrying on our trenches'.[26] By a strange stroke of fate, Berwick would not see the conclusion of the siege, and just ten days after the fighting for the bridgehead he was killed outright, decapitated by a chance roundshot while inspecting the siege trenches. He had been warned not to linger at a certain exposed spot but typically ignored the advice, although it was never certain whether the deadly projectile involved was from an Imperial or a French piece. Marshal Villars, still hobbling about with his mangled leg held in an iron brace since his wounding at Malplaquet, remarked when he heard of the instant death of his old comrade-in-arms '*Cet homme a toujour été heureux* [He always had luck that one]'. The Marquis d'Asfeld took up the command of the operations in the fallen marshal's stead, and in his capable hands the siege went on with hardly a missed beat.

Eugene was still at Heilbronn, joined on 5 June by 16,000 Hanoverian and Prussian troops, not all of whom behaved too well on the march to the campaign. This reinforcement was encouraging, and two weeks' later he felt strong enough to cross the Neckar, passing Adelshofen and pressing on to Bruchsal which was reached on 26 June. There he learned from von Wuttgenau that there was little likelihood of maintaining the defence of the fortress much longer, as the French breaching batteries had done their work, and a storm was likely to be attempted if no submission was offered by the garrison. Eugene went to scout the French dispositions for himself, and closed up to their lines on 1 July, cautiously drawing his army alongside the water meadows of the Rhine, with his left flank resting on Neudorf and the right at Waghäusel, and in this way effectively challenging the French to come out and fight. Amongst the troops, waiting with Eugene to see what would happen next, was the young Crown Prince Frederick of Prussia, sent by his less-than-doting father to experience war at first hand. The gouty

Frederick-William's cautionary advice to Eugene was that his wilful son should, 'Not be allowed to get any higher opinion of his own importance than he already has'.[27] The Prussian king's own arrival in the camp, to see for himself what was happening and with a suitably substantial entourage, just added to the difficulties of the supplying the campaign with yet again no commensurate increase in bayonet strength. It was apparent that the French were in a strong position, and Eugene lacked numbers, even with the welcome reinforcements that had recently joined. It had taken considerable diplomatic pressure by Vienna to obtain these troops for service on the Rhine, and they had to be employed with care. The emperor was not helpful, urging Eugene on to great things that were quite evidently not achievable, and although several of his generals, veteran and stalwart Seckendorff amongst them, urged him to risk everything and attack d'Asfeld, an attempt was made instead to divert the Rhine and flood out the French siege works. The hot, dry summer weather did not help, and before this could be done to any real effect, von Wuttgenau submitted on 18 July 1734, rather than face a storm 'sword in hand', with a subsequent sack and pillage of the town.

Eugene had little option but to fall back to Bruchsal on 24 July, from where he sent in a reinforcement to the garrison commander of Mainz. On 8 August he moved the army to the small town of Trebur, with flanks secure on the Rhine and the Main, ready to threaten the flank of the French as they approached Oppenheim. D'Alsfeld, finding himself thwarted by these well-judged manoeuvres, pulled back in the direction of Worms, while Eugene moved to Heidelberg on 19 August, looking for the chance to fall on one or other of the temporarily dispersed French marching columns. Neither commander, it seemed, was able to outwit or outmarch the other, and no further decisive engagement took place before the close of the campaign season with the cold months of October. Eugene had all along been concerned at the possibility that Bavaria might openly declare for the French in the conflict, threatening the rear of his army, and this was particularly likely should he suffer a heavy defeat in open battle. This caution, combined with a pronounced lack of numbers, may be seen in the constrained moves he made while attempting to lift the siege of Phillipsburg, and in the subsequent manoeuvres against d'Asfeld. As it was, although the loss of the fortress was certainly regretted, things could have been far worse given the situation he faced when the campaign opened. The garrison under von Wuttgenau had held out for a very creditable 58 days, and the French campaign, in the process, had been brought to a halt at time of peril for the ill-prepared Imperial forces along the course of the Rhine.

It had been a difficult year for Austria, with a collapse in Italy and the defeat of General Königsegg at Gnastalla, the loss of the Milanese and Tuscany, and both Naples and Sicily occupied by Spanish forces.[28] Eugene returned to Vienna, no longer the thrusting commander of Zenta, Turin and Peterwardein, but an elderly man, sick and in low spirits, and his advice to Emperor Charles was simple, to end the war on the best terms possible. The emperor, however, still hoped for intervention by the Maritime Powers, assistance which most observers could plainly see would not be forthcoming, but the recovery of Naples and Sicily featured heavily in his calculations, and other than at the negotiating table, this could only be accomplished if Great Britain was involved. The way ahead could not be seen with clarity, so that over the winter all the senior ministers in Vienna were required to give their 'reasons in writing' for continuing the war, or not. Many urged peace, as did Eugene once again, but Charles was doggedly determined to wring whatever advantage could be had from a fresh campaign, however unlikely that outcome might seem. So it was that Eugene, still not recovered to health, was sent back to command the Imperial troops at Bruchsal on the Rhine in May 1735, and despite the emperor's exhortations to assume the offensive, a strictly defensive posture was again the only practical course open. This was particularly so as indiscipline in the army amongst both officers and men had been rife in Eugene's absence. Desertions amongst the unpaid troops had increased, Prince George of Hesse had in disgust marched away his contingent of excellent troops, contrary to his instructions, and other veteran commanders such as Duke Charles-Alexander of Württemberg and General Seckendorff were at loggerheads with one another. This must have all seemed to be depressingly familiar, but despite his own growing infirmity, Eugene did what he could to cover the Rhine frontier. Late in August he received a contingent of stalwart Russian troops to augment his strength, but rather inexplicably they were recalled almost immediately, and marched away. Eugene really could undertake little, explaining in a letter to Charles that he could not on any account risk an action 'On which the security of the Monarchy depends'.[29]

In fact, Cardinal Fleury was careful not to press matters too much further, as that might have at last inclined Great Britain and Holland to get involved, and what France, Spain and Savoy had already gained was enough for the time being. The summer passed without decisive movement by either army on the Rhine, although Eugene felt strong enough to send Seckendorff with a corps to watch the river from Mannheim to Coblenz. Peace preliminaries were presented by Fleury in October 1735, and found to be a model of restraint, the cardinal having lost nothing of his subtle touch so that there was little that Vienna could do but to accept what was offered. Now, Naples and Sicily were to be granted to Don Carlos (Spanish troops occupied them already, of course), a portion of the Milanese was ceded to Savoy, and in return Tuscany and Parma were to be returned to Vienna. The key gain from Fleury's viewpoint was that Duke Francis-Stephen was required to give up Lorraine to the deposed Stanislaus Leszczynski, and accept the restored Duchy of Tuscany instead. Leszczynski having failed in his attempt to remain King of Poland, this would have to suffice for him instead, and on his death Lorraine would revert to France. Louis XV, in return, again acknowledged the Pragmatic Sanction, and with it the proposal, long mooted in Vienna, that

Francis-Stephen should marry Archduchess Maria-Theresa. From the point of view of Charles and the House of Habsburg, things might have been worse, and the succession question appeared to be settled, but the disappointment arising from a clear series of defeats in an unfortunate and avoidable war was there all the same, and some of this attached itself to Eugene and his comparative lack of success, although striving always with inadequate means.

Turning points in history are often only apparent after the event, and this proved to be so in the mid-1730s. The loss of Lorraine to French influence and eventual rule was notable and perhaps inevitable, so that Vienna could no longer realistically pose as the Holy Roman Empire's protector of the Rhine frontier against French ambitions. Much of what had been striven for in Italy and gained at great cost had been signed away, while Great Britain and Holland had, despite solemn treaty obligations, kept well out of things. Austria had been shown to be ill-prepared for war and lacking firm allies, and the sombre last act of Eugene's long military career showed this with depressing certainty. For all that, his careful handling of the campaign against Berwick, when the French were in such overwhelming strength, was to his credit, and that Vienna should have done so modestly well under the treaty terms agreed for peace, when seen against its almost complete lack of success on the battlefield, indicated that not all had been in vain. Still, an overly extended Austrian Empire, as it had stood after the victories in Italy and against the Ottomans on the plains of Hungary, had proved to be without solid substance, and it would in future years be prey to the aggressive ambitions of neighbouring states, Prussia, Saxony, Bavaria and Russia, and even Constantinople, with whom it was thought, good relations had been carefully constructed.

'Feeble in mind and body',[30] and finding it difficult to speak without coughing, Eugene slipped from the scene, and was too frail in February 1736 to attend the long-delayed marriage between Archduchess Maria-Theresa and Duke Francis-Stephen. In their union lay the foundations for the attaining of her father's cherished ambition for her succession to the Imperial throne, albeit only after years of war. That all lay far ahead, and mercifully could not be foreseen, so that the wedding was celebrated in appropriate style. On 20 April, Eugene was hail enough to enjoy a small lunch party, and then attend a convivial supper with a few friends and a quiet game of cards at the home of Gräfin Batthyány. He felt unwell as the game proceeded and left early, breathing with difficulty, and was taken back to the Winterhof Palace by an old comrade, Count Sylva Tarouca, the Portuguese ambassador to the Imperial court. After refusing some medication offered by his valet, he was put to bed, saying that the morning would be soon enough for the draught. Prince Eugene died in his sleep that night, apparently quite peacefully, at the grand age for the period of seventy-two years, six months and three days. Happily for an old and weary warlord bearing the scars of many battles, it could be said that 'His life was glorious and his death was easy'.[31]

Emperor Charles was distraught when he was told, and declared perceptively that 'The fortunes of the Empire have perished with Prince Eugene'.[32] State mourning was ordered, and the body in an open casket lay in state in the Winterhof for three days, while all the bells of the city tolled for an hour each day. He was clad in his simple red uniform as a colonel of dragoons, his first official military appointment when, long ago as a young man in a hurry and with a way to make in the world, he had ridden splendidly to war and entered the service of Emperor Leopold. His field marshal's baton lay at his side, along with his sword, and the ermine-trimmed cap sent by the pope after the Peterwardein victory. The guard around the body was provided by officers of the prince's own Kufstein Regiment of Dragoons, as curious Viennese filed past to stare and pay their respects. Eugene's heart was removed, as was the custom, and sent to the family tomb in Turin, while after a magnificent funeral procession held on 26 April 1736, his remains were interred in St Stephen's Cathedral. This was the passing of a great man, all acknowledged this, and the cortège with Eugene's riderless horse with reversed boots in the stirrups took three hours to make its way through the packed streets of Vienna. Emperor Charles and the entire court were in attendance on foot, richly attired in the favoured Spanish style, but officially incognito as protocol required, for Eugene had not been a member of the Imperial family. The simple stone coffin, laid in the crypt of the cathedral and engraved with a bas-relief depicting the capture of Belgrade, was topped by a pyramid bearing the prince's name.

The reigning House of Savoy appeared to have no interest, and so no close family member attended the proceedings, Eugene's eldest and only surviving nephew having died the previous year. He had never bothered to draw up a will, but it was decided that his 52-year-old niece, Victoria, who he had never met, should inherit everything except property in Hungary which reverted to the Crown. She quickly sold off whatever she could, much of the art collection being acquired by the new Duke of Savoy. Eugene's death was widely noted as marking the passing of an era, and Horace Walpole in London reflected a generally held view that 'During the last thirty years of his life, even the reminder of what he had been kept things in some order, as his very yes or no during his sounder age, had kept them in the very best'.[33] He may well be held responsible for rash and expensive failures such as Cassano and Denain, but, for all his imperfections, the Eugene of Zenta, Blenheim, Turin, Peterwardein and Belgrade was undoubtedly the best field commander the Austrian Habsburgs would ever have at their disposal, and his like would not be seen again in Europe.

The acknowledgment that is due, and widely given, to Eugene's extraordinary and successful partnership with Marlborough does not lessen the standing of either man, for the duke himself said that the two would never differ over who deserved the most credit on any one day. Each stands secure in military reputation and renown, and while together victorious at Blenheim, Oudenarde and Lille,

Eugene was not beside Marlborough when he triumphed at Ramillies in 1706, just as in that same gloriously hectic summer he rode alone to save Turin. Yet, over all those great and famous passages of arms, lies the memory of the almost legendary days in the valley of the middle Danube basin and on the plains of Hungary, where astonishing successes over the Ottomans affected the course of European history as few others ever did, deeds that demand the utmost attention and admiration. That Eugene did not, on careful examination, face the overwhelmingly daunting odds that are so often quoted, matters little, for the victories were absolute in fact and in effect, and established the foundations for the military, social and economic shape of a vast area of south-eastern Europe delivered from Ottoman hegemony and overlordship. Furthermore, had he failed, then a reinvigorated Sublime Porte, as was briefly seen in the years immediately following his death, would very likely have sought to wind the clock back to the 1690s and Europe's future would have taken on a very different aspect. That this did not happen was due to Eugene, and his almost unique genius as a commander. Warlord is surely not too strong an accolade to bestow, and as no official representative of his own family, the royal House of Savoy, attended his funeral, Prince Eugene remained in death what he had become in life, an Austrian Hero.

The Holy Roman Empire, the Austrian Empire and the Habsburg Monarchy

The Holy Roman Empire was divided into ten Circles for administrative purposes, and these comprised Bavaria, Austria, Franconia, Swabia, the Upper Rhine, the Lower Rhine, Burgundy, Westphalia, Lower Saxony and Upper Saxony. Within these Circles the individual rulers of the constituent states had almost absolute control over their own affairs, although acknowledging allegiance to the elected emperor (by long custom a Habsburg in Vienna). The scope for friction between the Habsburgs and other increasingly self-confident constituent parts of the Empire was obvious.

> [The Emperor] could neither wage war, make alliances, nor conclude peace on behalf of the Empire without their consent. They were not bound to provide him with an army, nor with any significant amount of money [but] the princes were free to contract alliances as they saw fit, provided that these were not contrary to the interests of the Empire as a whole.[1]

The elective process for the supreme Imperial position was in the hands of the nine most prominent rulers (the electors) in the Empire, at the Imperial Diet or electoral college – the Prince-Archbishops of Cologne, Mainz and Trier, and the King of Bohemia (coincidentally a Habsburg), the Count Palatine, the Duke of Saxony, the Elector of Bavaria and the Margrave of Brandenburg (soon to be known as the King in Prussia). Hanover would eventually be allowed to join the electoral college, on payment to Vienna of a huge subsidy, and so, the elector's cherished role and status could clearly be bought, and perhaps sold.

The eldest son of the emperor was accorded the title the King of the Romans, and his election to the throne by the Imperial Diet once the father died was largely a matter of form, although the various electors would have to be assured of their own privileges along the way. Archduke Joseph enjoyed this automatic process on the death of Emperor Leopold, but in 1711 his younger brother Charles, not having been made King of the Romans, had to wait on the convenience of the other electors. There was no implicit provision for a female candidate to take the Imperial throne, hence the complex provisions of the Pragmatic Sanction enacted by Emperor Charles on behalf of his eldest daughter, so that Maria-Theresa could become empress alongside her husband.

The rapid expansion by Austria into Hungary and along the line of the Danube, accelerating after the victory outside Vienna in 1683, inevitably exercised a powerful gravitational pull upon the attention of the Habsburgs, with the creation of what became a much-enlarged Austrian Empire. Accordingly, the Habsburg ruler in Vienna was simultaneously the elected leader of the largely German-centred Holy Roman Empire, the hereditary ruler of the Austrian Empire, and also of the Habsburg Monarchy courtesy of wearing the crowns of Bohemia and Hungary, although these two honours were always dependent upon the support of the local nobility, whose own long-held rights and jealously guarded privileges had to be confirmed at every step. As Austria had no king or queen, the Habsburgs coined the titles Archduke and Archduchess instead.

Notes

Title Page
1. Shakespeare, W., *Henry IV*, Act I, Part II, Scene 3.

Chapter 1
1. Henderson, p. 7.
2. Henderson has it that Olympia Mancini aspired to the king's hand in marriage, but Fraser is clear that it was Marie. See Fraser, pp. 50–2.
3. The Comte de Soissons was sent to London to conduct the negotiations leading to the marriage of King Charles II's sister, Henrietta-Anne, to Louis XIV's brother, Philippe, Duc d'Orleans.
4. Henderson, p. 7.
5. Malleson, p. 12.
6. Henderson, p. 11.
7. Malleson, p. 13.
8. Henderson, p. 13.

Chapter 2
1. Ingrao, p. 60.
2. Stoye, *The Siege of Vienna*, p. 52.
3. Goodwin, p. 174.
4. Wheatcroft, *The Enemy at the Gate*, p. 65.
5. Goodwin, p. 177.
6. Stoye, *The Siege of Vienna*, p. 52.
7. MacMunn, p. 38. Pikes had fallen out of use in the Austrian army by 1683. See Lloyd, pp. 91–2, also Chandler, *The Art of Warfare in the Age of Marlborough*, p. 80.
8. Horsley, p. 415.
9. Goodwin, p. 173.
10. Ibid., p. 144.
11. Murphey, pp. 48–9.
12. Duriegl, p. 8.

13. Henderson, p. 19.
14. Ingrao, p. 77.
15. Wheatcroft, p. 173.
16. Goodwin, p. 233.
17. Malleson, p. 24.
18. Stoye, *Marsigli's Europe*, p. 45.
19. Henderson, p. 29.
20. Malleson, p. 35.
21. Arneth, Vol. I, p. 452
22. Malleson, p. 44.
23. Ibid., p. 50.

Chapter 3

1. McKay, p. 42.
2. Ibid.
3. After the defeat at Zenta, the splitting of the Ottoman army on two sides of the Tisza was seen as an obvious and appalling error by the sultan. However, that is to be wise after the event, as any crossing of a wide water obstacle had risks, and the Ottoman infantry were strongly entrenched to provide a stout rearguard for the baggage train to get over before following in due course. All should have been well, but for the ruthless driving energy shown by Eugene.
4. Murphey, p. 72. Ottoman commanders would often leave their heavier artillery pieces behind to avoid slowing the movement of the field army, the success of which often depended upon rapid movement. If a major siege had to be undertaken, then the pieces would be called forward at the appropriate time. Whether an enlarged artillery park would have helped save the sultan's army at Zenta can never be known, but in all likelihood the haul of guns taken by Eugene would just have been larger.
5. Henderson, p. 42.
6. McKay, p. 45. Some reports have it that the grand vizier was murdered by his own mutinous troops.
7. Anon., *Feldzuge von Prinz Eugen von Savoyen*, Vol. I, p. 52.
8. Chandler, *The Art of Warfare in the Age of Marlborough*, p. 302, for details. MacMunn, Henderson and McKay all seem to be in error here.
9. Henderson, p. 43.
10. Ibid.
11. McKay, p. 46.
12. Spielman, p. 179.
13. Goffman, p. 231.

14. Ibrahim Pasha, the Ottoman surveyor working with Count Marsigli, was worried that the sultan would think he was giving too much away. Marsigli was sympathetic to the concern and made much fuss about having to relinquish quite indefensible Imperial outposts, to ease the difficulty.

Chapter 4

1. Spielman, Appendix 3.
2. Henderson, p. 54.
3. Symcox, p. 67.
4. McKay, p. 59.
5. Ibid.
6. Langallerie, p. 161.
7. Kamen, p. 60.
8. McKay, p. 60.
9. Malleson, p. 84.
10. Shoberl, p. 65.
11. Wolf, p. 518.
12. Malleson, p. 85.
13. McKay, p. 62.
14. Churchill, Book 1, pp. 471–81.
15. St John, Vol. 1, p. 194.
16. Ibid., p. 195.
17. Malleson, p. 93.
18. Arneth, Vol. I, p. 171,
19. Anon, *Feldzuge des Prinzen Eugen von Savoyen*, Vol. I, p. 113.
20. Malleson, p. 99.
21. Chandler, *The Art of Warfare in the Age of Marlborough*, p. 302.
22. Murray, Vol. I, p. 30.
23. Heller, Vol I., p. 505.
24. Lediard, Vol. I, p. 201.
25. McKay, pp. 67–8.
26. Ibid., p. 89.
27. Ibid., p. 68.
28. Malleson, p. 102.

Chapter 5

1. McKay, p. 68.
2. Arneth, Vol. I, p. 525.
3. Braubach, Vol. I, p. 28.

4. Chandler, *The Art of Warfare in the Age of Marlborough*, p. 80. By the early 1700s most armies in Europe had adopted a platoon firing technique, which was more effective than the previous method of firing by whole ranks at a time.

5. Ingrao, pp. 91 and 110–11.

6. Arneth, Vol. II, p. 222.

7. Palatine – 'an appointed officer having the same authority within a certain district as would be exercised elsewhere by a sovereign lord.' (*Oxford English Dictionary*, 1911, p. 874).

8. Stoye, *Marsigli's Europe*, p. 248. Count Luigi Marsigli, as the second-in-command at the time of the capitulation, was spared but dismissed from the Imperial service.

9. Henderson, p. 74.

10. Arneth, Vol. II, p. 231.

11. The appointment of Marlborough to command the Anglo-Dutch armies when on campaign was controversial, as he was comparatively inexperienced when viewed against other veterans, particularly Dutch, but it proved to be an inspired choice.

Chapter 6

1. Coxe, *Memoirs of John, Duke of Marlborough*, Vol. I, pp. 148–53.

2. Henderson, p. 96.

3. McKay, p. 78.

4. Churchill, Book 1, p. 732.

5. Arneth, Vol. I, p. 242.

6. McKay, p. 80.

7. Churchill, Book 1, p. 775.

8. Henderson, p. 101.

9. Churchill, Book 1, p. 772. Marlborough to the Prince of Hesse, 10 June 1704 'He [Eugene] is going to command on the Rhine where his presence is indeed necessary.'

10. Coxe, *Memoirs of John, Duke of Marlborough*, Vol. I, p. 166.

11. Churchill, Book 1, p. 821.

12. McKay, p. 84.

13. Henderson, p. 104.

14. Churchill, Book 1, p. 829.

15. Henderson, p. 104.

16. Churchill, Book 1, p. 833.

17. Ibid., pp. 837–8.

18. Chandler, *Military Memoirs*, p. 41.

19. Ibid., p. 165.
20. Ibid., p. 166.
21. Verney, p. 133.
22. Murray, Vol. I, p. 401.
23. Trevelyan, *Select Documents for Queen Anne's Reign*, p. 130.
24. Murray, Vol. I, p. 391.
25. Verney, p. 136.
26. Pigaillem, p. 106
27. Chandler, *Military Memoirs*, p. 172.
28. Coxe, *Memoirs of John, Duke of Marlborough*, Vol. I, p. 211.
29. Murray, Vol. I, p. 391.
30. Churchill, Book 1, p. 865.
31. Coxe, *Memoirs of John, Duke of Marlborough*, Vol. I, p. 214.
32. Churchill, Book 1, p. 865.
33. Arneth, Vol. I, p. 274.
34. St John, Vol. I, p. 291.
35. Trevelyan, *Select Documents for Queen Anne's Reign*, p. 166.
36. Malleson, p. 124.

Chapter 7

1. Pierre de Lucas, Comte de la Roche d'Allery, was another hero of the defence of Vienna in 1683. Vendôme's attack on Verrua was stubbornly resisted with heavy casualties on both sides, including six senior French officers.
2. Anon, *Feldzuge des Prinzen Eugen von Savoyen*, Vol. VII, p. 102.
3. Henderson, p. 118.
4. Chandler, *The Art of Warfare in the Age of Marlborough*, p. 303.
5. Henderson, p. 118.
6. Coxe, *Memoirs of John, Duke of Marlborough*, Vol. II, p. 251.
7. Henderson, p. 119.
8. Coxe, *Memoirs of John, Duke of Marlborough*, Vol. I, pp. 356–7.
9. Ibid., p. 364. This thought contrasts nicely with the resentment Vendôme felt at what he regarded as neglect by Louis XIV while rebuilding his armies after Blenheim in 1704. The defeat of Villeroi at Ramillies in the summer of 1706, of course, only made things worse.
10. Ingrao, p. 113.
11. The ruthlessness of the Danish cavalry at Ramillies may have been due, at least in part, to reports of the mistreatment of their countrymen taken prisoner at Calcinato.
12. McKay, p. 99.
13. Paoletti, p. 243.

14. St John, Vol. I, p. 344.
15. Pevitt, p. 72.
16. Churchill, Book 2, p. 174.
17. Malleson, p. 143.
18. Langallerie, p. 315.
19. Paoletti, p. 234.
20. Langallerie, p. 315.
21. Shoberl, p. 99.
22. Pevitt, p. 73.
23. Langallerie, p. 315.
24. Ibid.
25. Chandler, *The Art of Warfare in the Age of Marlborough*, p. 304.
26. Coxe, *Memoirs of John, Duke of Marlborough*, Vol. I, p. 459.
27. Paoletti, p. 261.
28. Murray, Vol. III, pp. 139–40.
29. Ibid., p. 150.
30. Wolf, p. 546.

Chapter 8

1. Churchill, Book 2, p. 220.
2. Ingrao, p. 114, for interesting comments on this controversial treaty, and the degree to which it aided, or hindered, the allied effort overall. Without the withdrawal of French troops from Italy, the assault on Toulon, so enthusiastically pressed by the Maritime Powers, could not have proceeded, which may not after all have entirely been a bad thing.
3. Murray, Vol. III, p. 390.
4. Anon., *Feldzuge, den Prinzen Eugen von Savoyen*, Vol. IX, p. 774.
5. McKay, p. 104.
6. Tindal, p. 450.
7. Visé, p. 8.
8. Churchill, Book 2, p. 251.
9. Paoletti, p. 276.
10. Churchill, Book 2, p. 251.
11. Visé, p. 14. Some accounts do assert that the French strength in Toulon was not that great when the allies arrived, and much might have been achieved by an early assault. See Coxe, *Memoirs of John, Duke of Marlborough*, Vol. II, p. 141: 'The garrison in Toulon scarcely exceeded 8,000 men . . . Such an effort would doubtless have been crowned with success.'
12. Ibid., p. 46.
13. Churchill, p. 253.

14. Visé, p. 42.
15. Coxe, *Memoirs of John, Duke of Marlborough*, Vol. II, p. 147.
16. Visé, p. 54.
17. Langallerie, p. 341.
18. Henderson, p. 145.
19. Ibid., p. 146.
20. Trevelyan, *England under Queen Anne*, Vol. II, p. 308.
21. T'Hopff, p. 340.
22. Churchill, Book 2, p. 274.
23. Henderson, p. 147.
24. Coxe, *Memoirs of John, Duke of Marlborough*, Vol. II, pp. 142–3.
25. Ibid, p. 150. A rather ungenerous comment from Wratislaw, as Victor-Amadeus had always to be aware of the exposed posture of Savoy.

Chapter 9

1. Coxe, *Memoirs of John, Duke of Marlborough*, Vol. II, p. 152.
2. Ibid., p. 207.
3. Churchill, Book 2, p. 331.
4. Ibid., p. 336.
5. Ibid., p. 334.
6. Coxe, *Memoirs of John, Duke of Marlborough*, Vol. II, p. 240.
7. Chandler, *Military Memoirs*, p. 201.
8. St John, Vol. II, p. 27.
9. Churchill, Book 2, p. 349.
10. Ibid., p. 350.
11. Ibid.
12. Henderson, p. 157.
13. Malleson, p. 167.
14. St John, Vol. II, pp. 30–1.
15. Coxe, *Memoirs of John, Duke of Marlborough*, Vol. II, p. 270.
16. McKay, p. 118.
17. Petrie, p. 229.
18. St John, pp. 36–7.
19. Murray, Vol. IV, p. 129.
20. Churchill, Book 2, p. 425.
21. Murray, Vol, IV, p. 126.
22. Ibid., p. 177.
23. Churchill, Book 2, p. 435.
24. McKay, p. 116.
25. Henderson, pp. 165–6.

26. Coxe, *Memoirs of John, Duke of Marlborough*, Vol. II, p. 320.
27. Duffy, *The Fortress in the Age of Vauban and Frederick the Great*, p. 38.
28. McKay, p. 117.
29. Arneth, Vol. II, p. 39.
30. Chandler, D. (ed.), *Journal of John Deane, 1704-1711*, 1984, p. 74.
31. Petrie, p. 232.
32. Lediard, Vol. II, p. 405.
33. Arneth, Vol. II, p. 486.
34. Churchill, Book 2, p. 554.
35. Petrie, p. 237.

Chapter 10

1. McKay, p. 122.
2. Arneth, Vol. II, p. 69.
3. Churchill, Book 2, p. 575.
4. Ibid., p. 576.
5. Murray, Vol. IV, p. 520.
6. Churchill, Book 2, p. 577.
7. Henderson, p. 172.
8. David Chandler, *Marlborough as Military Commander*, p. 251.
9. Ibid., p. 257.
10. Horsley, p. 338.
11. Ibid., p. 339.
12. McKay, p. 125.
13. Chandler, *Journal of John Wilson*, p. 78.
14. Accounts of the casualties suffered at Malplaquet vary considerably, but there is no doubt that those in the allied army were far higher than amongst the French, and arguably negated much of the advantage gained with so much effort by Eugene and Marlborough on the day. In London, the political damage to Marlborough was substantial.
15. Chandler, *Journal of John Wilson*, p. 80.
16. McKay, p. 126.
17. Horsley, pp. 348–9,
18. Coxe, *Memoirs of John, Duke of Marlborough*, Vol. III, p. 51.
19. 'Nothing more is possible/Go no further' – reputedly a remark of Marshal Villars' tailor, when asked to let out his breeches to cater for an expanding waistline.
20. Murray, Vol. V, p. 267.
21. Ibid., p. 266.
22. Goslinga, p. 116.

23. Henderson, p. 189.
24. Ibid., p. 192.
25. Coxe, *Memoirs of John, Duke of Marlborough*, Vol. III, p. 288.
26. Ibid.
27. Trevelyan, *England Under Queen Anne*, Vol III, p. 218.
28. Horsley, p. 357.
29. Churchill, Book 2, p. 955.
30. Horsley, p. 358.
31. Ibid., p. 362.
32. Artistic depictions of Marshal Villars leading his troops to victory across the defences at Denain can only be highly imaginative, as his mangled leg held in an iron brace would not heal and continued to give excruciating pain.
33. Arneth, Vol. II, p. 256.
34. McKay, p. 141.
35. Horsley, p. 378.
36. McKay, p. 144.
37. Chandler, *Military Memoirs*, p. 229.
38. Arneth, Vol. II, p. 511.
39. Sturgill, p. 143.
40. McKay, p. 257.
41. Arneth, Vol. II, p. 342.
42. Coxe, *History of the House of Austria*, Vol. III, p. 96.

Chapter 11

1. Henderson, p. 223.
2. A new financial system put in place by Eugene's opponents at court collapsed under the strain of raising war subsidies, so an alternative, more to his liking, was substituted. See McKay, p. 161.
3. David Chandler gave the Ottoman strength at Peterwardein as 60,000, a far lower figure than most other accounts, but no indication of his sources. See Chandler, *The Art of Warfare in the Age of Marlborough*, p. 305.
4. The lavish provision of ammunition at Peterwardein is in contrast to the sixteen rounds per man issued to the French at Ramillies ten years earlier. See Falkner, *Marlborough's Wars*, pp. 96–7.
5. McKay, p. 162.
6. OstA-Kriegsarkiv, *Deutsche Geschichte in Dokumentes, Prinz Eugen* (nd).
7. McKay, p. 162.
8. Shoberl, p. 291.
9. Malleson, p. 229.
10. Horsley, p. 404.

11. Ibid., p. 419. Reports on the strength of Khálil Pasha's army vary widely, with both Malleson and McKay silent on the subject. Henderson (p. 227) says 'certainly numbering over 200,000', but this is suspect, as there was no way, even with the excellent Ottoman administration on campaign, that such a host could be maintained in the field in such a war-ravaged region. What is not in question, however, was that the Ottoman army outnumbered that of Eugene before the walls of Belgrade, but the disparity is arguably nowhere near what is often claimed. See Murphey, *Ottoman Warfare* for interesting comments on this.
12. Horsley, p. 420.
13. McKay, p. 165.
14. Horsley, p. 429.
15. Shoberl, p. 186.
16. Horsley, p. 441.
17. Ibid., p. 446.
18. Ibid., p. 456.
19. Ibid., p. 458.
20. Chandler, *The Art of Warfare in the Age of Marlborough*, p. 219.
21. Braubach, Vol. III, p. 460.
22. Henderson, p. 230.
23. Goodwin, p. 239.
24. Malleson, p. 250.

Chapter 12

1. Kamen, p. 119.
2. The Farnese family line in Parma, and that of the Medicis in Tuscany, were both about to fail.
3. Cassels, p. 26.
4. McKay, p. 174.
5. Falkner, *Fontenoy, 1745*, for more details on the complex dynastic, political and military manoeuvring that led to the war for the Imperial throne.
6. Henderson, p. 234.
7. Spanish customs, dress and ceremony were increasingly favoured at Charles's court in Vienna.
8. Henderson, p. 238.
9. Arneth, Vol. III, p. 516.
10. The Southern, or Austrian, Netherlands were incapable of being defended, other than with the aid of the Maritime Powers. An expensive distraction, when attention in Vienna was focussed both on the affairs in south-eastern Europe, in Italy, and later by the difficulties of the succession of Archduchess Maria-Theresa as Empress.

11. Chandler, *Military Memoirs*, p. 232.
12. McKay, p. 209.
13. Kamen, p. 133.
14. Henderson, p. 225.
15. Ibid., p. 251.
16. McKay, p. 217.
17. By the 1729 Treaty of Seville, the terms of the Treaty of Utrecht were confirmed.
18. Arneth, Vol. III, p. 574.
19. McKay, p. 223.
20. Duffy, *Wild Goose and Eagle*, p. 28.
21. Henderson, p. 277.
22. McKay, p. 233.
23. Ingrao, p. 131.
24. Petrie, p. 333.
25. Malleson, p. 251.
26. Petrie, p. 334.
27. Henderson, p. 283.
28. The valiant Claude Mercy, although blind and deaf, led his troops in this dismal final campaign in Italy, and was felled by a musket ball while in the saddle.
29. Arneth, Vol. III, p. 464.
30. McKay, p. 241.
31. Ibid., p. 242.
32. Malleson, p. 258.
33. Coxe, *History of the House of Austria*, Vol. II, p. 193.

Appendix
1. Cassels, p. 23.

Bibliography

Anon., *ÖstA-Kriegsarchiv – Feldzuge des Prinzen Eugen von Savoyen*, 1876–81 (20 vols and atlas).

_____, *ÖstA-Kriegsarchiv – Deutsche Geschichte in Dokumentes; Prinz Eugen von Savoyen*, n.d.

_____, *The Life and Military Actions of Prince Eugene of Savoy*, 1736.

Armstrong, E., *Elizabeth Farneze, the Spanish Termagant*, 1892.

Arneth, A., *Prinz Eugen von Savoyen*, 1858 (3 vols).

Banks, J., *The History of Prince Eugene of Savoy*, 1741.

Benedikt, H., *Kaiseradler über dem Apennin. Die Österreicher in Italien 1700 bis 1865*, 1964.

Braubach, M., *Prinz Eugen von Savoyen*, 1965 (5 vols).

Brunner, O., *Österreich und die Walachie während des Turkenkrieg vor 1683-1699*, 1930.

Burrell, S (ed.), *Amiable Renegade, Memoirs of Captain Peter Drake*, 1960.

Busbecq, O., *Turkish Letters* (tr. E. Forster), 1927.

Carutti, D., *Vittorio Armadeo II*, 1856.

Cassels, L., *The Struggle for the Ottoman Empire, 1717-1740*, 1966.

Chandler, D., *The Art of Warfare in the Age of Marlborough*, 1976.

_____ (ed.), *Military Memoirs, Captain Robert Parker and the Comte de Merode-Westerloo*, 1968.

_____(ed.), *The Journal of John Wilson, 1694-1727*, 2005.

Churchill, W., *Marlborough, His Life and Times*, 1947 (4 vols in two-book reprint edition).

Coxe, W., *Memoirs of John, Duke of Marlborough*, 1843 (3 vols).

_____, *History of the House of Austria*, 1847 (6 vols).

Duffy, C., *The Fortress in the Age of Vauban and Frederick the Great*, 1985.

_____, *The Wild Goose and the Eagle*, 2019 (revised).

Düriègl, G., *Vienna 1683*, 2003.

Falkner, J., *Great and Glorious Days, Marlborough's Battles*, 2002.

_____, *Arnold Joost van Keppel, 1st Earl Albemarle* (Oxford Dictionary of National Biography), 2004.

_____, *Marlborough's Wars, Eye-Witness Accounts*, 2005.

_____, *The War of the Spanish Succession, 1701-1714*, 2015.

_____, *Fontenoy, 1745*, 2019.

Fraser, A., *Love and Louis XIV*, 2006.

Goffman, D., *The Ottoman Empire and Early Modern Europe*, 2002.

Goodwin, J., *Lords of the Horizons*, 1998.

Goslinga, S. van., *Mémoirs, Relatifs a la Guerre de Succesion, 1706-1709, et 1711*, 1857.

Greiner, C., *Der Turkenlouis – Markgraf Ludwig von Baden-Baden, 1655-1707*, 1989.

Harris, S., *Sir Cloudesly Shovell, Stuart Admiral*, 2001.

Hegyi, K., *The Ottoman Empire in Europe*, 1989.

Heller, F. (ed.), *Militarische Correspondenz*, 1848 (2 vols).

Henderson, N., *Prince Eugen of Savoy*, 1964.

Horn, E., *François Rákóczi II*, 1906.

Horsley, W. (tr and ed.), *The Chronicles of an Old Campaigner, 1692-1717*, 1904.

Hüttle, L., *Max Emmanuel, Der Blaue Kurfust*, 1976.

Ingrao, C., *The Habsburg Monarchy, 1617-1815*, 2000 (2nd edition).

Kamen, H., *Philip V of Spain, the King who Ruled Twice*, 2001.

Kreutel, R. (ed.), *Kara Mustafa vor Wien*, 1955.

_____, *Im Reiche des goldenen Apfels*, 1957.

Langallerie, M., *Memoirs of the Marquis de Langallerie*, 1710.

Lediard, T., *Memoirs of the Duke of Marlborough*, 1736 (3 vols).

Lloyd, E., *Vauban, Montclamert, Carnot, Engineer Studies*, 1987.

MacMunn, G., *Prince Eugene, Twin Marshal with Marlborough*, 1934.

Malleson, G., *Prince Eugene of Savoy*, 1887.

McKay, D., *Prince Eugene of Savoy*, 1977.

McNeill, W., *Europe's Steppe Frontier, 1500-1800*, 1964.

Murphey, R., *Ottoman Warfare, 1500-1700*, 1999.

Murray, G (ed.), *Letters and Despatches of the Duke of Marlborough*, 1845 (5 vols)

Nicolle, D., *The Armies of the Ottoman Turks*, 1983.

Nouzille, J., *La Campagne decisive du Prince Eugene en Hongrie (1697)*, 2020.

Odenthal, J., *Österreichische Türkenkrieg, 1700-1718*, 1938.

Paoletti, C., *Italy, Piedmont and the War of the Spanish Succession, 1701-1712*, 2021.

Parvev, I., *Habsburgs and Ottomans between Vienna and Belgrade, 1683-1739*, 1995.

Petrie, C., *The Marshal, Duke of Berwick*, 1953.

Pevitt, C., *The Man who would be King, Philippe Duc d'Orleans*, 1997.

Pigaillem, H., *Blenheim 1704, Le prince Eugene et Marlborough contre la France*, 2004.

Roblot, C., *Les Gloires de Toulon, 1707*, 1880.

Rothenburg, G., *The Austrian Military Border in Croatia, 1527-1747*, 1960.

Sautai, M., *La Manoeuvre de Denain*, 1902.

Shoberl, F. (tr), *Memoirs of Prince Eugene of Savoy*, 1811.

Spielman, J., *Leopold I of Austria*, 1977.

St John, B. (tr and ed.), *The Memoirs of the Duke of St Simon*, 1876 (3 vols).

Stoye, J., *The Siege of Vienna, 1683*, 1964.

_____, *Marsigli's Europe, 1680-1730*, 1994.

Sturgill, C., *Marshal Villars and the War of the Spanish Succession*, 1965.

Symcox, G. (tr & ed.), *War, Diplomacy and Imperialism, 1618-1763*, 1974.

_____, *Victor-Amadeus II of Savoy*, 1985.

Tepley, K., *Türkische Sagen und Legenden um die Kaiserstadt Wien*, 1980.

T'Hoff, T, van (ed.), *The Correspondence of Marlborough and Hiensius*, 1951.

Tindal, N., *The Continuation of Mr Rapin's History of England*, Vol. XVI, 1757.

Trevelyan, G., *Select Documents for Queen Anne's Reign, 1702-1707*, 1929.

_____, *England under Queen Anne*, 1932 (3 vols).

Verney, P., *The Battle of Blenheim*, 1976.

Visé, J. de., *The History of the Siege of Toulon* (tr A. Boyer), 1708.

Wheatcroft, A., *The Habsburgs*, 1995.

_____, *The Enemy at the Gate*, 2008.

Williams, B., *The Whig Supremacy, 1714-1760*, 1962.

Wolf, J., *Louis XIV*, 1968.

Wright, W., *Ottoman Statecraft*, 1935.

Index